Iftā' and Fatwa in the Muslim World and the West

Iftā' and Fatwa in the Muslim World and the West

Edited by
Zulfiqar Ali Shah

The International Institute of Islamic Thought
London • Washington

THE INTERNATIONAL INSTITUTE OF ISLAMIC THOUGHT, 1435 AH/2014 CE

THE INTERNATIONAL INSTITUTE OF ISLAMIC THOUGHT
P.O. BOX 669, HERNDON, VA 20172 USA
www.iiit.org

LONDON OFFICE
P.O. BOX 126, RICHMOND, SURREY TW9 2UD, UK
www.iiituk.com

ISBN 978-1-56564-483-0 Paperback

Contents

About the Contributors

Imad-ad-Dean Ahmad (president, Minaret of Freedom Institute, Bethesda, MD), holds a PhD in astronomy and astrophysics (University of Arizona, 1975). He is a senior lecturer at the University of Maryland, and teaches a course on Islamic religion, history, and civilization at Wesley Theological Seminary (Washington, DC). He is the author of *Signs in the Heavens: A Muslim Astronomer's Perspective on Religion and Science* (Beltsville, MD: amana publications, 2006) and *Islamic Rules of Order* (Beltsville, MD: amana publications, 2008), co-editor of *Islam and the West: A Dialog* (American Muslim Foundation, 1998) and co-author of *Islam and the Discovery of Freedom* (Beltsville, MD: amana publications, 1997). His address on "Islam, Commerce, and Business Ethics" was published in Nicholas Capaldi, *Business and Religion: A Clash of Civilizations?* (Salem, MA: M & M Scrivener Press, 2005)

Mahmoud Ayoub* (faculty associate in Islam and Christian-Muslim Relations, Hartford Seminary, Hartford, CT) holds a PhD in the history of religion (Harvard University, 1975). From 1988 to 2008, he was a professor and director of Islamic Studies, Department of Religion, Temple University, Philadelphia. He has also taught at the University of Pennsylvania, the Pacific School of Religion (Berkeley), San Diego State University, the University of Toronto, and McGill University. Among his publications are *Redemptive Suffering in Islam* (The Hague: Mouton, 1978), *The Qur'an and Its Interpreters*, vols. 1 & 2 (Albany: State University of New York Press, 1984-92), *Dirāsāt fī al-'Alaqāt al-Masīḥīyah al-Islāmīyah* (*Studies in Christian-Muslim Relations*) vols. 1 & 2 (2000), and *Islam: Faith and History* (Oxford, UK: Oneworld, 2004). His articles have appeared in *The Muslim World*, *The Journal of the American Oriental Society*, *The Bulletin of the Institute of Middle Eastern Studies* (Tokyo), *Islamochristiana* (Rome), and many other journals and books.

Abdessamad Belhaj (assistant professor of Arabic and Islamic Studies, Pázmány Péter Catholic University, Budapest; visiting lecturer at Catholic University of Louvain, Belgium) holds a PhD in arts and humanities (Islamic studies; Mohammed V University, Morocco, 2001) and a PhD in political and social sciences (Catholic University of Louvain, Belgium, 2008). He specializes in Islamic theology, philosophy, Qur'anic studies, and Islamic law, and serves on the Editorial Advisory Board of *Futūḥ al-Buldān: Sources for the Study of Islamic Societies*.

Alexandre Caeiro (assistant professor, Center for the Study of Contemporary Muslim Societies, Qatar Faculty of Islamic Studies, Hamad Bin Khalifa University, Doha) holds a PhD in religious studies (University of Utrecht, the Netherlands, 2011). He has taught at Utrecht University, Friedrich-Alexander-Universität Erlangen-Nürnberg, and

* Prof. Ayoub contributed to discussions during the seminar as a senior scholar.

Cairo University. He is the author of *The "Muslim Question" in Europe: Integration Debates and Muslim Responses* (accepted at Amsterdam University Press: 2013) and *The Chaos of Fatwas: Rethinking Religion and Politics in the Arab World* (under preparation). His research interests include the relation between religion and politics in Europe and the Arab World, Islamic law in the modern world, and transformations of religious authority.

Kenneth Honerkamp (professor, Department of Religion, University of Georgia) teaches Modern Standard Arabic as a second language and in-depth textual study for advanced students. He holds a PhD in religion (University of Aix-en-Provence, France, 1999) and graduated from al-Qarawiyyin University of Morocco. Among his publications are *Rasā'il Sufiyah al-Abī 'Abd al-Raḥmān al-Sulamī* (*Four Unedited Epistles by al-Sulami*; 412/1021), *Manāqib Imām al-Shādhilī by 'Abd al-Nūr al-Amrānī* (*Biogragphy of Hassan al-Shadhili dating from the 14th Century*), and *Spiritual Alchemy: Master and Disciple - The Letters of Ibn Abbad of Ronda* (1332-90) (*Rasā'il al-Kubrā*). He is involved in researching Arabic manuscripts, particularly those found in the less-often-referred-to manuscript collections of Morocco. He conducts research in the fields of Islamic law and the integral relationship of the Shari'ah and Sufism.

Vinay Khetia (PhD candidate, religious studies, McMaster University, Hamilton, ON, Canada) specializes in Islamic intellectual history and Shi'ism, with a focus on demonstrative jurisprudence and devotional literature. His doctoral dissertation focuses on Twelver Shi'i Liturgy as a unique expression of Shi'i piety and devotional theology. He is currently preparing an annotated translation of Shaykh al-Mufid's (d. 1022) *Al-Fuṣūl al-'Ashrah fī al-Ghaybah* (Ten Chapters Related to the Occultation).

Moustafa Kassem holds an MA in business administration (City University of New York) and is an MA student in Islamic law (Umm al-Qura University, Makkah). He has lectured at Fordham University (New York) and Effat University (Jeddah).

Abdulaziz Sachedina (professor and IIIT Chair in Islamic Studies, Ali Vural Ak Center for Islamic Studies, George Mason University, Fairfax, VA) holds a PhD in Islamic studies (University of Toronto, 1976). He is the author of *Islamic Messianism* (Albany: State University of New York Press, 1980), *The Just Ruler in Shiite Islam* (New York: Oxford University Press, 1998), *The Islamic Roots of Democratic Pluralism* (New York: Oxford University Press, 2001), *Islamic Biomedical Ethics: Theory and Application* (New York: Oxford University Press, 2009), *Islam and the Challenge of Human Rights* (New York: Oxford University Press, 2009) and numerous articles in academic journals. He is co-author of *Human Rights and the Conflicts of Culture* (Columbia: University of South Carolina Press, 1988) and translator of Al-Sayyid Abu al-Qāsim al-Musawi al-Khu'i, *The Prolegomena to the Qur'an* (New York: Oxford University Press, 1998). He is conducting research and writing on Islamic law, ethics, and theology (Sunni and Shi'i) with a focus on social and political ethics (e.g. interfaith and intra-faith relations, Islamic biomedical ethics, and Islam and human rights).

Abdullah Saeed (Sultan of Oman Professor of Arab and Islamic studies and director, the National Centre of Excellence for Islamic Studies, Asia Institute, University of Melbourne, Australia) holds a PhD in Islamic studies (University of Melbourne, Australia, 1992). He is the author of *The Qur'an: An Introduction* (London and New York: Routhledge, 2008), *Islamic Thought: An Introduction* (London and New York: Routledge, 2006), I*nterpreting the Qur'an: Towards a Contemporary Approach* (London and New York: Routledge, 2006), *Freedom of Religion, Apostasy, and Islam* (Aldershot, UK and Burlington, VT: Ashgate, 2004), *Islamic Banking and Interest: A Study of the Prohibition of Riba in Islam and Its Contemporary Interpretation* (Leiden and New York: E.J. Brill, 1996), *Islam in Australia* (Crows Nest, Australia: Allen & Unwin, 2003), and *Essential Dictionary of Islamic Thought* (Australia: Seaview Press 2001). His research focus is the negotiation of text and context, *ijtihād* and interpretation, and the reform of Islamic thought. His publications cover Qur'anic hermeneutics, Islam and human rights, the reform of Islamic law, Muslim communities in Australia, and Islam and the freedom of religion. One of his major research works resulted in the six-volume *Qur'an-Related Literature in Indonesia*.

Zulfiqar Ali Shah (executive director, Fiqh Council of North America; religious affairs director, Islamic Society of Milwaukee) received his PhD in theology and religious studies (University of Wales) and has taught at the International Islamic University Islamabad, the University of Wales, the University of Northeast Florida, and St. Thomas University. A former president of the Shari'ah Scholars Association of North America (SSANA), he has authored *A Study of Anthropomorphism and Transcendence in the Bible and Qur'an: Scripture & God in the Judeo-Christian & Islamic Tradition* (Herndon, VA: IIIT, 2012), *Astronomical Calculations and Ramadan: A Fiqhi Discourse* (Herndon, VA: IIIT, 2009), and several scholarly articles and books on a variety of subjects. His areas of interest are comparative religions, *tafsīr*, Islamic theology and philosophy, comparative *fiqh*, Islamic history, and Islamic civilization.

Introduction

IIIT's Summer Institute for Scholars held its seminar on "*Iftā'* and Fatwa in the Muslim World and the West: The Challenges of Authority, Legitimacy, and Relevance" on July 11-20, 2011, at its headquarters in Herndon, VA. A host of world-renowned scholars from various schools of thought, academic backgrounds, and hermeneutical dispositions participated in a total of fifteen sessions.

A sort of consensus seemed to emerge that the processes of *iftā'* (formulating a fatwa) and then issuing a fatwa are in a chaotic situation both in the Muslim world and the West. There are problems related to competency, expertise, specialization, intellectual and juristic stagnation, blind imitation, interdisciplinary disconnect, proliferation, authority, legitimacy, acceptance, and cultural relevance, just to mention a few.

In the formative classical period of Islamic jurisprudence (the rise of the Abbasids in 750 to the fall of Andalusia in 1492), the well-known scholars not only possessed the intellectual skills required for analytical reasoning, they also had a broad general knowledge of the fields relevant to their cultural contexts in which they issued their edicts. Contemporary knowledge is categorized into so many specializations and sub-specializations that one person or one group of scholars cannot possibly master all of them and develop a comprehensively consistent legal methodology or juristic tradition. The problem is compounded by the fact that Muslim jurists seldom enroll in secular universities to equip themselves with modern research tools. They are at a loss to study the ever increasing technically sophisticated scientific fields, and the secular social scientists or technology experts seldom study the Shari'ah and its underlying principles.

This dichotomist bifurcation perhaps poses the greatest hindrance as well as challenge to the process of developing an up-to-date, relevant, and applicable jurisprudence. Fatwa is defined as applying the Shari'ah to existing realities. A viable fatwa, therefore, requires a knowledge of the Shari'ah as well as local customs, cultural realities, individual and communal implications, and other relevant matters. Perhaps the biggest challenge in today's formulation of fatwas is the above-mentioned bifurcation, which engenders an idealism that lacks practicality and relevance.

The confusion is intensified by the lack of a hierarchical religious authority, especially among Sunnis; the lack of coordination between different areas of expertise and territorial regional juristic bodies; the proliferation of fatwas through media; the unprecedented social, political, economic, and technical changes; and, most importantly, the lack of professional training, openness, courage, creativity, and analytical reasoning among the majority of traditional Muslim jurists. There is a visible sense of loss and intellectual bankruptcy among the legal as well as the theological tradition of the twenty-first-century ummah. Muslim jurists are trying to solve complicated modern problems with the ancient tools of hazy analogy, imitation, and outmoded *madhhab*-bound legal methodologies while practically closing the doors of *ijtihād* (innovative analytical reasoning) in an effort to safeguard the tradition and originality.

But there were problems even with the original juristic tradition, which was formulated and fixed during the first three Islamic centuries. There was so much political tumult and social turmoil going on during those years that the jurists' legal outlook and thinking processes could not have escaped their surroundings. Their staunch fatwas against apostasy and blasphemy reflect that period's geopolitical realities.

Muslims of the prophetic and *rāshidūn* eras adhered closely to the authentic texts due to their sincerity, piety, prophetic training, and temporal proximity to the revelation. Then the context started impacting how the authentic texts were understood, interpreted, paraphrased, and implemented. The transition from *khilāfah* to kingship changed the socio-cultural realities, and the iron hands of the Umayyad and Abbasid rulers left their imprints upon the legal and juristic traditions. These traditions are never formulated in a vacuum anyway, for they respond to corresponding cultural, political, socioeconomic, and epistemological realities.

This was also the period when Muslims developed a sense of Islam's superiority over all other religious traditions, especially Judaism and Christianity. They divided the world into *dār al-Islām* and *dār al-kufr*, and the latter was assessed as *dār al-ḥarb*. Many Qur'anic texts and hadith reports were contextualized in light of this supremacist ideology. A number of generic texts were specified, and a number of particular texts were generalized with the help of mostly circumstantial textual and contextual evidence that changed the probable texts into categorically pinpointing meanings, interpretations, and implications. Many weak *aḥādīth* were implied to substantiate these new-found categorical implications, and the whip of *ijmā'* (consensus), along with political repercussions, was used to silence opposition or difference.

The hierarchical authority of such fundamental Islamic sources as the Qur'an was sometimes compromised by pinpointed precise impositions based upon hadith reports or the claims of *ijmā'*, while those prophetic reports and claims of *ijmā'* in themselves were questionable. As a result, a great deal of dust gradually settled over the original legal tradition. Gender, sectarian, political, theological, and at times regional subjectivities were – and still are – manifestly visible in certain quarters of our juristic tradition.

Both the Muslim and non-Muslim worlds have drastically changed. The new geopolitical and scientific realities belonging to our rapidly changing world demand a fresh look at some aspects of the established juristic tradition. The world can no longer be categorized into *dār al-Islām* and *dār al-kufr*, for it has become a small village that is shared and often governed by non-Islamic traditions. A new universally accommodating and pluralistic outlook, rather than the old supremacist attitude, is necessitated by this on-the-ground reality. The *maqāṣid al-Sharī'ah* approach is better suited to these trying times than the oft-followed traditional analogical (*qiyāsī*) approach.

During the past few decades, a great effort has been made to formulate a consistent globally relevant *maqāṣidī* approach; however, this is still in the formative stage. Muslims living in minority settings are usually inclined toward it due to their unique problems and contexts. And then there are the problems of authority, precision, relevance, and acceptance. Resolving them requires tremendous institutionalized research, concerted efforts, large financial and intellectual resources, and, first and foremost, the courage to face modern problems head on without shrugging them off or sweeping them under the rug.

Existing juristic bodies are largely unable to realize this dream due to reasons beyond their control or capabilities. In the long term, the minority tradition (*fiqh al-aqallīyah*) may well become the preferred Muslim discourse (*fiqh al-awlīyah*) because of its underlying ethical principles, creativity, practicality, relevance, and legitimacy.

The way forward involves a systematic fresh look at and a re-evaluation of the old fatwas, as well as the issuance of new ones with a *maqāṣidī* outlook that are relevant to the ever-changing global realities. Such a process requires a consistent legal methodology that is formulated and developed by a consensus among qualified Muslim jurists with interdisciplinary backgrounds, perhaps using the US Supreme Court model. The fully articulated methodology should give credence to such universal and overarching Qur'anic principles as human dignity, justice, fairness, human equality, gender equity, pluralism, social justice, and morality. This would require a detailed discussion and a comprehensive treatment of the Shari'ah's true objectives, as well as a broad consensus about them.

The Qur'anic text will have to be given priority over all other sources of the Shari'ah, and the hadith and *fiqhī* texts must be subservient to it and its established overarching principles. Even the heavily contextualized Qur'anic passages should be reinterpreted in light of contemporary contexts using analytical reasoning, while giving ample consideration to local, regional, national, and international norms, customs, and contexts. The Hadith corpus and its interpretation should also be contextualized. Muslim tradition has done an amazing job in differentiating between the Qur'an's Makkan and Madinan chapters and with the reasons for the revelation (*asbāb al-nuzūl*); however, the same passion and preciseness is mostly missing in the Hadith literature. Not only should this literature be studied and interpreted in light of the gradual developmental process through which the prophetic mission passed, but the variables should also be differentiated from the constants. Additionally, the cultural and geopolitical milieu, as well as the social contexts of the past fatwas and their issuers (muftis), should be given a great deal of weight while reevaluating the legal tradition and its particulars.

Jurists are products of their worldview, culture, religious outlook, sectarian and theological beliefs, sociopolitical milieu, and framework of meaning. They are, therefore, conditioned by the very same factors. These surrounding elements are part and parcel of one's thinking process and are, quite naturally, reflected through one's ideas, perceptions, outlooks, and understanding of things. Consequently, they influence one's interpretations of the Qur'an and Sunnah.

We need to distinguish clearly between God's literal word (viz., the Arabic text of the Qur'an) and the human interpretations embodied in the countless multi-layered and multi-faceted exegetical as well as legal works. Any arbitrary imposition of human ideas, agendas, and inclinations upon the revealed text is an act of textual violence. We must mold our lives in light of the Qur'anic guidance and not twist the Qur'anic text or its meanings to make them conform to our needs, agendas, and ulterior motives.

As the Qur'an speaks to people of all ages, times, genders, ethnicities, cultures, and aptitudes, it often employs the most comprehensive terms so that it will remain eternally relevant. Most of its imprecise, non-categorical (*mutashābihāt*) verses come under this category, for they may be interpreted in multiple ways. While this flexibility enables them to respond to the needs of various societies and cultures, it never violates the message's original philosophy, intent, and congeniality. A sensible, balanced, and true understanding of these terms will always keep Muslims within the Shari'ah's established parameters, but may provide them with multiple choices when it comes to acting upon them in one's practical life.

There is fatwa and there is *taqwā*, the spectrum's two limits. A balanced and middle approach is always needed and appreciated by the majority. Muslim scholarship needs to build a consensus about these seemingly divergent passages, reports, and fatwas in light of contemporary realities and provide proper guidance so that the ummah does not undergo undue hardship and unnecessary division.

This does not mean that the Qur'anic or prophetic message or intent must be diluted or attenuated. What it does mean is that we must accept them as the most important guiding principles of our lives, but avoid imposing our ideas or perceptions upon them. The motto and guiding principle of this legal reformation should be "Let the Qur'an and authentic *aḥādīth* speak for themselves, and let them be the guides." I will insert a word of caution here, however. The Qur'anic text is the only divinely authorized text that has not been corrupted or experienced external intrusion. The Hadith corpus cannot come close to this absolute authority and authenticity due to historical witnesses of possible intrusions, corruptions, fabrications, and concoctions.

The early hadith compilers did a wonderful job of sifting through the corpus and separating the authentic and genuine from the fabricated, weak, or less authentic reports. But it seems that more emphasis was placed on authenticating the report's chain(s) of narration (*isnād*) than its actual content (*matn*). Today, equal efforts are needed to reconcile the content with the well-established overarching Qur'anic principles in light of reason and morality. The Prophet was sent not only to serve as the best ethical model, as the Qur'an states, but also to perfect the moral values, as he himself stated in an authentic hadith. His actions, statements, approvals, and teachings can never violate his established mottos of the best ethical and moral standards.

The contents of the hadith and *sīrah* should be revisited in light of the ethical and moral parameters. Reason, wisdom, common sense, and morality should be the cornerstones of this revision process. Positive criticism of the tradition is constructive, for this activity helps keep it relevant, vibrant, forward-looking, and alive. This process of critical revision and realignment will make things easy for contemporary Muslims, which is one of the Shari'ah's established principles and a much needed commodity today.

Abdullah Saeed, in his paper "Textual Challenges to the Death Penalty for Apostasy in Islam and the Question of Freedom of Religion," emphasizes the need for Muslims to move away from the classical-era law of apostasy (*riddah*) and its associated death penalty, and toward a concept of religious freedom that agrees with its contemporary understanding. The paper argues that neither the Qur'an nor the Prophet's actual practice provide any strong support for executing apostates. This penalty, which developed during Islam's early centuries, functioned as an important mechanism not only to suppress Muslims' religious freedom but also their intellectual freedom, particularly as regards theological debates. Given the weak classical legal position on the death penalty, Saeed argues that contemporary Muslims need to challenge this position by relying on the Qur'an, the Prophet's actual practice, and the views of a range of early and modern scholars in addition to supporting the modern understanding of religious freedom expressed in the Universal Declaration of Human Rights and other major international human rights documents.

Imad-ad-Dean Ahmad states, in his "Shuratic *Iftā'*: The Challenge of Fatwa Collectivization," that one of the primary challenges to juristic development right now is the specialization of knowledge, a reality that has made issuing legal opinions more difficult than ever before. Among the contributing factors are the amount of available data, the sophistication required to understand it, the varied cultural contexts in which juristic decisions are to be applied, the jurists' increasing distance from the textual sources' original languages and context, and the complex social conditions to which these decisions are to be applied. A new methodology has been suggested: collectivizing the process of issuing fatwas. This is based on the realization that since no single scholar can master all of the knowledge necessary to solve the modern world's many pressing issues, some mechanism of collective *iftā'* is necessary.

Ahmad considers the rationales for this posited approach, as well as some objections and obstacles. He suggests that rather than developing a totally new collective methodology, Muslims should combine the traditional concept of *shūrā* (consultation) with the modern scientific methodologies of peer review and the new developments in online communication. This would allow them to implement techniques that could use the latest technological and scientific developments to preserve the fundamental principles of juridical development. This process supplements the classical texts with the discoveries of scientific inquiry; provides a way to include social and physical scientists, along with scholars of the traditional disciplines; restores the separation between the government and scholarship of early Islamic society; and avoids the sectarianization of institutions. After outlining how the results can be made available to civil and political society, he applies this envisaged approach to two particularly difficult issues: calendar reform and embryonic stem cell research.

In his "Minority *Fiqh* as Deliberative *Ijtihād*: Legal Theory and Practice," Abdessamad Belhaj explains that Islam considers deliberation an essential characteristic of transmitting, interpreting, and teaching religious knowledge. During the ummah's formative period, studying and reflecting on the Qur'an was a collective undertaking. The idea of holding scientific circles in mosques originated from those early Muslims who gathered around a scholar to learn and share knowledge. In the classical era of Muslim learning, scholars developed deliberative methods to communicate knowledge of the Qur'an and Sunnah, such as recitation, dictation, assignment of a lesson, and collective memorization.

In particular, *iftā'* evolved as a collective scientific activity of diverging opinions, consultation, and discussion. Such deliberation was particularly helpful in generating and developing *madhāhib* (legal schools). Deliberation is not concerned with the law's operative aspects alone (e.g., institutions, processes, communication, and contestation), but is also involved in very basic legal concepts (e.g., norms, reasoning, and customs). Above all, it intervenes as a process of formulating law through argumentation, constructed rules, and consensual meanings. In jurisprudence, this approach can be described as the difference-consensus process through which jurists tried to deal with multiple juridical opinions and complex realities. In various times and places, these difficulties compelled them to adopt a collective approach to resolve legal issues.

Within the context of Muslims living in the West, Belhaj submits that the deliberative *ijtihād* pursued by minority *fiqh* is a symbolic form of collective action. He first discusses its theoretical background, both as seen by legal theorists and the jurists of minority *fiqh*, and then defines the concept of minority fiqh and introduces its formulators in some detail. Subsequently, the function of this type of *fiqh* within the Muslim public space in the West is treated. In closing, he analyzes the hijab as a deliberative form of *iftā'*.

Alexandre Caeiro's "Ordering Religion, Organizing Politics: The Regulation of the Fatwa in Contemporary Islam" focuses on the recent proliferation of urgent calls for regulating the production of fatwas (*ḍawābiṭ al-fatwā*, *tanẓīm al-iftā'*). Perhaps the most prominent call was articulated in The Amman Message in July 2005, in which some 200 Muslim scholars outlined, at the request of King Abdallah II of Jordan, the conditions necessary for issuing legitimate fatwas. Several subsequent high-profile international conferences were devoted to this issue, media muftis began to reflect upon the dilemmas of issuing fatwas on satellite TV and the Internet, and newspapers and magazines across the Muslim world began to carry articles and op-eds on the need to organize *iftā'*. It seems that some type of diagnosis is widely shared, one that cuts across the usual lines of religious and political orientation, by state and non-state actors, be they traditional ulama, Islamists, or secularists: The production of fatwas has been so deregulated that it can no longer be controlled. The ensuing proliferation has led to "chaos" (*fawḍā*), which is causing perplexity (*ḥīrat*) among Muslims and thus ranks as one of the contemporary ummah's major quandaries.

He suggests that the diagnosis of "chaos" is less self-evident than is often assumed. While acknowledging that the contemporary situation poses various challenges to religious authority, the article argues that the urgency underlying these calls is shaped by a specific understanding of the fatwa's functions, that contradictory religious opinions have been a feature of the Islamic tradition since the very beginning, and that they have not always been perceived as an embarrassment. The author further argues that conflicting fatwas no longer pose a primarily theological or legal problem, but rather raise a political-ideological dilemma.

Caeiro starts by reconstructing very briefly some features of what he calls the "narrative of chaos" and focuses on two of its most prominent features. He then details the approach of Yusuf al-Qaradawi, a prominent Islamic scholar whose interventions in many ways problematize the assumptions underlying this narrative. He concludes by offering some remarks that link the two sides of the discussion on *fawḍā* to the concerns outlined above.

Moustafa S. Kassem, in his "Fatwa in the Era of Globalization," analyzes the etymology of fatwa and its Qur'anic and *fiqhī* usage. He talks about its special position in the Islamic religion and culture, defines the qualifications that a mufti should possess, and talks about who validates those qualifications. He discusses the Internet's role as it relates to this particular activity, while concentrating more upon the future of fatwa in the era of globalization. In closing, he addresses the possible future challenges posed by the Internet and globalization for scholars and institutions.

In his "Al-Qushayri's Fatwa and His *Risālah*: Their Relevance to Intra-Islamic Dialog Today," Kenneth L. Honerkamp argues that at a time when suicide bombers are targeting Sufi shrines in India and Pakistan and some western scholars and numerous present-day Muslims see Sufism as an extraneous growth having little to do with Islam's authoritative sources or as a sectarian development that occurred at a given point in Islamic history, the relevance of al-Qushayri's fatwa, issued in 436/1044, cannot be stressed enough. His fatwa and subsequent imprisonment and exile from his hometown exemplify the sociopolitical ramifications of what is most commonly assumed to be a pronouncement of a juridical or legal nature. The *Risālah* itself reveals the existence of a virtue-based ethical discourse of formative Sufism that delineates a strategy for attaining both wisdom and an intimate knowledge of God. Honerkamp refers to this discourse as being a facet of fatwa founded upon correct comportment (*fatwā akhlāqī*).

Al-Qushayri wrote this lengthy essay for the Sufis of his time to remind them of Sufism's inherently ethical nature and to vindicate the authenticity of its Islamic roots by proving that its foundational principles were drawn from the Qur'an and Sunnah. His fatwa and *Risālah* complement each other and offer those seeking an understanding of the human spirit a testimony to humanity's timeless spiritual quest and the textual sources, as well as the interpretive and analytic methodologies, from which it is drawn.

The *Risālah* also represents the confluence of two seminal Islamic traditions: (1) the tradition of intellectual textual discourse derived from the foundational elements of Islamic spirituality, namely, the Qur'an and Sunnah, in conjunction with the texts transmitted from generation to generation by the scholarly elite who dedicated themselves to preserving and transmitting the prophetic example; and (2) with an oral tradition that was an integral facet of the textual tradition. The *Risālah* presents these complete and with individual chains of transmission.

There is a current tendency to compartmentalize the Islamic discourse into the realms of jurisprudence, theology, and mystical ethics (Sufism). Yet the training and expertise that al-Qushayri brought to bear in his works, as well as the legacy he left to future generations, testify to his roots in the narration and collection of hadith, Shafi'i jurisprudence, and Ash'ari *kalām*. The *Risālah al-Qushayrīyah* contextualizes the importance of maintaining intra-Muslim dialog along the broadest possible lines that excludes none of the areas of the traditional discourse and includes new ones as well.

Vinay Khetia, in "The Guardians of Islamic Marriage Contract and the Search for Agency in Twelver Shi'a Jurisprudence," examines the Imami debate over whether a mature female virgin of sound mind needs her *walī*'s (guardian - her father, grandfather, great-grandfather, etc.) approval to get married. If she marries without his consent, would this be an act of *zinā* (fornication)? Where does legal agency (*istiqlālīyah*) lie? Contemporary jurists are of two opinions: This agency is shared (*tashrīk*) between them or belongs to the woman (*istiqlāl al-bint*). He focuses on the works of two contemporary jurists – Ayatullah al-Sayyid Abul Qasim al-Khui's *Mabānī al-'Urwah al-Wuthqā* (representing the *tashrīq* position), and his student Ayatullah al-Sayyid Sadiq al-Ruhani's *Fiqh al-Sādiq* (representing the woman's agency) – and also considers some Sunni positions. On the principle of *mukhālafah li al-'āmmah*,

Shi'a scholars resolve contradictory positions by rejecting the one that is closer to the Sunni position on the premise that it was an act of dissimulation. In conclusion, he considers the social function of compatibility (*kafā'ah*) and the prohibition of preventing the woman's marriage (*a'adl*).

Abdulaziz Sachedina's "Islam, Healthcare, and Spirituality" looks into how *iftā'* works in a new field like ethics, which has been regarded as a totally secular field of inquiry. The hospital culture is generally regarded as a secular culture in which ethical norms are derived only from human reason and experience, a practical ethics. Virtue ethics is the foundation of all ethics, but ethics here means the practical reasoning that leads to a conclusion about the rightness or wrongness of the decisions we pursue. It is quite relative, because each decision is made on a case-by-case basis, albeit based on a given culture's absolute values. The paper mainly seeks to answer the question: "What is the justification for me to do what I am doing?" This is the course of action followed by the *fuquhā'*: "Why am I making the decision the way I am making it (*fiqh al-istighlālī*)?" Western secular bioethics are being taught in Muslim hospitals and clinics, although Muslims are mainly interested in fatwas. When a patient's family refers to a fatwa, however, the doctors listen but make the decision themselves since there is no patient empowerment. In the western setting, bioethics is about patient empowerment. While a fatwa might influence a decision, it is not necessarily part of the process.

Some Muslims have translated western bioethics into Arabic, Persian, and other languages. Muslim students are taught the same four principles of bioethics as their counterparts in the West, including autonomy, which has little meaning in Muslim culture's communitarian context. The United States experienced a public uproar against the authoritarian medical profession that led to patient empowerment. This paper's main thrust is to seek what makes bioethics Islamic, based upon Islam's foundational religious goals, in order to develop fatwas, the raw material, into a full-fledged bioethical system.

The International Institute of Islamic Thought hopes that the papers in this volume shed some light on a subject that impacts the lives of individuals as well as societies in both Muslim-majority and Muslim-minority lands. *Iftā'* and fatwa will continue to be of concern to scholars and practitioners, hopefully informed by the discourse in this volume.

Zulfiqar Ali Shah
Executive Director
Fiqh Council of North America

Textual Challenges to the Death Penalty for Apostasy in Islam and the Question of Freedom of Religion

Abdullah Saeed

Abstract

This paper emphasizes the need for Muslims to move away from the classical Islamic law of apostasy (*riddah*) and the death penalty associated with it and toward a concept of religious freedom that accords with contemporary understandings of religious freedom. It argues that neither the Qur'an nor the Prophet's *actual practice* provide any strong support for such a punishment. This penalty developed in classical Islamic law during Islam's early centuries and functioned as an important mechanism to suppress the Muslims' religious and intellectual freedom, particularly in relation to theological debates. Given this inherent weaknesses, I assert that Muslims now need to challenge this position by relying on the Qur'an, the Prophet's actual practice, and the views of a range of early and modern scholars, as well as support the understanding of religious freedom as expressed in such major international human rights documents as the Universal Declaration of Human Rights (UDHR).

The Concept of Religious Freedom

Any discussion of religious freedom needs to refer to a standard with which Muslims, Christians, Jews, Buddhists, Hindus, and others are generally comfortable. One such standard appears to be provided by Article 18 of the United Nations' Universal Declaration of Human Rights (UDHR):

> Everyone has the right to freedom of thought, conscience and religion. This right includes freedom to change his religion or belief and freedom, either alone or in community with others and in public or private, to manifest his religion or belief in teaching, practice, worship and observance.[1]

This article emphasizes several aspects of this right: to have or adopt a religion, to change religion, to practice a religion, and to teach a religion. These elements, by and large, appear to be similar to the rights emphasized in the Qur'an and demonstrated in the Prophet's actual practice in relation to religious freedom.

Muslims have historically been reasonably tolerant of religious minorities in their midst, and even of theological differences among themselves. From the time of the Prophet, they have lived in multi-religious societies and their interactions with non-Muslims (e.g., Christians, Jews, Buddhists, or Hindus) have been accepted as normal. Both the Qur'an and the Prophet recognized the need to allow people to choose their own religion and to prohibit forced conversion. For example, the Qur'an recognized that Jews and Christians were "People of the Book," and the Prophet and his political successors allowed them to follow their religious traditions, norms, and laws under Muslim rule. These same provisions were extended to the Zoroastrians[2] and Hindus with whom the Muslims came into contact, which reveals how the latter viewed the question of religious freedom even in Islam's early days.

Many examples also exist of the tolerance of "unorthodox" views in the midst of Muslim societies: The famous poet Abu al-Ala' al-Ma'arri (d. 1058) attacked key religious beliefs and practices in his poetry, yet remained unharmed and died a natural death. Among his sayings critical of religion include:

> They all err—Muslims, Jews,
> Christians, and Zoroastrians:
> Humanity follows two world-wide sects:
> One, man intelligent without religion,
> The second, religious without intellect.[3]

His attacks on religious practices can also be easily discerned here:

> O fools, awake! The rites you sacred hold
> Are but a cheat contrived by men of old,
> Who lusted after wealth and gained their lust
> And died in baseness—and their law is dust.[4]

The free-thinking philosopher, physician, and alchemist Muhammad ibn Zakariyyah al-Razi (d. 925 or 935) also publicized his equally unorthodox (and some would say "heretical") views and was not harmed. Even a figure like al-Ghazali (d. 1111), whose ideas were controversial during certain periods of his later life, remained unharmed. These are only a few of the many examples of tolerance in early Muslim societies. More importantly, mainstream Muslim "creeds" adopted this tolerant approach toward Muslims who, in their view, did not follow mainstream positions in theological matters. The famous Creed of Imam Tahawi says:

> We do not declare anyone among the people of our *qiblah* a disbeliever for any sin, as long as he does not deem it lawful...[5]
>
> People of mortal sins among the community of Muhammad (peace be upon him), will not abide in the Fire forever, as long as they are monotheists....[6]
>
> We do not specify anyone among them to be in either Paradise or in the Fire. We also do not accuse any of them of disbelief, idolatry, or hypocrisy, as long as none of that manifests from them.[7]

The religious tolerance that characterized many pre-modern Muslim societies, moreover, seems to have been more widespread than in many non-Muslim-majority countries during that same period of time. The history of Christian Europe, particularly between the twelfth and sixteenth centuries, for example, includes many inquisitions and forced conversions of large numbers of Muslims and Jews in Spain and elsewhere,[8] a practice Muslim jurists and theologians held to be incompatible with Islam.

The Importance of Religious Freedom

Religion, one of the most important aspects of humanity, has always been part of human history. In fact, few communities have been without it. Religious identity, furthermore, remains one of the most important aspects of an individual's identity. Religion and faith are ingrained in the human psyche, and religious tradition is an integral aspect of the lives and identities of the vast majority of human beings.

For these reasons, freedom of religion is now considered a fundamental and universal right according to the Universal Declaration of Human Rights (UDHR) and similar documents, such as the International Covenant on Civil and Political Rights (ICCPR) and the European Convention on Human Rights (ECHR), as well as such Islamic human rights documents as the Cairo Declaration on Human Rights in Islam.[9] Some recent Muslim thinkers, among them Sayyid Qutb (d. 1966), argue that this freedom is perhaps the most important right for any human being and that denying it to anyone is like stealing one's humanity.[10]

Restricting religious freedom can have negative individual and collective consequences that can lead to conflict, rebellion, instability, and a lack of social cohesion. Without such freedom, most contemporary multi-religious societies, which encompass many religious traditions, could not function harmoniously. On the other hand, religious freedom tends to be associated with a range of positive social benefits, including gender equality, low military spending, a strong economy, and good health.[11] Although one cannot argue that it is the cause of such benefits, their association with religious freedom is significant.[12]

The Reality in Muslim-Majority Countries Today

Unfortunately religious freedom, as described in Article 18 of the UDHR, is seldom apparent in many Muslim-majority countries, many of which restrict it to a similar extent as do China, Russia, North Korea, Myanmar/Burma, and several others.[13] Some Muslim-majority countries impose severe restrictions on Muslims by criminalizing what their religious establishments consider to be blasphemy, heresy, apostasy, and even criticism of the dominant orthodoxy. In such countries, non-Muslims also face a range of restrictions as regards proselytization; the possession or importation of religious materials, which can lead to the confiscation of personal religious items; the public practice of non-Muslim religions; placing strict limits on building or renovating non-Muslim places of worship; government monitoring of religious activities; raiding private services; and sometimes harassing or even imprisoning non-Muslim religious leaders or believers. All of this continues to occur despite the tradition of Muslim societies, which have historically tended to be remarkably open and tolerant toward non-Muslims.[14]

Many Muslims have difficulty with the modern understanding of freedom of religion, as expressed in Article 18 of UDHR, which includes the freedom to change one's religion, based on the belief that Islam prohibits apostasy (*riddah*) and punishes it with death. Despite this, at the state level most Muslim-majority countries have ratified the International Covenant on Civil and Political Rights (ICCPR), which includes its own Article 18 on religious freedom:

> Everyone shall have the right to freedom of thought, conscience and religion. This right shall include freedom to have or to adopt a religion or belief of his choice.

Responding to the problem of endorsing the freedom to change one's religion, several Muslim-majority countries that have ratified this document have lodged reservations against this article, stating that it conflicts with their understanding of Islam and the Shari'ah. Bahrain's reservation includes the statement "as not affecting in any way the prescriptions of the Islamic Shari'ah,"[15] and Pakistan declares that its "provisions... shall be so applied to the extent that they are not repugnant to the Provisions of the Constitution of Pakistan and the Shari'ah laws."[16]

Despite such reservations, Muslims have been and continue to participate in human rights debates at the international level, including those dealing with freedom of religion. For instance, during the debate over the UDHR's draft of Article 18 and prior to its adoption in 1948, Lebanon's Christian delegate insisted on including a phrase that affirmed the freedom to change one's religion. The Pakistani delegate, an Ahmadi, saw no problem with the phrase. The Saudi delegate, however, objected on the grounds that it violated Islamic principles.[17]

Sensitivities Surrounding Apostasy

Many contemporary Muslims believe that apostasy and its associated penalty is a fundamental aspect of Islam that cannot be changed. They perceive those who argue for any form of religious freedom that includes such a freedom as being against Islam, the Shari'ah, and fundamental Muslim values.

Given the issue's sensitive nature, Muslim scholars who write about apostasy and argue for freedom of religion often face difficulties in Muslim societies. When Shaykh Taha Jabir al-Alwani, for example, completed his *Lā Ikrāha fī al-Dīn* (*There Is No Coercion in Matters of Religion*), some of his colleagues at the International Institute of Islamic Thought (IIIT) advised him not to publish it. As he was at that time the institute's president, they warned him that the book could have a significant negative impact on both the institute and how other Muslims perceived it. Listening to their advice, he published it only after his term had ended.[18] Although he is a well-known traditionally trained scholar, one who is well-respected internationally for his scholarship in Islamic jurisprudence and was living in the United States at that time, al-Alwani was very aware that he could potentially experience a backlash for challenging this particular traditional perspective.

Unsurprisingly, the challenges for Muslims in Muslim-majority countries are even greater. When Salman Taseer, then governor of Pakistan's Punjab province, questioned the country's blasphemy law, which functions like an apostasy law as far as Muslims so accused are concerned, he was assassinated by one of his own bodyguards in January 2011.[19] In Pakistan, the murderer was widely praised for standing up in defense of "Islam." Fatwas were issued that condemned Taseer and supported his assassin.

Publications critical of apostasy laws can easily be banned. My own book (co-authored with Hassan Saeed), *Freedom of Religion, Apostasy, and Islam*, was banned in the Maldives in 2008. Again, this is indicative of the kind of consequences faced by Muslims who choose to challenge the status quo in regard to apostasy law.

Understanding Apostasy

In classical Islamic law, apostasy means reverting from Islam to unbelief in Islam, whether by intention; by an action that removes one from Islam; or by a statement, be it in the form of mockery, stubbornness, or conviction.[20] Classical Islamic law has many definitions for apostasy, among them[21] denying God's existence or attributes; denying a particular messenger or that he is truly a messenger; or denying one of the fundamentals of religion, for instance, that there are five obligatory prayers (*ṣalāt*) in a day or declaring prohibited (*ḥarām*) something that is clearly permissible (*ḥalāl*) or vice versa; or worshipping an idol.[22] Although these ways are clear as regards the person's intention, many statements and actions that are not so clear can nevertheless be used to accuse a Muslim of committing apostasy.

The Qur'an refers to apostasy several times but provides no specific worldly punishment. Instead, it suggests a severe punishment in the next life. Some *aḥādīth*, however, mention it and seem to specify the death penalty. Moreover, early Sunni and Shi'i jurists were in general agreement about what apostasy broadly entailed and that it should be punished by death.

Key Textual Challenges

Despite this long-held traditional position, several scholars today, myself included, now argue that apostasy laws carrying the death penalty need to be reconsidered. While a great deal of evidence supports this position, this paper only focuses on three: (a) the Qur'an's silence, (b) hadith texts and the question of reliability, and (c) problems with the claim that this punishment is based on consensus.

The Qur'an's Silence

The Qur'an condemns apostasy in no uncertain terms, but specifies no worldly penalty for it. Apostasy is mentioned in several verses (e.g., Q. 2:217, 5:54, and 16:106); however, none of them stipulates a penalty for it in this life despite condemning the apostate in very harsh and unequivocal terms.[23]

S. A. Rahman, former chief justice of Pakistan, in his excellent *Punishment of Apostasy in Islam*, points out this Qur'anic silence despite the fact that it mentions apostasy no less than twenty times.[24] Selim el-Awa, a well-known jurist from Egypt who discusses apostasy at length, agrees, citing this complete silence and stating that the evidence contained within the Sunnah is open to interpretation.[25] Mahmud Shaltut analyzes the relevant Qur'anic evidence and concludes that apostasy carries no temporal penalty because it speaks only of punishment in the hereafter.[26]

Moreover, verses like Q. 2:217 and 3:86-97 clearly envisage a natural death for the apostate.[27] The following passage seems to offer a strong argument against the death penalty for apostasy:

> Those who believe, then disbelieve, then believe again, then disbelieve and then increase in their disbelief – God will never forgive them nor guide them to the path. (Q. 4:137)

The implication here is unmistakable. The text would hardly entertain the prospect of repeated belief and disbelief if death were the prescribed punishment for the initial act.

Hadith Texts and the Question of Reliability

Given that the Qur'an is Islam's most important and authoritative text, the fact that it provides no support for the death penalty, despite referring to apostasy, is significant. Evidence to support such a penalty therefore has to be found elsewhere. Jurists usually found it in the Hadith corpus, which contains such *aḥādīth* as "Whoever changes his religion, kill him"[28] and several similar texts. A number of these are found in those Hadith collections that Sunnis consider authentic, such as those compiled by al-Bukhari (d. 870) and Muslim (d. 875). Many contemporary Sunnis usually do not allow the authenticity of these *aḥādīth* to be questioned, although both past and recent scholars have questioned the authenticity of at least some of them.

In the following pages I will present several arguments in relation to the *aḥādīth* that have been advanced by scholars who support freedom of religion as expressed in the UDHR's Article 18, particularly with regard to the issue of death penalty for apostasy.

Those *aḥādīth* that appear to support such a penalty and are attributed to the Prophet seem to contradict many Qur'anic verses on religious freedom.

The Qur'an is particularly clear that religious choice is individual and personal and that people can choose to follow God's way or not. Most importantly, it clearly prohibits any coercion in matters of faith. Some Muslim scholars, including many classical jurists, have argued that those verses that support religious freedom have been "abrogated." However, close to 100 verses are broadly supportive of religious freedom. How can such a large number of them be abrogated by one or two verses that may or may not be relevant to the issue at hand, or by a small number of *aḥādīth* (such as "Whoever changes his religion, kill him")? The abrogation argument is hard to support, and emphasis should be placed, in my view, on the broad thrust of the verses that support religious freedom, individual choice, and non-coercion.

The *aḥādīth* most often quoted in support of the death penalty are problematic in other ways as well. For example, the hadith "Whoever changes his religion, kill him" is notably general and ambiguous. If one were to take it literally, anyone who converts from any religion can be killed, such as a Christian who converts to Islam. Such a position is obviously absurd.

Classical jurists frequently encountered such ambiguity in the Qur'anic and hadith texts; they were often quite comfortable with sidelining certain texts in favor of others, and interpreting or reinterpreting them. This ambiguity enabled them to interpret texts in specific ways and thereby extend Islamic law beyond the texts themselves or restrict the scope of meaning of particular texts.

Prominent jurists, among them Abu Hanifah, Malik, and Shafi'i, sometimes had to lay aside certain texts and rely on others in their legal decisions. As a result, certain ambiguous texts had to be clarified or interpreted[29] and certain general texts also had to be particularized. The concept of textual ambiguity has been central to the development of Islamic law. In fact, some of the earliest jurisprudential works, like Shafi'i's *Risālah*, rely heavily upon it. This accounts for his analysis of *bayān* (roughly translated as "making clear the meaning" of the substance of Qur'anic communication[30]) and the methodological insights he provides. The Islamic legal tradition provides tools to deal with such questions. But while they are useful, some contemporary Muslim scholars argue that we need to develop them further. This is an area to which contemporary Muslim scholars have much to contribute.

While *aḥādīth* are a critically important part of Islam's tradition, they need to be approached with care and some degree of caution. Although hadith collectors and scholars have provided us with the results of their work in determining these accounts' authenticity and reliability, Muslims today perhaps also need to build on this and develop further ideas and methodological tools.

In some cases, questions about the long-accepted authenticity of some *aḥādīth* may have to be asked afresh. For instance, although "Whoever changes his religion, kill him" exists in Bukhari's collection, there are questions about the reliability of certain people in its chain of transmission, at least in the best known version. This is the one attributed to Abd Allah ibn Abbas (d. 687), the Prophet's cousin, by his slave/student Ikrimah (d. 723), although it seems to have been widely circulated by Ayyub al-Sakhtiyani (d. 749), one of Ikrimah's students in the second Islamic century.[31]

In hadith scholarship, Ikrimah's role as a key source raises some questions. Some notably senior scholars who were his contemporaries considered him to be a liar. For example, Ali ibn Abd Allah ibn Abbas, the son of Ibn Abbas, to whom Ikrimah attributed it, accused Ikrimah of lying about his father. Similarly, Sa'id ibn Jubayr viewed Ikrimah unfavorably, as did Sa'id ibn al-Musayyab, who apparently told his slave, "Do not tell lies about me, as Ikrimah tells lies about Ibn Abbas."[32] Although Bukhari accepted *aḥādīth* narrated by Ikrimah, Muslim, the other equally important hadith scholar, did not. Thus there is evidence to suggest that Ikrimah was unreliable and that his hadith can be questioned. Admittedly this hadith has several versions, but many are considered "weak."[33] In other words, the authenticity of the hadith most frequently quoted to support the death penalty for apostasy can be placed under considerable suspicion, at least as far as the best known version is concerned. Al-Alwani's examination of it and its different versions is particularly helpful in this regard.[34]

Another issue is that hadith (as *sayings* attributed to the Prophet) used to support his penalty contradict Prophet Muhammad's *actual practice*. Apostasy or conversion out of Islam existed in the Prophet's time. In fact, several Muslims left Islam immediately after his famous "Night Journey" to Jerusalem and then to heaven (known as *isrā'* and *mi'rāj*, respectively): they questioned how the Prophet could go to Jerusalem and return to Makkah in one night when such a journey usually took several weeks. Similarly, some of the Muslims who migrated to Abyssinia when persecution became unbearable became Christians.[35] The Qur'an also makes many references to hypocrisy (*nifāq*) and the hypocrites (*munāfiqūn*) in Madinah who were, for all practical purposes, apostates. Interestingly, none of them were executed. No evidence suggests that the Prophet considered such a punishment or, more importantly, that he actually ordered it applied to those who simply changed their faith.

Assuming that "Whoever changes his religion, kill him" and other similar hadith are reliable and authentic, one must understand the *context* in which the Prophet may have said them. Admittedly some contemporary Muslim scholars object strongly to "context" when interpreting Qur'anic or hadith texts, arguing that the text's dictates should be followed literally.[36] Others argue that understanding the "context" is essential for a proper understanding. Such debates are, of course, nothing new. Classical commentators on the Qur'an, for example, addressed context in a somewhat limited way, such as through the occasions of the revelation (*asbāb al-nuzūl*). Similar limited attempts were made in relation to hadith literature as well. Although jurists considered "context" to some extent, their conception of it was often limited. Modern debates on context, including the socio-historical context, are comparatively sophisticated and are likely to have, in the future, a significant impact on the interpretation of texts like the hadith in question.

Al-Alwani noted that "Whoever changes his religion, kill him," if authentic, was probably associated with a range of conspiracies against Muslims at the time. For example, certain sections of the People of the Book in Madinah were encouraging Muslims to return to their former religions in order to undermine the community. He suggested that these apostates and their associated conspiracies would have provided the specific context for such a saying.[37]

Although this explanation is plausible, the context in which the Prophet and the Muslims were living should be considered as well. The Muslims were based largely in Madinah, and the Prophet was attempting to establish the first Muslim community there despite various internal and external threats to its existence. As far as he was concerned, people were divided into two clear groups: (a) Muslims and their allies from among the People of the Book, and (b) their enemies, largely from outside Madinah. Given that this division was based primarily on one's religious identity, a Muslim who returned to the religion of the "enemy" would be required to leave the community and join the enemy. Conversion would not allow much space in which an ex-Muslim could function as a normal member of the community because at the time one's religious identity was deeply connected to one's political identity. Given the existing state of war, an apostate would also have to take up arms and fight the Muslims. If so, killing an enemy combatant would be perfectly legitimate based on the norms of that time. If the Prophet urged the killing of apostates, the above saying would most likely have been uttered in this context.

One hadith attributed to the Prophet, also considered authentic, is directly linked to this communal division. It refers to those who leave their religion and separate themselves from their community.

> The Prophet, peace be upon him, said: "The blood of a Muslim who confesses that there is no god but Allah and that I am the messenger of Allah, cannot be

> shed except in three cases: a life for life; a married person who commits illegal sexual intercourse; and the one who turns renegade from Islam (apostate) *and leaves the community of Muslims* [author's emphasis]."[38]

Indeed, in their discussions about this hadith, apostasy, and the death penalty, a number of jurists have identified a close connection between leaving Islam and fighting the community. For example, al-Marwadi discussed apostasy in the context of fighting rebels.[39] The Hanafi jurist Sarakhsi (d. 1096) also argued that female apostates should not be put to death because they do not take up arms and fight the community.[40]

The context has changed significantly in our times, however, for in a modern nation-state there does not need to be a conjunction between one's religious identity and political identity. In multi-religious societies like the United States, for example, people of different faiths can live side-by-side and be citizens regardless of their religion. Given the constitutional guarantee of religious freedom, conversion is easy and is not necessarily tantamount to rejecting citizenship.

Problems with the Claim That This Punishment Is Based on Consensus

The second most important argument is the supposed consensus (*ijmā'*) among Muslim jurists for the death penalty.[41] The belief is that if such a consensus exists, then contemporary Muslims have no authority to challenge it. In challenging this argument, three points can be noted.

First, no scholarly consensus about what actually constitutes "consensus" exists. Muslim jurists have proposed many conceptions of it and how it should be reached. Some believe that only the Companions' consensus should be considered authoritative, others believe that it is the consensus of scholars, and still others believe that it is the consensus of the entire Muslim community. Other related issues, such as when and how consensus should take place, are also subject to heated debate and controversy.

Second, even if one accepts that consensus cannot be challenged, there is no consensus on the death penalty for apostasy. Even the Companions did not agree on this. Umar ibn al-Khattab was informed at least once that a provincial governor had killed one or more apostates. He did not support this action; rather, he said that the transgressors should have been fed and imprisoned in the hope that they might return to Islam.[42] Umar did not indicate that the governor had applied a punishment of God and the Prophet. Instead, he distanced himself from what the governor had done. Similarly, two key scholars, Ibrahim al-Nakha'i (d. 726) and Sufyan al-Thawri (d. 778) also advocated that apostates be encouraged to return to Islam forever. This indicates that they envisioned no worldly punishment, and certainly not the death penalty, for apostasy.[43]

Third, there is no agreement on whether the death penalty is a prescribed (*ḥadd*) or discretionary (*ta'zīr*) punishment under Islamic law. While some schools consider it a *ḥadd* punishment, others believe it should be left to the ruler's discretion.[44] These views indicate a lack of consensus about apostasy, even concerning the nature of the punishment. It also raises the question of why jurists supported it so strongly, given the absence of a Qur'anic text, any strong basis for it in the Prophet's actual practice, and the problems with the hadiths used to support it.

The Influence of the Sociopolitical Context

At this stage, it is important to return to the context in which the jurists of the first three Islamic centuries were functioning. Capital punishment was apparently common in early Islam after 660, when the last of the Prophet's first four political successors died. It was particularly apparent under Mu'awiyyah ibn Abi Sufyan (d. 680), Yazid ibn Mu'awiyyah (d. 683), and Abd al-Malik ibn Marwan (d. 705). In fact, under them capital punishment for political crimes seems have to become the norm. For example, when Abd al-Malik sent al-Hajjaj ibn Yusuf (d. 714) in 694 as a governor to pacify the rebellious Iraqis, who were agitating against the state and challenging his authority, al-Hajjaj went to the mosque, summoned the people of Kufa, and told them:

> A lot of turbans and beards are visible here but very soon they are going to be wet with blood. Many heads are present in this assembly, which will soon be chopped off. Amir al-Mu'minin Abdul Malik examined his quiver and selecting the hardest and the most deadly arrow, shot it at you, in other words, he imposed me on you as your ruler. I will remedy all your ills and lack of discipline and straighten you out completely.[45]

This threat to kill any anti-state agitator and challenger of the caliph's authority was addressed to all Muslims, including scholars and the pious. Moreover, numerous reports describe the bloodshed that occurred during and immediately after the Abbasids' rise to power in the mid-eighth century.

This was also the period during which Islamic law was taking shape, *aḥādīth* were being collected, and Islamic disciplines were being developed. Jurists were exploring principles of the law and how they were going to develop it. All of these developments were occurring in an environment in which capital punishment for political crimes was common and often ordered by rulers without the involvement of a judge (*qāḍī*).[46] These jurists would have found it perfectly natural to accept the overall ethos of their time. Of course, they would have been deeply concerned about killing people for political crimes, but they would have considered it natural to take a firm line on issues like apostasy, which they seem to have viewed as a religious and a political crime, and to apply the death penalty.

This was also the period during which Muslims developed the idea that Islam was superior to all other religions, an idea that became particularly evident in the creeds that developed during the fourth, fifth, and sixth Islamic centuries. Scholars saw a need to make a clear separation between Muslims and non-Muslims (including the People of the Book) and to highlight Islam's superiority. This appears to have led to the reasoning that any challenge to its superiority through apostasy would result in dishonoring the Muslims and thus should be punished with death.

Support for Religious Freedom in Islamic Tradition

Rethinking the death penalty should start with what the Qur'an actually has to say: People have free choice in matters of faith. Examples of this include:

> The truth [has now come] from your Sustainer: let, then, him who wills, believe in it, and let him who wills, reject it (Q. 18:29)

and,

> Whoever chooses to follow the right path, follows it but for his own good; and whoever goes astray, goes but astray to his own hurt; and no bearer of burdens shall be made to bear another's burden. (Q. 17:15)

These verses affirm that accountability is personal and individual as opposed to a group, community, or state matter.

According to the Qur'an, everyone will stand alone before God on the Day of Judgment, a day on which every person will be concerned only with oneself. The Qur'an even reminded the Prophet that he was not responsible for the decisions of others:

> To me [shall be accounted] my doing, and to you, your doings: you are not accountable for what I am doing, and I am not accountable for whatever you do. (Q. 10:41)

Forced conversions are therefore counter to the Qur'anic understanding of personal freedom. The Qur'anic verses "There is no coercion in matters of faith" and "whoever wants to believe, believe" negate the very idea of coercion.

Strong historical evidence also supports the tolerance of religious or theological difference. As noted earlier, history has produced many examples of Muslims who refused to follow the orthodox line and of non-Muslims who refused to enter Islam. It appears that Muslims generally left such people alone and tolerated them. More importantly, little evidence exists to support the idea that past Muslim governments were concerned about this penalty or had implemented it on a large scale, despite the fact that apostasy has always existed. Only a relatively few high-profile cases of alleged apostasy are widely known (e.g., the case of the mystic Mansur al-Hallaj [d. 922] and the Mughal prince Dara Shikoh [d. 1659]). Often one can see that political considerations were behind such cases, with the label of "apostasy" given to justify the killing. The core concern of many Muslim governments was to ensure their population's stability and manageability, and at times they used the law of apostasy to remove those who they perceived as threats to these goals, rather than simply because of their alleged apostasy.

Conclusion

Given the difficulties associated with the issues surrounding the meaning, authenticity, and context of the texts under discussion, it is important to take into account certain considerations and principles when reading those texts that have a bearing on our understanding of religious freedom.

First, the Shari'ah's broader objectives (*maqāṣid al-Sharī'ah*) may need to be redefined and reworked to be suitable for our contemporary context. Indeed, as protecting religion is one of its objectives, this concept should be broadened to include understandings of religious freedom that fit contemporary expectations. Second, there is a need to retain a clear sense of the hierarchy of texts. The Qur'an must remain the first authority, followed by the Hadith literature, not the other way around. Third, although a linguistic analysis of texts provides a starting point for understanding their meaning, this should not be the end of the process. Many jurists and scholars have only analyzed key texts linguistically and undertaken no further analysis, an approach that perhaps causes them to miss important messages contained in the text. Clearly, understanding why the Qur'anic and hadith texts exist plays an important role in our understanding of them. The broader social, historical, intellectual, and cultural contexts in which they were revealed or produced can be taken into account when trying to determine their meaning.

Fourth, there is a need to critically evaluate the hadiths' chains of transmission to determine their reliability. Equally important is that the texts' proposed meanings must make sense, be reasonable, and be based on what we know about the Prophet. Fifth, the difficulties associated with consensus suggest caution when determining the meaning based on any claims of consensus in the Islamic legal tradition.

There are many other reasons why the law of apostasy (including the death penalty) should be reconsidered: It is counterproductive and serves no useful religious, spiritual, ethical, or moral purpose; it reduces belief and religion to a political act that is devoid of spirituality; it generates religious hypocrisy wherever it is enforced; it kills Muslim creativity; and it allows authoritarian regimes to support establishments that curtail Muslims' intellectual and political freedom and their ability to discuss vital Islamic issues all in the name of protecting Islam. Such restrictions conflict with contemporary understandings of universal human rights and damage the reputation of both Islam and Muslims. They also conflict with the conception of religious freedom rooted in the Qur'an, one that was proclaimed 1,400 years ago, well before the UDHR.

Endnotes

1. Article 18, Universal Declaration of Human Rights. Adopted by the UN General Assembly on December 10, 1948. Available at http://www.un.org/en/documents /udhr/.
2. Yohanan Friedmann, *Tolerance and Coercion in Islam: Interfaith Relations in the Muslim Tradition* (Cambridge: Cambridge University Press, 2003), 73-74.
3. Humanistic texts, "al-Ma'arri," n.d., http://www.humanistictexts.org/al_ma% 27arri.htm.
4. Ibid.
5. Hamza Yusuf, *The Creed of Imam Al-Tahawi* (Berkely: Zaytuna Institute, 2007), 64.
6. Ibid., 68.
7. Ibid.
8. Khalid Baig, "On Religious Tolerance" (April 27, 2001), http://articles.youngmuslims. ca/outreach-and-invitation/on-religious-tolerance/.
9. "Cairo Declaration on Human Rights in Islam," adopted at the Islamic Conference of Foreign Ministers, Cairo, 1990, http://www.unhcr.org/refworld/publisher, ARAB,,,3ae6b3822c,0.html.
10. Sayyid Qutb, *Fī Ẓilāl al-Qur'ān* (Cairo: Dar al-Shuruq, 1996), 1:291.

11. See B. J. Grim, "God's Economy: Religious Freedom and Socio-Economic Wellbeing," in *Religious Freedom in the World*, ed. P. Marshall (Lanham, MD: Rowman and Littlefield Publishers, 2008), http://crf.hudson.org/articledocs/Gods Economy.doc.
12. Ibid.
13. Theodore Malloch, "Free to Choose: Economics and Religion" (paper presented at the World Trends in Religious Freedom conference, the Hudson Institute, July 9, 2007), http://crf.hudson.org/articledocs/FreetoChoose.doc, p. 1.
14. Baig, "On Religious Tolerance."
15. Reservation lodged with the Secretary-General on December 4, 2006 by Bahrain, following its accession to the Covenant on September 20, 2006. See "United Nations Treaty Collection, Status of Ratifications: International Covenant on Civil and Political Rights (2011)," http://treaties.un.org/Pages/ViewDetails.aspx?src=TREATY&mtdsg_no=IV-4&chapter=4& lang=en.
16. Ibid.
17. Ann Elizabeth Mayer, *Islam and Human Rights: Tradition and Politics* (Boulder: Westview Press, 1991), 164. See also the discussions in Johannes Morsink, *The Universal Declaration of Human Rights: Origins, Drafting, and Intent*, (Philadelphia: Pennsylvania University Press, 1999), 24-25 .
18. Taha Jabir al-Alwani, *Lā Ikrāha fī al-Dīn*, 2d ed. (Herndon, VA: International Institute of Islamic Thought, 2006), 12.
19. See news reports, e.g., "Death Sentence for Killer of Pakistan Governor," ABC News, October 1, 2011.
20. Abd al-Rahman al-Jaziri, *Min Kitāb al-Fiqh 'alā al-Madhāhib al-Arbā'ah* (Beirut: Dar al-Fikr, n.d.), 5:422-23; Wahbah al-Zuhayli, *Al-Fiqh al-Islāmī wa Adillātuhu* (Damascus: Dar al-Fikr, 1997), 6:184; Abu Bakr al-Jaza'iri, *Minhāj al-Muslim* (Cairo: Maktabat al-Kulliyat al-Azhariyyah, 1979), 535.
21. Zuhayli, *Al-Fiqh al-Islāmī*, 6:183; Jaza'iri, *Minhāj al-Muslim*, 535; Jaziri, *Min Kitāb al-Fiqh*, 5:422-27.
22. Abu Muhammad Ali ibn Ahmad ibn Sa'id ibn Hazm, *Al-Muḥallā*, ed. Ahmad Muhammad Shakir (Cairo: Maktabat Dar al-Turath, n.d), 11:408-16.
23. Subasi, "The Apostasy Question," 2. (Citing S. M. Zwemer, *The Law of Apostasy in Islam* [London: 1924].)
24. Mohammad Hashim Kamali, *Freedom of Expression in Islam* (United Kingdom: The Islamic Texts Society, 1997), 91.
25. Mohamed Selim El-Awa, *Punishment in Islamic Law* (Indianapolis: American Trust Publications, 1982), 54-55.
26. Kamali, *Freedom of Expression*, 91. Citing Mahmud Shaltut, *Al-Islām: 'Aqīdah wa Sharī'ah* (Kuwait: Matabi' Dar al-Qalam, n.d.), 292-93; Nu'man Abd al-Raziq al-Samara'i, *Aḥkām al-Murtadd fī al-Sharī'ah al-Islāmīyah* (Beirut: Dar al-Arabiyyah, 1968), 114.
27. Rudolph Peters and Gert J. J. de Vries, "Apostasy in Islam," *Die Welt des Islams*, New Series 17, no. 1 (1976-77): 14.

28. Abu al-Abbas Shihab al-Din Ahmad al-Qastallani, *Irshād al-Sārī lā Ṣharḥ Saḥīḥ al-Bukhārī* (Beirut: Dar al-Fikr, 1990), 14:396.
29. See relevant sections in Muhammad Baltaji, *Manāhij al-Tashrī' al-Islāmī fī al-Qarn al-Thānī al-Hijrī* (Cairo: Dar al-Salam, 2004).
30. Imam Muhammad ibn Idris al-Shafi'i, *Al-Risālah fī Uṣūl al-Fiqh* (Treatise on the Foundations of Islamic Jurisprudence), tr. Majid Khadduri (Cambridge: The Islamic Texts Society, 2008), 67.
31. Al-Alwani, *Lā Ikrāha*, 123.
32. Ibid., 127.
33. Ibid.
34. Ibid., 123-39.
35. Ibid., 101-04.
36. Abdullah Saeed, *Interpreting the Qur'an: Towards a Contemporary Approach* (Abingdon: Routledge, 2006), 116-25.
37. Al-Alwani, *Lā Ikrāha*, 118.
38. Bukhari, *Saḥīḥ al-Bukhārī: The Translation of the Meanings of Saḥīḥ al-Bukhārī*, Arabic-English trans. Muhammad Muhsin Khan, rev. ed. (Ankara: Hilal Yayinlari, 1976), 1012. Also see Abdullah Saeed and Hassan Saeed, *Freedom of Religion, Apostasy, and Islam* (Aldershot, UK: Ashgate Publishing, 2004), 59.
39. Al-Mawardi, *The Ordinances of Government*, tr. Wafaa H. Wahba (Reading, UK: Garnet Publishing, 1996), 60-71.
40. Muhammad ibn Ahmad al-Sarkhasi, *Al-Mabsūṭ* (Beirut: Dar al-Ma'rifah, n.d), 10:109.
41. See relevant sections in Baltaji, *Manāhij al-Tashrī' al-Islāmī.*
42. See the discussion in Mahmoud Ayoub, "Religious Freedom and the Law of Apostasy in Islam," *Islamochristian = Islāmīyat Masīḥīyat* 20 (1994): 75-91.
43. Kamali, *Freedom of Expression*, 91.
44. Saeed and Saeed, *Freedom*, 56. Citing al-Jaziri, *Min Kitāb al-Fiqh*, 5:8.
45. Akbar Shah Najeebabadi, *History of Islam* (Riyadh: Dar al-Salam, 2001), 2:154.
46. Saeed and Saeed, *Freedom*, 67.

Bibliography

Alwani, Taha Jabir al-. *Lā Ikrāha fī al-Dīn*. 2d ed. Herndon, VA: International Institute of Islamic Thought. 2006.

Australian Broadcasting Corporation. "Death Sentence for Killer of Pakistan Governor." ABC News, October 1 , 2011.

Ayoub, Mahmoud. "Religious Freedom and the Law of Apostasy in Islam." *Islamochristian = Islāmīyat Masīḥīyat* 20, (1994): 75-91.

Baig, Khalid. "On Religious Tolerance," April 27, 2001, http://articles.youngmuslims.ca/outreach-and-invitation/on-religious-tolerance, accessed October 17, 2011.

Baltaji, Muhammad. *Manāhij al-Tashrī' al-Islāmī fī al-Qarn al-Thānī al-Hijrī*. Cario: Dar al-Salam, 2004

Bukhari. *Ṣaḥīḥ al-Bukhārī: The Translation of the Meanings of Ṣaḥīḥ al-Bukhārī, Arabic-English trans*. Translated by Muhammad Muhsin Khan, rev. edn. Ankara: Hilal Yayinlari, 1976.

El-Awa, Mohamed Selim. *Punishment in Islamic Law*. Indianapolis: American Trust Publications, 1982.

Friedmann, Yohanan. *Tolerance and Coercion in Islam: Interfaith Relations in the Muslim Tradition*. Cambridge: Cambridge University Press, 2003.

Griffel, Frank. "Toleration and Exclusion: Al-Shāfiʻī and al-Ghazālī on the Treatment of Apostates." *Bulletin of the School of Oriental and African Studies* 64, no. 3 (2001).

Grim, B. J. "God's Economy: Religious Freedom and Socio-Economic Wellbeing." In P. Marshall (ed.) *Religious Freedom in the World*. Lanham, MD: Rowman and Littlefield Publishers, 2008, http://crf.hudson.org/articledocs/GodsEconomy.doc, accessed 17 October 2011.

Humanistic texts, "al-Maʻarri," n.d., http://www.humanistictexts.org/al_ma%27arri.htm, accessed October 17, 2011.

Ibn Hazm, Abu Muhammad Ali b. Ahmad b. Saʻid. *Al-Muḥallā*. ed. Ahmad Muhammad Shakir. vol. 11. Cairo: Maktabat Dar al-Turath, n.d.

Islamic Conference of Foreign Ministers, Cairo Declaration on Human Rights in Islam. Adopted at the Islamic Conference of Foreign Ministers, Cairo, 1990, http://www.unhcr.org/refworld/publisher,ARAB,,,3ae6b3822c,0.html, accessed October 17, 2011.

Jaza'iri, Abu Bakr al-. *Minhāj al-Muslim*. Cairo: Maktabat al-Kulliyat al-Azhariyyah, 1979.

Jaziri, Abd al-Rahman al-. *Min Kitāb al-Fiqh ʻalā al-Madhāhib al-Arbāʻah*. Beirut: Dar al-Fikr, n.d.

Kamali, Mohammad Hashim. *Freedom of Expression in Islam*. Kuala Lumpur: Berita Publishing, 1994.

Kohler, Kaufmann and Richard Gottheil. "Apostasy and Apostates from Judaism," n.d., http://www.jewishencyclopedia.com/view.jsp?artid=1654&letter=A#ixzz1b05oQpva, accessed October 17, 2011.

Malloch, Theodore. "Free to Choose: Economics and Religion." Paper presented at the World Trends in Religious Freedom conference, Hudson Institute, July 9, 2007, http://crf.hudson.org/articledocs/FreetoChoose. doc, accessed October 17, 2011.

Mawardi, al-. *The Ordinances of Government*. Trans. Wafaa H Wahba. Reading: Garnet Publishing, 1996.

Mayer, Ann Elizabeth. *Islam and Human Rights: Tradition and Politics*. Boulder: Westview Press, 1991.

Morsink, Johannes. *The Universal Declaration of Human Rights: Origins, Drafting, and Intent*. Philadelphia: Pennsylvania University Press, 1999.

Najeebabadi, Akbar Shah. *History of Islam*, vol. 2. Riyadh: Darussalam, 2001.

Peters, Rudolph, and Gert J. J. De Vries. "Apostasy in Islam." *Die Welt des Islams*, New Series, 17, 1/4, 1976-1977.

Qastallani, Abu al-Abbas Shihab al-Din Ahmad al-. *Irshād al-Sārī lā Sharḥ Saḥīḥ al-Bukhārī*. Beirut: Dar al-Fikr, 1990.

Qutb, Sayyid. *Fī Ẓilāl al-Qur'ān*. vol 1. Cairo: Dar al-Shuruq, 1996.

Saeed, Abdullah and Hassan Saeed. *Freedom of Religion, Apostasy, and Islam*. Aldershot: Ashgate Publishing, 2004.

Saeed, Abdullah. *Interpreting the Qur'an: Towards a Contemporary Approach*. Abingdon: Routledge, 2006

Samara'i, Nu'man Abd al-Raziq al-. *Aḥkām al-Murtadd fī al-Sharī'ah al-Islāmīyah*. Beirut: Dar al-Arabiyyah, 1968.

Sarakhsi, Muhammad b. Ahmad al-. *Al-Mabsūṭ*. Beirut: Dar al-Ma'rifah, n.d.

Shafi'i, Imam Muhammad b. Idris al-. *Al-Risālah fī Uṣūl al-Fiqh* (*Treatise on the Foundations of Islamic Jurisprudence*). Translated by Majid Khadduri, Cambridge: The Islamic Texts Society, 2008.

Shaltut, Mahmud. *Al-Islām: 'Aqīdah wa Sharī'ah*. Kuwait: Matabi' Dar al-Qalam, n.d.

Subasi, Turgut. "The Apostasy Question in the Context of Anglo-Ottoman Relations 1843-44." *Middle Eastern Studies* 38, no. 2 (2002).

United Nations Treaty Collection. "Status of Ratifications: International Covenant on Civil and Political Rights." http://treaties.un.org/Pages/ViewDetails.aspx?src=TREATY&mtdsg_no=IV-4&chapter=4&lang=en, accessed October 17, 2011.

United Nations General Assembly. "Universal Declaration of Human Rights. Adopted by the UN General Assembly 10 December 1948." http://www.un.org/en/documents/udhr/, accessed October 17, 2011.

Zuhayli, Wahbah al-. *Al-Fiqh al-Islāmī wa Adillatuhu*, vol. 6, Damascus: Dar al-Fikr, 1997.

Zwemer, S. M. *The Law of Apostasy in Islam*. London, 1924.

General Discussion

- Some people are forced to feign apostasy: "except for him who is coerced but his heart is full of faith" (Q. 16:106). *Lā ikrāha fī dīn* was revealed in the following context: A young man was converted by some Christian oil merchants from Syria. His father asked the Prophet if he would be held accountable for not preventing this event. The hadith in question is Abbasid propaganda against the Alawis and should not be considered a hadith at all. The alternative hadith gives only three cases in which capital punishment is authorized; moreover, it does not use any cognate of *riddah*.
- The Uraynah tribe is a complicating factor. Were they killed for apostasy or *ḥirābah* (war on society)? Bukhari has a chapter on *ḥirābah* but not on *riddah*. There is also the following account: Mu'adh ibn Jabal once found a Jew who had converted to Islam and then apostatized. He insisted that this person should be killed on the spot. Umar ruled that he should have been given three days to repent and then be killed if he did not do so.

- What is the downside of religious freedom? Most of the Ten Commandments are religious prescriptions that limit religious freedom. For Evangelists, religious freedom means the right to proselytize anywhere in the world.
- Zaffarullah Khan was Pakistan's representative during the debate on the declaration of human rights. Jamil Barudi, a Lebanese Christian, represented Saudi Arabia.
- In her Freiberg Lecture, Patricia Crone said that Muslims love to talk about these things but have yet to implement them.
- Rather than speculate on why the jurists accepted this hadith, we should ask what they are trying to achieve when they incorporate it into their *fiqh*.
- The Qur'an is clear about God's punishment of apostasy on the Day of Judgment. The only question is whether it is punishable by people in this life.
- Umar used to beat an unrepentant alcoholic who converted to Christianity. Later on he exiled him. The man joined the Byzantine army, and Umar swore he would no longer exile people. Thus there is no doubt that he was defending the death penalty against traitors.
- Having the freedom to convert is better than encouraging hypocrisy. This was the case in Madinah, and the Prophet is the best example for us.
- Both Shafi'i and Maliki jurists said this hadith is vague, as it seems to require killing Christians who become Muslims. We need to address the other hadith, because it does suggest that an apostate could be killed.
- The Prophet punished treason rather than apostasy.
- A new book by IIIT on authenticating hadith may be very helpful. Bukhari focused only on the chains of transmission, which at that time was the primary concern.
- Historically, the hadith were peripheral compared to the emphasis we find today.
- Bukhari and Muslim are really *fiqh* manuals organized topically.
- There was a hadith movement in early Islam with tension between its adherents and other jurists, but over time they came to dominate. The question is the confusion between hadith and Sunnah.
- The distinction between hadith and Sunnah was addressed in a previous IIIT summer institute. Imam Malik was concerned with the living Sunnah, the practice of the people of Madinah, rather than with hadith *per se*. His book is not one of the *Sittah* (viz., the six Sunni hadith collections).
- How should legislators in Muslim countries deal with converts to Christianity who become propagandists against Islam?
- What do we think about hegemonic discourses? How do questions of religious freedom connect with geopolitical concerns?
- Was the punishment for *riddah* or for actions by the apostates, not just as combatants, but as spies?
- A hypocrite makes a better spy than an apostate.
- There is a hadith that the blood of Muslims can be spilled in only three cases: a married person who commits adultery, a murderer, and one who forsakes his religion and the community to take up arms against Allah. There are two categories

of those who forsake Islam: one who is born Muslim and a convert. The Zaydis believe that both classes should be killed immediately; however, the Ibadis say the woman must be sentenced to life in prison so that she might repent.

- Although the so-called *riddah* wars are used as evidence for killing apostates, it is a misnomer. Umar disagreed with Abu Bakr's decision to fight these wars, for some rebels were renegades while others were simply tax resisters.
- We love freedom of religion when we are the minority, less so when we are the majority. Without religious freedom, the authorities control everything in the name of religion; however, the advice that the Prophet received from God was only to communicate His message. Reciprocity and freedom of belief should be for all.
- Contemporary debates are colored by how Muslims see their position vis-à-vis the rest of the world. It is about our pride, not just simply a theological or legal matter. It was heavily political even in the historical debates.
- Apostasy may well be about treason or other political acts, particularly in the early period of Madinah, but not so much later on.
- Imam Malik distinguishes the Sunnah from hadith in clear terms. Shafi'i takes the hadith as the clear statement of the Sunnah.
- The Qur'an uses the term *īmān* for belief and makes a clear distinction from Islam. This is about freedom. The lack of freedom is the problem we confront in the Muslim world.

Shuratic *Iftā'*: The Challenge of Fatwa Collectivization

Imad-ad-Dean Ahmad

Abstract

One of the primary challenges to the process of juristic development in the modern world is the specialization of knowledge, for this has made the issuance of legal opinions more difficult than ever before. Among this challenge's contributing factors are the amount of data available, the sophistication required to understand it, the variations in the cultural contexts in which juristic decisions are applied, the jurists' increasing distance from the original languages and contexts of the textual sources, and the complexity of the social conditions in which the decisions are to be applied. A new methodology has been suggested: collectivizing the process of issuing fatwas. The argument has been made that since no single scholar can master all of the knowledge necessary to arrive at a decision on a number of pressing issues, some mechanism of collective *iftā'* is necessary.

We consider this argument, as well as some objections and obstacles to it. We suggest that rather than developing a totally new collective methodology, we combine the traditional concept of *shūrā* (consultation) with the modern scientific methodologies of peer review and new developments in online communication. This approach will allow us to implement techniques that take advantage of the latest technological and scientific developments to preserve the fundamental principles of juridical development. This process supplements the classical texts with the discoveries of scientific inquiry, provides a way to include social and physical scientists along with scholars of traditional disciplines, restores the separation between state and scholarship of early Islamic society, and avoids the sectarianization of institutions. After discussing how the results can be made available to civil and political society, we illustrate the issue by examining such particularly difficult contemporary issues as calendar reform and embryonic stem cell research.

Introduction

In the classical era of Islamic jurisprudence – from the rise of the Abbasids to the fall of Andalusia – the best scholars were those who not only possessed the keen intellect required for clear original and analytical reasoning, but who had a broad general knowledge of each field that might bear on their legal reasoning. The rate of developing new knowledge has risen exponentially in recent centuries, and there has been a dearth of "Renaissance men" since, well, the Renaissance. Today, specialists who master the intricate details of particular fields of knowledge far outnumber those who have a broad general knowledge. And even the best of these latter scholars can specialize in a few fields at most, and thus must rely on other specialists for detailed knowledge of other fields. This extreme specialization, a hallmark of modernity, poses one of the primary challenges to juristic development today and makes the issuance of legal opinions (*iftā'*) more difficult than ever before.

Some suggest that since no single scholar can possibly possess all of the knowledge needed for engaging in *ijtihād* on issues that require significant technical knowledge in specialized fields, we must develop a new methodology for collectivized *iftā'*. This paper explores the arguments for fatwa collectivization, the particular challenges faced while formulating this collectivization, and solutions to overcome the ensuing obstacles and objections. While no one person can master all the fields of knowledge existing today, anyone engaged in *iftā'* in any capacity must have a basic understanding of many disciplines, among them research methodology, textual analysis, and the physical and social sciences.

Historical Perspective

We do not intend to engage in a detailed historical review, but rather to present a brief summary with some highlights that may put the problem into a historical perspective. We will then consider how circumstances have changed and what modifications of the existing methodology are necessary.

As always, it is best to begin by defining our terms. A *fatwa* is a non-binding legal opinion, and *iftā'* is the process of issuing such opinions. The resulting legal opinion must be distinguished from the binding legal judgment (*qaḍā*) issued by a judge (*qāḍī*). The judge is concerned with legal disputes, while the mufti provides jurisconsultation on issues ranging from ritual to family relations to political questions. The mufti, who implements the *iftā'* and issues the fatwa, may be of two kinds: (1) a *mujtahid*, one who is qualified to engage in original legal thought and issue fatwas, based on his/her own reasoning, derived from the sources of Islamic law, and (2) one who is not qualified to that extent, but who is well-versed in the analysis of the earlier *mujtahids* (a *muqallad*) and thus must cite the sources for his/her fatwa.[1]

Interestingly, some of the issues with which contemporary *iftā'* deals have been present from the earliest times, including "fatwa shopping" and evaluating the mufti's competence.[2] As the overwhelming majority of such opinions were delivered orally, there is no record of them.[3] This is not a problem, however, because most of them dealt with routine non-controversial matters and were prompted only by the fact that the questioners' low level of literacy prevented them from looking up the answers themselves. In such an environment, the paucity of the written record posed no problem.[4] While issues of *fiqh* and *iftā'* overlap, the former's development is distinguished by its formal systematic evolution. *Iftā'*, which is directed at answering particular real-world inquiries, is often unrecorded.

Over the centuries, changes in the environment (political and scholarly at first, and then technological) altered the institutions of *iftā'*: "Before the eleventh century CE a *muftî* was simply someone who issued fatwas, knowledge and recognition by the scholarly community were the only prerequisites for a muftî. Beginning in the eleventh century a public office of *muftî* was affixed to the private vocation of *iftā'*."[5] This office became increasingly politicized until, under the Ottomans, the chief mufti, the "*shaykh al-Islām* [was] appointed and dismissed only by the Sultan," who "depended on the secular authority [of] the qāḍîs to execute his judgments."[6]

Over the last couple of centuries, muftis have increasingly asserted a right not to be bound by *taqlīd* to earlier fatwas. Further, the administrative structures of the colonial powers and the subsequent postcolonial regimes' usurpation of *iftā*'s functionality shifted the muftis' focus from questions of daily life to areas of "anti-colonial resistance and … the struggle for national independence."[7] Muftis must now wrestle with the challenges posed by various aspects of modernity as well.

At the same time, there has been an exponential rise in the amount of human knowledge and in the degree of specialization in the proliferating fields of knowledge. How can a mufti answer a question about medical ethics, for example, if he has no grasp of the medical issues involved and no comprehension of the discourse of ethicists within the medical profession? If he has no familiarity with the available technical information and none of the sophistication required to understand it, he must either make wild guesses or accept the advice of technical advisors. But these advisors, in turn, may have no familiarity with the Qur'an and Sunnah. Those of us living in the West are confronted with additional problems: immigrant and/or foreign muftis who are unfamiliar with the cultural context in which their juristic decisions are to be applied. Throughout the world, problems are posed by the jurists' increasing distance from the textual sources' original languages and contexts, as well as by the complex social conditions in which their rulings are to be implemented.

Obstacles and Objections to Collectivization

Some have posited that many of the problems alluded to above may be addressed by collectivizing *iftā'*. Since no single scholar can master all of the knowledge necessary to formulate a realistic and appropriate ruling, some mechanism of collective *iftā'* has been declared necessary. Let's consider these arguments, along with some objections and obstacles.

Setting aside for the moment what these mechanisms might be, let's consider the abstract benefits of having multiple participants in the process. How are more heads better than one? By allowing multiple parties to collaborate in the decision, the group engaged in *iftā'* benefits from the complementarity of its members' knowledge. Medical researchers with no knowledge of Qur'anic Arabic, Arab grammarians with no knowledge of medicine, bioethicists unschooled in Islamic history, political theorists with no knowledge of hadith, and classically trained Islamic legal scholars who have no experience in modern scientific research can compensate for one another's weaknesses. Such collaboration can also provide a context for each other's contributions in addressing particular problems that might, in theory, be resolved by a hypothetical al-Azhar graduate in Islamic studies who had won the Nobel prize in medicine, had such a person existed.

Attractive as this fantasy may be, serious objections arise when we try to imagine the most appropriate mechanism. Let's imagine that a committee has been appointed to deal with embryonic stem cell research. Let's ignore the problems posed by its size. For the sake of argument, let's assume that every conceivable relevant discipline is represented. If the committee members form a deliberative body modeled on a Parliament, how will their relative areas of strength be integrated into the deliberative and decision-making processes? Qualified *mujtahid*s will object to giving any role whatsoever to medical technicians and would relegate them to the status of non-voting advisors to be consulted for technical information. Medical experts may well feel that their insights are not sufficiently understood by religious legal experts, who are incapable of integrating them into a coherent fatwa.

Another problem we must confront is the scope of such committees' mission. Is their mandate revolutionary or evolutionary? Are they to weave an entirely new understanding of the Shari'ah, one that would replace the old *fiqhī* schools? Are they required to hew as closely as possible to precedent and thus merely tweak old fatwas by the smallest quanta necessary to meet the challenges posed by the questions asked? For example, when a resident of Vancouver (Canada) complains that the old fatwas on when to begin and end fasting cannot be implemented because the classic definitions of *ishā'* and *fajr* times do not obtain, should he/she be told to break the fast at the local maghrib time (8:17 p.m. on Ramadan 1 of this year) and similarly a resident of the Hague be told to begin to fast at dawn time at the Hague of 2:03 a.m.? Or should everyone at his/her longitude adopt the *maghrib* and *fajr* times of the latitude of Makkah, 6:50 p.m. and 4:22 a.m., respectively?

Modes of Collectivization

When we consider how to collectivize a traditionally individualized process, we should begin by identifying the two modes of collectivization that may be brought to bear: the "parliamentary mode" and the "academic research mode" of interaction among the members of the collective.

In the parliamentary mode, those identified as participants engage in a formalized debate on such questions as may be put to them by proposing fatwas. As is customary for such debates, each proposal's merits are discussed; amendments are put forward and considered; and votes are taken on the proposed amendments, substitute amendments, modifications, alterations, and so on until a majority (or some super majority), as may be required, can agree upon its final form.

Such an approach, however, has enormous drawbacks. As mentioned above, there will be a debate as to who is entitled to vote in such a discussion. Some members of the deliberative body will be more equal than others, in the sense that the latter may be allowed to participate but not to vote. While formulating amendments, political compromises may be made and the final fatwa may be a hybrid that is fully endorsed by few, if any, of the constituent body's members. However, it is the only end product that the parliamentary process can formulate. In other words, what should be a legal process will be politicized. The similarity of such a method to parliamentary legislation evokes the famous dictum that those who like legislation, like those who like sausage, should never see it being made.

The alternative mode, that of academic research, calls for the *mujtahid* to develop his/her opinion in an iterative fashion and then submit it for expert review at each iteration. It is subjected to peer review at every step, and the relevant suggestions are incorporated into the next iteration. Further, the publication of such fatwas allows competitors to publish alternative fatwas informed by the work of their peers. The drawbacks to this mode are that it is slow and does not guarantee that competing fatwas will be dropped. I think that these drawbacks are an acceptable price to pay for a process that promises to match the success of modern scientific research (which is also slow and often results in competing models) in arriving at the truth. One must recall that competing fatwas are a common feature in Islamic history. Those who require an instant fatwa may have to be content with an individualized fatwa and forgo the advantages of collectivization.

A Proposed Mechanism

Rather than develop a totally new collective methodology, we suggest combining the traditional concept of *shūrā* with the modern scientific methodologies of peer review and the new developments in online communication. Such an approach will enable us to implement techniques that take advantage of the latest technological and scientific developments to preserve the fundamental principles of juridical development. This process supplements the classical texts with the discoveries of scientific inquiry, provides a way to include social and physical scientists along with scholars of traditional disciplines, restores the separation between state and scholarship of early Islamic society, and avoids the sectarianization of institutions.

I use OCI to signify an *online collaborative iftā'* to designate this proposed method, for it combines academic research with the expert review capabilities of the latest technology, while preserving the benefits of an evolutionary approach that remains linked to traditional methods. The wiki technology, best known for its implementation in Wikipedia, is a popular method of online collaboration. The work of an initial drafter is published online, after which approved collaborators can alter and/or add to it. But this approach is plagued by "thrashing," defined as people who hold different perspectives repeatedly changing one another's material. Therefore, I do not propose it as a viable OCI method. My proposal is closer to what is called a "collaborative Q&A site," such as those powered by the online technology known as stackoverflow.[8]

An OCI site can be established, and the general public can post questions for which they desire a fatwa. The resulting responses of first-draft fatwas will be posted to a closed audience of reviewers, and then revised by authorized peers and commented upon by a broader circle of experts who can comment upon (but not change) the posted text. Once a fatwa has been refined and assumed its final form, it will be available to the general public for reading and further comments. Nothing in this model prevents competing fatwas from being published in response to a single inquiry. Although mechanisms for combing or reconciling such fatwas could be put in place, the possibility of admitting multiple solutions (even if mutually exclusive) must be retained if we are to avoid sectarianism. If, for example, there is a Sunni and a Shi'i answer to a particular inquiry, there is no reason not to publish both of them. The traditions to which they belong would be clearly identified in order to help non-experts select one of them.

Writers for the initial draft may either be *mujtahid*s who have some knowledge of the technical areas of expertise in the question, or technical experts who have some familiarity with the traditional texts on related issues. Commentators and editors may base their comments and amendments on technical, *maqāṣidī*, or traditional considerations, since it is desirable that the final product consider all of these. As with scientific peer review, those who issue fatwas need to fully consider all possible criticisms, although they may rebut any of them as well. As much of the debate over controversial points would be retained in the final fatwa, as is historically found in a well-written classical fatwa, all fatwas would conclude with *Allāhu a'lam* (God knows best).

Implementing this proposal will require cooperating teams of computer programmers and an administrative board to screen and appoint the fatwa writers, editors, and consulting experts. Propagating the results is built into the mechanism itself, as the Internet provides its own propagation. Such civil society institutions as mosques and Islamic federations can be motivated to use the resulting fatwa by giving them a role in the recruitment and administrative process. Muslim businesses can be invited to advertise on the site, thereby giving them an incentive to implement it in their operations. It is essential, however, that the academic integrity of the selection and review process be maintained. Constitutional safeguards must be in place in order to insulate operations from corruption (e.g., an advertiser seeking a fatwa favorable to a halal designation for a particular food or financial product). The prescription for such safeguards is beyond the scope of this paper.

Illustrated Applications

Calendar Reform

The Fiqh Council of North America (FCNA) has attempted to reform the Islamic calendar via the parliamentary mode of collective *iftā'*. One almost successful effort during June 2006 involved the official council members consulting with three non-member scientists: an engineer, a nuclear physicist, and an astronomer. These consultants presented their individual competing proposals for how to define the date of the *hilāl* crescent and were questioned by FCNA members. In turn, as these members made their *iftā'* arguments the scientists were allowed to comment and question them. A vote was taken to adopt the astronomer's proposal, the "Uniform Islamic Calendar for the Western Hemisphere" (UIC),[9] that the date of the new month be based on the convention of the astronomical new moon before sunset at Makkah.

However, within forty-eight hours FCNA reversed itself, out of session, and adopted the proposal of the nuclear physicist, who had privately lobbied its members after the session had ended. This called for adopting the convention of the new moon's birth at noon GMT, which would result in a one-day delay in the start of the Islamic month in about one case out of eight. The official position given on the FCNA website says only that "to determine a lunar Islamic calendar, a conventional point of reference must be used. The International Date Line (IDL) or the Greenwich Mean Time (GMT) may be used."[10] The very next year it changed its position again and adopted the European Council for Fatwa and Research's (ECFR) position: The conjunction must take place before sunset in Makkah *and* the moon must set after sunset in Makkah. This allowed the date to be one day *earlier* than that of the UIC about one time in eight, and, as regards FCNA's previous position, about one time in four.[11]

The above history reveals the politicization of *iftā'* to which a parliamentary approach is susceptible. The continual changing of position, not to mention the frequent failure to follow one's own fatwa (too well-known to require citation here), are among the problems of such an approach. How might events have unfolded if an OCI had been employed? A fatwa based on the UIC could have been the original draft, with the comments, questions, and criticisms of the consulting scientists and FCNA members annotated and debated online with the proposal's ongoing evolution. After this, it could have coalesced into a final form or, failing convergence, into two or three variations. It seems to me that even in the event of divergence, it is unlikely that we would have ended up with more than the three positions described above or that the evolution would have taken more than the five years that have passed since that original FCNA meeting in 2006 to arrive at the vague statement on the FCNA website cited above.

Embryonic Stem Cell Research

The Shi'i position on embryonic stem cell research is well established,[12] and research in Iran on the subject is reportedly well underway.[13] The American Muslim community was still wrestling with this issue as recently as 2010, when the Islamic Institute "convened a panel of experts, in cooperation with the Fiqh Council of North America (FCNA), the North American Council of Islamic Jurisprudence, the Graduate School of Islamic and Social Sciences (GSISS), and the International Institute of Islamic Thought (IIIT) ... consisting of medical doctors, scientists, and Islamic scholars" to deliberate "all aspects of this topic at length, in order to develop an Islamic perspective on stem-cell research."[14] Their conclusion was that such research is permissible, subject to certain conditions; however, they concluded: "It is an Islamic opinion subject to further enhancements in the case of scientific developments unknown to us at this time."[15]

An OCI could have started by stating the Shi'a position and allowing the consultants participating in the FCNA conference to make whatever comments and changes they wished. The unlimited varieties of areas of expertise that can be brought to bear in an OCI would make up for the lack of training in bioethics, which is a fact of life for those muftis who have dealt with this subject to date.[16] The worst-case scenario is that convergence would remain incomplete. But even in that case, the current state of opinion would be constantly updated and available to inquirers without needing to hold any further conferences. In other words, there would be a state-of-the-art fatwa available at all times.

Conclusions

We live in an era of high literacy, including computer literacy, when more and more Muslims can avail themselves of the ability to look up a fatwa rather than rely on oral delivery. This has exacerbated the problem of fatwa shopping on the demand side and the posting of fatwas of undetermined pedigree on the supply side. Creating a well-organized OCI would address both problems. Participants would receive a real-time as-needed education in the relevant areas of texts, *tafsīr*, context, science, and technology. A one-stop site for online fatwas would provide the opportunity for quality control on the demand side and a market deterrent to the proliferation of fatwa sites on the supply side (as Wikipedia and Google dominate the wiki encyclopedia and online search engine, respectively). Including all experts in the process would both deter sectarianism and enhance the fatwas' quality. The Internet's mass marketing aspects could facilitate education on *iftā'* as well as the propagation and adoption of the fatwas produced. Neither the ideas proposed here nor any form of collectivization can remove the need for participants in modern *iftā'* to have a basic understanding of multiple disciplines, including research methodology, textual analysis, and the physical and social sciences.

Endnotes

1. Brinckley Messick, "Fatwa: Process and Function," *The Oxford Encyclopedia of the Modern Islamic World*, ed. John Esposito (Oxford, NY: Oxford University Press, 1995), 10.
2. Ibid., 11.
3. Ibid., 10.
4. Ibid., 11.
5. Ahmad S. Dallal, "Fatwas: Modern Usage," *The Oxford Encyclopedia*, 13.
6. Ibid.
7. Ibid., 15.
8. See stackoverflow.com. Accessed July 17, 2011.
9. Imad-ad-Dean Ahmad, *A Uniform Islamic Calendar for the Western Hemisphere* (Bethesda, MD: Imad-ad-Dean, Inc., 1990).
10. FCNA, "Decision on Determining the Islamic Lunar Calendar," FCNA (December 5, 2010), http://www.fiqhcouncil.org/noḍe/13, accessed 5/26/2011.
11. This convention is identical to the Umm al-Qurra calendar used by Saudi Arabia as its civil calendar.
12. Megan Meyer, "Stem Cell Research Is Consistent with Shia Islam," *Muslim Voices* (December 9, 2009), http://muslimvoices.org/stem-cell-research-consistant-shiite-islam/, accessed May 26, 2011.
13. Washington Times, "Iran at forefront of stem cell research," *Washington Times* (April 15, 2009), http://www.washingtontimes.com/news/2009/apr/15/iran-at-forefront-of-stem-cell-research/?page=1, accessed May 26, 2011.
14. FCNA, "Embryonic Stem-Cell Research," *FCNA* (December 6, 2010), http://www.fiqhcouncil.org/noḍe/23, accessed May 26, 2011.
15. Ibid.
16. Abdulaziz Sachedina. "Islam, Healthcare, and Spirituality," IIIT Summer Institute on *Iftā'* and Fatwa in the Muslim World and the West: Challenges of Authority, Legitimacy, and Relevance (see pages 163-82 of this publication).

Bibliography

Ahmad, Imad-ad-Dean. *A Uniform Islamic Calendar for the Western Hemisphere.* Bethesda: Imad-ad-Dean, Inc., 1990.

Dallal, Ahmad S. "Fatwas: Modern Usage." In *The Oxford Encyclopedia of the Modern Islamic World.* Edited by John Esposito. Oxford: Oxford University Press, 1995.

FCNA. "Decision on Determining the Islamic Lunar Calendar," *FCNA,* December 5, 2010) http://www.fiqhcouncil.org/node/13, accessed May 26, 2011.

———. "Embryonic Stem-Cell Research," FCNA, December 6, 2010). http://www.fiqhcouncil.org/node/23., accessed May 26, 2011.

Messick, Brinckley. "Fatwa: Process and Function." In *The Oxford Encyclopedia of the Modern Islamic World.* Edited by John Esposito. Oxford: Oxford University Press, 1995.

Meyer, Megan. "Stem Cell Research Is Consistent with Shia Islam." In *Muslim Voices* (12/9/2009). http://muslimvoices.org/stem-cell-research-consistant-shiite-islam/. Accessed 5/26/2011.

Sachedina, Abdulaziz. "Islam, Healthcare, and Spirituality." IIIT Summer Institute on *Iftā'* and Fatwa in the Muslim World and the West: Challenges of Authority, Legitimacy, and Relevance. Herndon, VA: IIIT, 2014.

Stackoverflow.com, accessed July 17, 2011.

Washington Times. "Iran at Forefront of Stem Cell Research," *Washington Times,* April 15, 2009, http://www.washingtontimes.com/news/2009/apr/15/iran-at-forefront-of-stem-cell-research/?page=1, accessed May 26, 2011.

Discussion

Discussant: Muhammad Adam al-Sheikh
I believe that collective fatwas are very important for the reasons stated. When the Prophet was asked who would answer their questions after his death, he told to make a collective effort. *Hilāl* and *ḥalāl* are examples of areas identified by the Fiqh Council. Unfortunately fatwa shopping does exist. Some may ask you whether a boyfriend/girlfriend relationship or a *muṭ'ah* marriage is better? If you say both are *ḥarām*, you will be ignored. One can say that *muṭ'ah* is not allowed, but that at least you will not be subjected to *ḥadd*. Truly, *Allāhu a'lam*. It is the one part of any fatwa that is beyond debate. It is better to say "I don't know" rather than do *tahbīz*. As to FCNA, we invite Dr. Imad back.

Discussant: Jamal Barzinji
Whether a fatwa is binding depends on who's issuing it. I would like more of a discussion of the Sunni vs. Shi'i methods. I make a distinction between *shūrā* approach and collective fatwa. In Saudi Arabia they do consult with experts but they think they know more, so you should be advocating that the knowledge of the experts should be

binding. We assume that those who go into Shari'ah are inferior scholars, which is unfortunately true. Is it easier to teach a banker Islam or to teach an Islamist banking? I would like to see a degree in Shari'ah given only to those who have first earned an advanced degree in any other discipline. I would prefer a Supreme Court model. I worry about the control of advertisers. Dr. Taha took some really courageous positions in *maqāṣid al-Sharī'ah*. Since we lost him to Egypt, we have found no replacement. The Organization of Islamic Cooperation (OIC) would have been the right ones to take on this task. NASA can pinpoint the moon's location and phase at every second, so why doesn't our political leadership accept that? My suggestions are to (1) revive FCNA; (2) beef it up with experts in medicine, astronomy, and other fields; (3) encourage more scientists to take intensive courses in Shari'ah and expose our respectable scholars of Shari'ah to intensive courses of general knowledge and modern technology, because the brightest of them would appreciate this; (4) insist on the role of *maqāṣid* in taking us out of stagnation; and (5) exhibit pride in *fiqh al-'aqallīyāt*, which, *inshā' Allāh*, will become *fiqh al-awlawīyāt*.

Ahmad: I would be glad to consult with FCNA, whether they agree with me or not, so long as my views are not misrepresented. The binding fatwas that Dr. Jamal mentioned demonstrate the problems of state-scholar entanglement. The great early Islamic scholars were famous for refusing to cooperate with the government. Academic authority is different, because it a non-coercive authority derived from the listener's respect for the professor. The Shi'a do have a more structured system than the Sunnis, and they require the people to attach themselves to a scholar. But even their leading scholars, those like Ayatullah Sistani, allow people the flexibility to accept other scholars' decisions.

The experts' knowledge is binding in a way comparable to the peer review process. Scientific experts with no knowledge of Islamic law should be allowed input into the process, but should not be allowed to impede the output of the process. The same goes for so-called Shari'ah scholars with no knowledge of the matter in question. Dr. Jamal's suggestion of earning an advanced degree in anything else as a prerequisite for Shari'ah scholarship is fascinating, and perhaps would obviate the need for collective *iftā'*. But if not, I think it could be incorporated into my proposal so that those with editorial control over the published fatwas would have to be knowledgeable in both Islamic law and the relevant secular science(s).

I will have to give your proposal of a Supreme Court model serious thought; however, if you look at the United States Supreme Court, you will see it has not totally eliminated the problems of politicization. I also worry about the adverse impact of advertisers, but I think this can be dealt with constitutionally because the Internet is so inexpensive that you are not a slave to them. In any case, you always face the possibility of competition. Given this reality, I think that the objective of any site should be to have such a degree of quality and integrity that the most qualified scholars will be drawn to it. I don't have much faith in the OIC because of my concerns over politicization. Why NASA doesn't suffice is that there are some strictly Islamic concerns on which it has no opinion. For example, the Prophet did not take the science of his day into account. Those issues must be answered on grounds of *maqāṣid* rather than science.

General Discussion

- *Muṭ'ah* has nothing to do with fatwa; it is a *fiqhī* debate. All know it was practiced in the beginning, but disagree with whether it was abrogated. I would suggest fatwa institutionalization rather than collectivization. Some have proposed establishing research institutions to deal with these issues for *mujtahid*s to sign off on. Much of this paper could be incorporated into this. There is freedom, and we have to be careful what we call fatwa. One might jest that shuratic fatwa is a contradiction in terms. Whether we accept a legal opinion or not, we shouldn't call just any conclusion a fatwa.
- The objective of institutionalization has always been there, but the challenge of authoritarianism has always been there as well. Why has Dr. Taha's example not led to a tradition? The political culture and psychology has prevented it.
- There is a fear of chaos if everyone were to speak as a *faqīh*. What we need is area research. Expertise and authority need not clash.
- It is not just a question of competence; it is also a question of courage. One very respected scholar who has excellent positions on two highly controversial issues has declined to make them public because he fears that if he were to do so he would lose his following and position.
- Collective fatwa can lead to *ijmā'*. This happened in the sciences. The theory of relativity was shocking when it was first published, but now it is the consensus view. Peer review need not be a drawn-out process; but on controversial issues it will be. As regards those controversial issues that require an immediate answer, a questioner may have to be satisfied with an individual fatwa until the peer review process works itself out.
- It is not colonialism per se that causes fragmentation of knowledge, but the explosion of knowledge. Interdisciplinary study is a means of managing the fragmentation. There is a role for interdisciplinarians. Non-Muslims friends can have knowledge of Islam, but those who do not should be included in the discussion in an appropriate way.
- Are we talking about an approach to *iftā'* in the United States or on a global scale? Who is the audience? Is the inclusion of non-Muslim experts in Islamic studies problematic in the area of authority?
- The audience is initially Muslims living in the United States, but it doesn't end there. There is no problem with allowing non-Muslim experts in Islamic studies to have input, although to give them editorial control over fatwas would simply be inappropriate.
- People need to master the Shari'ah from the beginning of their lives. It can't be done in six months.

- Not master, but being able to pass the tests given to the graduates of these schools of Shari'ah. He will not master it, but he will have enough knowledge to challenge the graduates of those schools. The dismantling of the *awqāf* has been an obstacle to obtain the best brains. Brilliant scientists, doctors, and IT specialists with strong Islamic background can enroll in a twelve-month program of intensive study to gain access to that knowledge, know how to handle it, and have access to it. *Allāhu a'lam.*
- The Imam Association in Michigan is an interesting model for the collectivization of fatwas in the North American context. Iran shot down some of these ideas because each has his own *khums* and followers. Yet somehow they will sometimes issue a fatwa together. All the *marāji'* are represented on the council in Qom.
- The Shi'a may have remained truer to the academic model.
- It's striking how conservative the use of Internet has been in the case of fatwa. Does this election of participants not politicize the process? The presentation indicates confidence in the capitalist model, even to the point of allowing advertising on the site. Are there any limits? Also, what are the long-term consequences of academization? Will flexibility be lost?
- Selecting participants will politicize the process, but it need not be fatal. We have the same problem in selecting the editors of an academic journal. If an author submits a paper to an academic journal and a reviewer with an opposing position rejects it, the author has an opportunity to rebut the criticism and ultimately another editor or reviewer will resolve the issue. The site's constitutional structure must be established in a way designed to minimize the risks of politicization and commercialization. As to the long-term consequences, we may be returning to an earlier model. In the early days of Islam, the people who did this work were not political appointees, but those scholars whose ability to do it made them respected by their peers and those who brought them the questions. Nuances need not be lost. The paper outlines a structure in which there is a great deal of input from many sources. If one person says something is haram and another says it is makruh, a debate will ensue and the final fatwa should reflect its nuances.
- There should be a happy marriage of the *fiṭrah* of creation and the injunctions of *waḥy*. Finally certain scholars, when starting their research, say that some of their opinions are contrary to the common understanding and they are afraid to publish them while they are alive. This is very sad. Can we at least convince them to write them down while they are alive for publication after their death?
- We should weaken rather than strengthen this institution of non-enforceable fatwas. Science is not collective but individual. We should fear the loss of individual creativity.
- The first established council of collective *iftā'* was in Egypt. The European Council was created in this mold. Independence doesn't necessarily lead to openness. Look at the fatwas of Muhammad Hussein Fadlallah. Would the institutionalization of fatwa work in the American context, with its amazing ethnic, sectarian, and doctrinal diversity?

- Non-binding *iftā'* can be compared to dietary advice. Nutritionists can't stop anyone from eating junk food, but their advice is valuable. Rather than weaken the institutions of *iftā'*, the mission should be to strengthen the sense of individual responsibility among the people. American diversity is not a problem. Consider Kuhnian paradigm shifts. When you look at the immigrant community here it appears to be hopeless, but their children all know they cannot justify a position because their fathers do it, because their opponents can say the same thing.
- The contempt of people in the field for others who have not been in it from the beginning is a problem. Two non-ulama FCNA members make very valuable contributions. There are at least three kinds of *muṭ'ah*: temporary marriage, *muṭ'ah al-ṭalāq* (termination by unilateral divorce) which is Sunnah but not applied, and the fatwa of Bin Baz (marrying with the undisclosed intention of divorce).
- No priest would ask a Muslim his opinion on canon law, and no rabbi would ask his opinion on rabbinic law; Islam, however, is an open field.

Minority *Fiqh* as Deliberative *Ijtihād*: Legal Theory and Practice

Abdessamad Belhaj

Abstract

Deliberation is an essential characteristic of transmitting, interpreting, and teaching religious knowledge in Islam. During the Muslim community's formative period, the process of studying and reflecting on the Qur'an (*tadārus wa tadabbur al-Qur'ān*) was done collectively. Within the local context of Muslim communities living in the West, the deliberative *ijtihād* practiced by those involved in formulating minority *fiqh* is a symbolic form of collective action. This article examines several standpoints on deliberative *ijtihād*, namely, those of al-Alwani (who emphasizes epistemology and legal hermeneutics), al-Qaradawi (who tends to highlight the ummah's collective action, which faces challenges and carries on reforms), and Ibn Bayyah (who puts forward the public interest and decision sharing).

Relying on the public interest (*maṣlaḥah*) as being the core intent of Islamic law, minority *fiqh* develops a stronger concern for maintaining social ties in the West between Muslims and non-Muslims. Minority *fiqh* jurists perceive their task as providing a local western form of a universal deliberative *ijithād*, and insist that these councils of jurists be open to scholars of the natural and social sciences in order to uphold the concepts of community, consultation, and pluralism.

Introduction

Deliberation is an essential characteristic of transmitting, interpreting, and teaching religious knowledge in Islam. During the Muslim community's formative period, the process of studying and reflecting on the Qur'an (*tadārus wa tadabbur al-Qur'ān*) was done collectively. The idea of scientific circles (*ḥilaq al-'ilm*) in the mosques originated among those early Muslims who gathered together around a scholar to learn and share knowledge. In the classical age (ninth to eleventh centuries), scholars developed deliberative methods to communicate knowledge of the Qur'an and Sunnah, such as recitation (*qirā'ah*), dictation (*imlā'*), assignment of a lesson (*muḥāsabah*), collective memorization (*dhikr*), and many others.

In particular, the field of juridical opinions (*iftā'*) evolved as a collective scientific activity of divergence of opinion, consultation, and discussion. Thus, deliberation has been particularly helpful in generating and developing legal schools (*madhāhib*). Not just the operative aspects of law are concerned (e.g., institutions, processes, communication, and contestation), for deliberation is also involved in very basic legal concepts (e.g., norms, reasoning, and customs). Above all, it intervenes as a process of making law through argumentation (*khilāf*), constructed rules (*qawā'id*), and consensual meanings (*ijmā'*). In Islamic jurisprudence, this undertaking can be described as the difference-consensus process through which jurists tried to solve the problem of multiple juridical opinions and complex realities. In various times and places, these difficulties compelled them to use collective methods to solve legal issues.

Within the local context of Muslim communities living in the West, I argue that the deliberative *ijtihād* practiced by minority *fiqh* is a symbolic form of collective action. In this form, action is an application of a hermeneutical understanding based on an ethical concern and practical reasoning. In this way, jurists engage in an effective dialogue, both within and without their communities, to respond to challenging western realities. On the one hand, given that Islamic law is indivisible from Muslim identity and ethics, jurists consider respecting its legal provisions (*fiqh*) to be a matter of daily life. On the other, Muslims in the West have to cope with different legislations, ethical principles, and social practices of the non-Muslim societies in which they live.

In the following pages, I will first discuss deliberative *ijtihād*'s theoretical background, as seen by Muslim legal theorists and minority *fiqh* jurists, and then define the concept of minority *fiqh* and discuss its developers. Subsequently, I will treat its function within the Muslim public space in the West and close by analyzing the hijab as a deliberative form of *iftā'*.

Deliberative Ijtihād *in Islamic Law: A Theoretical Setting*

Modern scholarship has understood deliberative *ijtihād* (*ijtihād jamā'ī*) in several quite different manners. Certain scholars equate consensus (*ijmā'*) and deliberative *ijtihād*, where consensus stands for "a form of collective *ijtihād*."[1]

This position considers *ijmā'*, the third source of Sunni Islamic law, as the origin of deliberative *ijtihād*. Further, since *ijmā'* itself is based on the Sunni principle of consultation (*shūrā*), deliberative *ijtihād* can be traced back to consultation. The goal of both processes is to reach a compromise, since unanimous agreement is necessary to solve juridical cases. As failing to resolve such issues would be inappropriate, a majority agreement is considered the next best option. But if they fail to reach even that, their endeavor cannot be considered deliberative *ijtihād*.[2] Nevertheless, a major difference between these two undertakings has to be stated here: If *ijmā'* is conditioned by the jurists' unanimous consensus, which is almost impossible to achieve if we consider the contemporary world's diversity, deliberative *ijtihād* is based on the majority principle and therefore accessible.[3]

A second perspective looks at "fatwa-giving committees as a novel form of collective *ijtihād*."[4] Here, emphasis is placed on the experts' complementarity of knowledge as regards combining their efforts and balancing opinions. As such, deliberative *ijtihād* seeks to make *ijtihād* an outcome of the comprehensive examination of a specific matter. In particular, when compared to the efforts of an individual jurist, who tends to consider partially the balance of benefit and harm in a juridical case, this form of *ijtihād* has the advantage of weighing between them. At any rate, it produces an opinion that is stronger than the individual's opinion. Under current circumstances, it is almost infeasible for an individual to attain a level of expertise equaling that displayed by fatwa-issuing committees. However, such an opinion is not obligatory. Even if a juridical council proclaims a ruling, an individual jurist's divergent opinion is worth considering by those who would like to follow it.[5]

Finally, a few reformist scholars perceive deliberative *ijtihād* as being embodied in a legislative assembly.[6] Given that this process involves consultation, it is seen above all as a representative body of the community. Despite this apparent similarity, if in a democracy elected parliamentary members legislate within positive law, then jurists are legislating within Islamic law. Further, that which is legislated by a parliamentary majority becomes binding, whereas deliberative *ijtihād* does not. These three standpoints (viz., consensus, fatwa-issuing committees, and legislation) are in fact embedded meanings within deliberative *ijtihād*'s structure and function. Although it does not result in an absolute consensus, it does reach a compromise to which a majority of jurists agree. Second, in the contemporary context it takes the form of a fatwa-issuing committee. As for legislation, deliberative *ijtihād* plays a parallel role to assemblies that, in a majority of Muslim societies, are regulated by positive law.

Granted that no agreement has been achieved yet with regard to deliberative *ijtihād*'s scope and meaning, the discussion here is limited to jurists of minority *fiqh*. These jurists have developed a legal reasoning that looks at deliberative *ijtihād* as a general category or a pre-condition that frames minority *fiqh*. Among them, Taha Jabir al-Alwani (b. 1935) has dedicated a great deal of his intellectual project to discussing this form of *ijtihād* as a collective legal undertaking that is part of the ummah's unity. He begins with the complexity of crises, problems, and realities that Muslims need to resolve with a "complex light" (*nūr murakkab*). The latter could be brought in only by means of a collective effort. He makes a strong statement that "no organism or elite or sect is able to cope with this complex darkness alone."[7] Not only are the realities complex, but the social sciences that help us grasp them are also undergoing tremendous change and fragmentation. Both complex realities and knowledge should push jurists to assert the necessity of deliberative *ijtihād*.[8] In other words, as individual hermeneutics cannot understand complex realities and texts on its own, a sort of collective hermeneutics is necessary.

Deliberative *ijtihād* should rely on "the epistemological complementarity of fields of inquiry which evolve in one universal framework attempting at dealing with human as well as natural phenomena."[9] Thus the philologist who dives deep into the meanings of a legal text by reviewing its interpretations in different historical periods enriches the deliberative character of *ijtihād*. Similarly, the ethnologist, historian, and archaeologist would be as effective as the philologist in exploring certain aspects of the legal texts. For al-Alwani, the importance of similar interdisciplinary contributions is shown through such scholars as Ibn Battutah (d. 770/1368) and Ibn Khaldun (d. 808/1406).[10] In the final analysis, complementarity should bridge the gap between the fragmented sectors of knowledge. As such, and within its universal logic, this implies a plurality of inquiries.[11] Since the purpose is to deal with complex realities, al-Alwani calls on the community to implement this complementarity/plurality through specific organs that would bring ideas into effective action.

M. A. Zaki Badawi noted al-Alwani's engagement with deliberative *ijtihād* in his preface to the latter's *Towards a Fiqh for Minorities: Some Basic Reflections*. The preface asserts that "al-Alwani calls for collective *ijtihād* that invites experts from the various fields of social science to play a major part in formulating new ideas and developing new perceptions."[12] Al-Alwani substantiates this claim by emphasizing collective action in his *Issues in Contemporary Islamic Thought* (2005), where he reiterates the necessity for all members of the ummah to seek reform through "collective and concerted action."[13] He justifies using collective *ijtihād* to resolve the many difficulties of individual *ijtihād* and states that "we must adopt the principle of collective or institutional *ijtihād* based on diverse disciples and specialists outside the framework of current fatwa committees or *fiqh* councils."[14]

Whereas al-Alwani sees deliberative *ijtihād* from the perspective of epistemology and legal hermeneutics, Yusuf al-Qaradawi (b. 1926) perceives it as a form of collective action (*al-'amal al-jamā'ī*). He opines that collective action is needed now in the form of a complex jurisprudential structure that features a high level of contemporary scientific knowledge and issues its legal decisions after study and examination. In addition, it should have the benefit of courage and freedom from any governmental or people pressure. In his view, the ultimate purpose of any collective action is to serve and support Islam. He therefore calls for the establishment of collective organs[15] on the condition that they should go public because they can attain their objectives only when they are exposed to the public.[16]

Since these objectives are essential for the community and can be accomplished only through collective action, deliberative *ijtihād* is a duty and a necessity (*farīḍah wa ḍarūrah*): "Help one another to do what is right and good; do not help one another towards sin and hostility" (Q. 5:2).[17] He understands this verse and similar Sunnah texts as indicating that Muslims should gather together to be influential, and compares such action to mass production, since small-scale production is not competitive.[18] This is also a necessity, because reality forces Muslims to achieve major objectives, among them liberation from occupation, resistance to foreign danger, unification of the divided community, social justice, freedom, establishing consultative political systems, and human rights. Such tasks, he maintains, cannot be done via individual efforts.[19]

Lastly, Abd Allah ibn al-Shaykh al-Mahfudh ibn Bayyah (b. 1935) shares the same idea of deliberative *ijtihād* with these two scholars, although he differs with them in some aspects. For instance, he talks of deliberative fatwa (*al-fatwā al-jamā'īyah*; also *iftā' jamā'ī*), a form of collective consultation initiated by caliphs to consult the community's leaders and reach a consensual opinion. He refuses to call these deliberations *ijtihād jamā'ī*, since he defines *ijtihād* as the personal conviction of a *mujtahid* who strives to deduce a legal judgment. Ibn Bayyah establishes continuity between these early deliberations and the revival of Islamic law in the fourteenth and the fifteenth centuries.[20] In this regard, he asserts that "the Islamic world has revived the establishment of deliberative jurisprudential opinion through the establishment of international *fiqh* academies, whether official or independent and popular."[21]

Ibn Bayyah states that these councils should deal with those public issues that are crucial for the community. On the one hand, "they should deal with political issues dealt with in political systems: *shūrā*, democracy and women's participation. On the other, they might treat economic issues such as investing in multinational companies taking into account the corruption that taints these companies or the involvement in organizations such as the GATT."[22] Furthermore, he admits that so far they have focused "on some social issues like the relationship between men and women in terms of reciprocal rights and duties."[23] Markedly, he highlights the political aspect of deliberative fatwa as a "revival of the Prophet's companions' custom which consists in consulting the community (*jamā'ah*) in public affairs."[24] This was the case, he maintains, with Umar ibn al-Khattab (d. 23/644), who rejected the idea that only a few members could address the community's issues, regardless of their level of scientific knowledge.[25] Rather, the collectivity should solve these issues and take the public interest into account.[26]

For Ibn Bayyah, two specific constituents need to be considered when inquiring into these issues: (1) a broad knowledge of all aspects of reality and a holistic vision that observes its different angles. Thus, such councils must give political, social, and economic experts a major status without granting them too much authority to issue legal judgments, and (2) juridical council members should upgrade their ability to handle such issues in order to acquire a balanced vision between the macro and micro levels. Given that they should bear in mind the law's purposes without discarding individual texts, they must create a relative continuity and meanwhile establish the comprehensiveness of the purposes. In other words, they should seek the middle way (*wasaṭīyah*).[27]

So far, this article has examined several standpoints on deliberative *ijtihād*, namely, those of al-Alwani (who emphasizes epistemology and legal hermeneutics), al-Qaradawi (who tends to highlight the ummah's collective action that faces challenges and carries on reforms), and Ibn Bayyah (who puts forward the public interest and decision sharing). In my view, each one looks at a specific facet of deliberative *ijtihād* and therefore they do not contradict each other. Deliberative legal hermeneutics might lead to collective action that benefits the public or, inversely, decision sharing will create a collective action that influences, in its turn, legal hermeneutics. Before analyzing how these conceptions intervene in the perception of minority *fiqh*, I will define the latter's scope and meaning.

The Concept and Developers of Minority Fiqh

Based on what has been presented above, any application of deliberative *ijtihād* should be done within the framework of reviving the ummah. As such, it should take into account the balance among the universal Shari'ah, Muslim realities, and collective action. This section examines how minority *fiqh* came into existence as a deliberative *ijtihād* adapted to the western context.

The Concept. Minority *fiqh* (*fiqh al-aqallīyāt*) is a legal discourse that tries to respond to challenging private and public issues for Muslims living in the West. This concept is believed to have arisen first in 1994 when al-Alwani, an Iraqi Sunni jurist, sought to provide a legal framework for Muslims to participate in American elections.[28] Within the current literature, one can distinguish between legal reasoning and legal practice. As a form of legal reasoning, minority *fiqh* selects and emphasizes specific sources, procedures, and principles of Islamic law that are seen as promoting the Shari'ah's intents as opposed to its strict letter. As a form of legal practice, it is a set of legal opinions (fatwas) on specific problems that allow Muslims in the West to overcome everyday dilemmas.

The key element in both expressions is the attempt to reconcile Muslim law and ethics with the sociopolitical conditions facing these Muslims. Hence, minority *fiqh* is tailored for particular individuals and groups, whereas fatwas are meant to be specific to those involved. For this reason, it does not perceive its legal function as competing with traditional *fiqh*. Rather, it derives its references from the Shari'ah, which minority *fiqh* jurists consider to be general and universal, and focuses on principles and cases that provide indulgent answers to problems faced by minority Muslim communities.

With regard to its sources, minority *fiqh* has recourse to the primary sources of Sunni law, namely the Qur'an and Sunnah, consensus and analogy, as well as to such secondary sources as public interest, juristic preference, custom, and the opinion of a Companion.[29] However, it is highly selective when dealing with Muslim legal sources. One can look at this type of *fiqh* from both a closed-source and an open-source perspective. In the first case, minority *fiqh* seems to draw on a set of traditional sources and principles used in Islamic law for exceptional juridical cases, especially in forced situations or in the absence of specific religious texts. In this respect, one can compare it to a *fiqh al-ḍarūrah* (a jurisprudence of necessary cases) since it is dealing with exceptional cases (*ḥālāt istithnā'īyah*), for Muslims should normally live in Muslim lands. In this sense, necessity is the closed dimension of *fiqh al-aqallīyāt* for, as seen from this perspective, it is a legal process that reacts passively to those hardships facing Muslims in the West.

In particular, *maṣlaḥah* (public interest) is a central issue and approach here. Its theoreticians have argued that minority *fiqh* allows one to formulate a pragmatic and adaptive attitude toward western norms and institutions. Thus they often reiterate the idea that if interests change, the legal opinions should also change according to time, place, and circumstances. As a result, public interest opens legal reasoning and practice to interacting with the context, seeking simplicity, and pro-activeness. Inversely, as al-Alwani has stated, such *fiqh* "applies to a specific group of people living under particular conditions with special needs that may not be appropriate for other communities."[30]

Although its supporters underline the individual's role in legal awareness and application, it is predominantly a collective jurisprudence. Cases of individual jurists making legal decisions with reference to minority *fiqh* remain limited. The major role is played by two organs: the ECFR (European Council for Fatwa and Research) in western Europe and the AMJA (Assembly of Muslim Jurists in America) in North America. This deliberative character of *fiqh al-aqallīyāt* enables the development of a legal approach that considers three conditions: the legacy of majority *fiqh*, the social condition of Muslim minorities in the West, and Muslims' legal obligations toward the laws of western societies.

The Developers. The credit for laying the foundations for minority *fiqh* should perhaps be accorded to al-Alwani. In 1999, his "An Introduction to Minority *Fiqh*: Foundational Insights" ("*Madkhal ilā Fiqh al-Aqallīyāt: Naẓarāt Ta'sīsīyah*") offered the first results of his reflection on the new subsection of fiqh. One year later he published (in Arabic) *Toward a Minority Fiqh for Muslims* (*Fī Fiqh al-Aqallīyāt al-Muslimah*), in which he argues for the necessity of *ijtihād* for Muslims in the West. His main concern seems to be the kind of constructive relations Muslims living there should establish with their non-Muslim counterparts. It should be noted that he is, above all, a specialist in *uṣūl al-fiqh*, and thus his interest in minority *fiqh*'s theoretical aspects is obvious. His intellectual project seeks to construct a new *ijtihād* that relies on a Qur'anic methodology that interacts with the social and natural sciences. For him, minority *fiqh*'s purpose is to develop a set of methodologies that make Islamic law and ethics flexible enough to be applied to the western context. His views were made accessible in English after his *An Introduction to Minority Fiqh* was translated and published as *Towards a Fiqh for Minorities: Some Basic Reflections* (2004).

Less theoretical and critical, but far more focused on legal practice, the Egyptian jurist and preacher al-Qaradawi (b. 1926) has authored one of the major foundational texts of minority *fiqh*: *The Jurisprudence of Muslim Minorities: The Life of Muslims among Other Societies* (*Fiqh al-Aqallīyāt al-*

Muslimah: Ḥayat al-Muslimīn wasaṭ al-Mujtama'āt al-Ukhrā) (2001). In his legal understanding, minority *fiqh* is part of a series of books on *taysīr al-fiqh li al-muslim al-mu'āṣir* (facilitating *fiqh* for contemporary Muslims). He shares with al-Alwani the centrality of *ijtihād* in shedding new light on modern sociopolitical issues. Nevertheless, in developing his "modern *fiqh*," al-Qaradawi draws more on his legal experience as a mufti. His formula is to combine traditional *fiqh* with an emphasis on public interest and moderation. He is often led to accept concessions for modernity on such issues as women and the state. Additionally, he conceives his version of minority *fiqh* as complementary to his *Religious Minorities and the Islamic Solution* (*Al-Aqallīyāt al-Dīnīyah wa al-Ḥall al-Islāmī*), which deals with non-Muslims living in Muslim societies. Above all, in respect to his presence in western Europe, al-Qaradawi seems to be motivated by a concern about the Muslims' religiosity and especially their secularization.[31]

Other recent contributions mostly illustrate the same issues discussed by al-Alwani and al-Qaradawi. The Mauritanian jurist Abd Allah ibn al-Shaykh al-Mahfudh ibn Bayyah (b. 1935), who published *The Making of Fatwā and Minority Fiqh: Ṣinā'at al-Fatwā wa Fiqh al-Aqalliyyāt* in 2007, stands close to the latter's style. Other jurists, preachers, and thinkers, mainly from Lebanon, Egypt, Tunisia, and Morocco (e.g., Khalid Abd al-Qadir, Salah al-Din Abd al-Halim, Abd al-Majid al-Najjar, and Isma'il al-Hasani) popularize the subject mainly by sticking to the line of reasoning elaborated by the above-mentioned authors. However, most of the Arabic-language literature on this topic has no direct contact with Muslim minorities in the West. Thus, *fiqh* and society belong to two different realms. Some jurists try to replace the necessary social asset for this type of *fiqh* with a philological work of terms and sources of *fiqh al-aqallīyāt*. At this point in time, their methodology seems to be a set of *ready-to-wear* concepts and processes that they apply to any sort of *fiqh*. Accordingly, the deliberative link based on embodying *fiqh* in everyday life is completely absent.

ECFR decision 5/12, issued in 2004, stipulates that it attributes special importance to *fiqh al-aqallīyāt* since it leads to an understanding of the Muslim presence in non-Muslim countries and to the application of Islamic legal provisions in that reality. In addition, it has reiterated the authority of al-Alwani, al-Qaradawi, and Ibn Bayyah as well as agreed that this concept is valid insofar as it fixes this subject within the legal provisions related to minority Muslim populations.[32] The ECFR mainly uses two procedures to issue legal decisions for them: (1) providing legal opinions (*iftā'*) to those individuals or groups that ask a question (*mustaftī*) through any communication media. It should be noted that the rulings are not necessarily binding on the askers, for they can seek another opinion and choose the most convenient one, and (2) holding long collective deliberations on more controversial questions. Its decisions seem to seek western Muslims' positive participation without assimilation. Thus as a strategy of image improvement, it follows a more conciliatory line.

In the words of al-Najjar, the ECFR seeks to incarnate a sedentary, civic, and collective Muslim presence in Europe, as opposed to one that is accidental, individual, and circumstantial.[33] Nevertheless, this body often produces a *fiqh* that is, to a certain extent, adapted to the second kind. The latter is based on licentious laws and practices (*fiqh al-tarkhīṣ*), which is the type of *fiqh* most convenient for individual cases. He sees Europe's Muslims as primarily groups and individuals who have specific social links with their surrounding environment. This collective dimension should increase and strengthen in the future.[34] For this reason, minority *fiqh* has yet to produce a jurisprudence of foundation (*fiqh al-ta'sīs*) that would normalize their juridical status,[35] one that would treat their juridical cases as if they were a majority in a Muslim country.

Instead of dealing with the licit and the illicit in daily issues, major issues need to be tackled, including political participation and family matters. However, al-Najjar does not predict the end of minority *fiqh* once it becomes a jurisprudence of foundation; he simply appears eager to readjust the former's dependence on dispensation (*rukhṣah*) while it should be promoting the punctual application (*'azīmah*). If Europe's Muslims fail to transition toward a jurisprudence of foundation, there is a double risk: religious practice will weaken, and they will not be in a position to transmit Islam's message or be a cultural partner with non-Muslim Europeans.[36]

Similar to other juristic deliberative *fiqhī* bodies in the Muslim world that rely on collective *ijtihād*, legal diversity characterizes the ECFR's deliberations. One of its immediate outcomes is eclecticism, which is typical of juristic councils comprised of members with different juristic backgrounds from the Muslim world.[37] No prominent ECFR founders or authorities were born or raised in Europe. Since most of them live in the Muslim world, the ECFR reflects a variation on modern Islamic jurisprudence, seen within the projects of *fiqh* renewal.

Minority Fiqh within the Muslim Public Space in the West. Hitherto, we have examined minority *fiqh*, from its genesis to its maturity, as an application of a new deliberative *ijtihād*. Furthermore, its theoreticians and institutions helped to provide solid foundations for it. Be that as it may, any new juristic effort is stimulated by the society in which the jurisprudence evolves.

Like any other hermeneutic tradition, Muslim legal hermeneutics necessarily responds to a given human condition. Therefore, minority *fiqh* is expected to achieve its goals inasmuch as it interacts with the West's deliberative environment. Moreover, because of these societies' fragmentation of authority, especially of religious authority, minority *fiqh* becomes a Muslim voice in the public debate on Muslim issues.

Increasingly, many Muslim scholars and institutions have come to realize that one cause of their fragmented authority is modernity.[38] Granted that in any public space legal pluralism is recognized by religious authorities, one could speak of a *deliberative religiosity*, by which I mean controversial religious practices that become part of the public debate and subject to the admitted differences of "authorized" interpretations.[39] I subscribe to Robert Justin Lipkin's framing of this concept as a "religious argument that plays a full role in the public square."[40]

In addition to social conditions that enhance fragmentation, other hermeneutic factors make the process of *iftā'* in the West a multi-part one. A particular question arises with reference to the law/fact dichotomy in Islamic jurisprudence. In this regard, Muslim American scholar Sherman A. Jackson establishes an opposition between the ability to understand the scripture's implication (Qur'an and Hadith), which belongs to the authority of law and the ability to verify the reality of those elements that refer to the authority of fact.[41] In other words, just because a principle is universally Islamic does not imply that its particularization has been put correctly. He makes the point that if "a jurist states such and such is permissible or impermissible because of the existence of this or that fact, it remains the right – indeed the responsibility – of individual Muslims to ascertain for themselves (or through other qualified determiners of specific facts), whether or not these facts actually exist."[42] Thus, when it comes to deciding how Islamic law is going to be applied, individual Muslims have to prolong their deliberation on the matter at hand, either independently or with other Muslim authorities.

Since *fiqh* in the West is a locus of interplay between texts and facts, it has to keep the balance between the fatwa-makers and the audience. A new study on a mosque in southern France shows that questions and answers have the same significance in determining a Muslim ethical space. *Fiqh* deliberations became the result of "multivocal authorship, authority as answerability and casuistic reasoning."[43] The jurist uses the question and answer genre to teach his audience the tenets of Muslim ethics. Rather than preaching, he develops a practical reasoning that focuses on behaviors and constructs his authority as "inherently dialogical and based in his relationship to the mosque community."[44] In this intellectual meeting, the audience is expected not only to listen, but also to challenge the imam's premises or even reject some of his conclusions. This interchange leads to a "collective ethical reflection, if not necessarily democratic endeavor."[45] The two dynamics of *fiqh*, the universalization of laws and the particularization of facts, establish the authority of Muslim ethos but also enhance the public's importance. The jurist must listen carefully to local voices in order to keep the discussion going until a consensus is reached.

Similarly, the public interventions of British Muslims with reference to 9/11 show how Muslims access the British "dialogical network" by expressing their reaction in the same or similar utterances of "a performative discourse that inscribes them in the inclusive category of those who condemn the terrorist attacks."[46] Thus, the capacity of western European societies to include Muslim minorities relies on the latter's ability to access these societies by means of the "Western cultural code." In this respect, L. Swaine noted that:

> Muslims seem to be fully able to take part in democratic deliberation, and that they violate no commandments of their faith by so doing"[47]:.. "Muslim minorities support liberty of conscience and religious liberty for all....via respectful argumentation and reasoning in public fora and also through the examples that they set in public and private life, in their interactions with others.[48]

Consequently, western Muslims are likely to shape any political construction in the West, inasmuch as they willingly promote the core interests of the societies in which they live. In particular, they would not have to expect Muslims in the West to follow the Shari'ah scrupulously, while aspiring to achieve a proactive role in the western political sphere. The only applicable requests, M. Benhanda reminds us, "are those made within the limits of public reason that is to say, claims are valid only when they rely on reasons consistent with the view of the person and society."[49] In other words, political liberalism allows Muslims to lead their own religious life but requires them to adhere, in an absolute manner, to its system of values on a universal basis.[50] The confrontation between liberalism and Islamic law becomes clear when a certain matter of consensus within Islamic juridical schools, such as inheritance rules, is discussed in the West.[51] For this reason, minority *fiqh* seems disposed to avoid "no through road" fatwas and tends to consider western societies' values and interests as well.

In this regard, A. March compares many of its thinkers to western theorists of discourse and deliberation who "reject an antagonistic, conflictual, zero-sum form of *da'wah* and debate in favor of something more collaborative and open-minded."[52] Likewise, A. Caeiro argues for "a complex deliberative process that underlies the European Council for Fatwa and Research"[53] and describes the ECFR project as an attempt to "imagine an Islamic counter-public."[54] To be accurate, this project seeks to shape an imagined Islamic counter-public. However, it has to accept the extreme fragmentation of the western Muslims' religious sphere.

For instance, conservative Muslims contest the legitimacy of minority *fiqh* and criticize several points in its reasoning. They rely on traditional *fiqh*, which has limited recourse to customs in making laws and is restricted to cases in which scriptural regulations are missing. When the scriptural regulations are founded on custom, legal provisions can be changed when the custom changes. Thus, conservatives criticize especially al-Qaradawi's fatwa that a Muslim woman living in the West can remain married to a non-Muslim (forbidden by a Qur'anic regulation). If he relies on weighing interests and finds a stronger interest for Islam in maintaining social ties in the West between Muslims and non-Muslims, conservatives reject this pragmatic reasoning on the grounds that western reality should not be the source of legislation. On the contrary, western societies are just as subject to the authority of Islamic law as are Muslim societies.[55] In other words, conservatives reject the idea of integration within western societies and, therefore, any principle that could enable them, under Islamic terms, to interact with these societies.

Inasmuch as minority *fiqh* is a legal discourse that aims at affirmative action, its proponents do not worry about such criticism. Rather, they focus on the complex Muslim reality of western European societies, wherein the major concern is the weakening religiosity among young Muslims. Thus, their legal process focuses on preserving Muslim identity, predication, relations with non-Muslims, and providing legal knowledge. As such it is, so to speak, a missionary *fiqh* (*fiqh da'wah*). In many respects, minority *fiqh* appears to be a way to establish communication links among Muslims over daily matters and to prevent their overwhelming secularization in the West. Many critical European Muslim voices do not accept the involvement of Islamic universities (e.g., al-Azhar) or Muslim *fiqh* councils in committees of fatwas and in the making of minority *fiqh*. Nevertheless, the pluralism and deliberation that characterize the ECFR and AMJA sessions could, if opened to young European Muslims, play a significant role in the life of these Muslims. Furthermore, any development of minority *fiqh* should consider the public space in the West and work in accordance with it.

It has been stated that the fragmentation of religious authority in the western Muslim public space has made minority *fiqh* jointly share this space with other Muslim representatives. In addition, the deliberative characteristics of western societies allowed this *fiqh* to critically assess the claims and arguments of its western opponents. Finally, its proponents show little interest in the conservatives' rejection of it as an innovation that alters the nature of Islamic law. Consequently, it represents a contribution to the development of a Muslim legal culture and a step toward the community's integration. In sum, *fiqh* in the West functions mainly as a counterculture that contests certain western values. In contrast, European societies say that their norms are not to be "offended" and thus demand uniformity. Muslim legal culture could eventually find its place as a legitimate part of western culture, provided that it is allowed to enter the public debate.

Case Analysis: Deliberating the Hijab. The dynamics of fragmentation and pluralism mentioned above help shape the scope of religious authority. As a result, diverging religious standpoints and multiple voices over religious questions coexist in the Muslim religious field in western Europe. In the following, I highlight the deliberative character of these communities' participation in the public space via the headscarf debate. The latter also illustrates the will, so to speak, of Muslim authorities and individuals to negotiate their integration in western European societies.

I suggest beginning with the case of a Muslim employee in the German state of Hessen, who appealed the notice at the Labour Courts of Appeal at Hessen to end her contract because of her hijab. The Federal Labour Court finally accepted her claim.[56] However, as M. Rohe has asserted, the solution is "probably not to be found, only, in the sphere of law."[57] For the most part, western societies view the hijab as a matter of culture, values, and biases. The democratic and humanitarian values of its legal order, in addition to the associated beliefs concerning it (e.g., the persecution of women and religious fundamentalism) are fundamental to the western sensitivity.[58] In other words, persuasion should not be individual in courts, case by case, for the hijab could give rise to an infinite number of cases. Rather, interaction should be done with the European public, admitting the need for constructing a public order in which Muslims should be allowed to participate in the construction of society and culture.

Although *sunnah* provides a model of Islamic law and ethics, its many principles and rules can be applied in various ways. For instance, a tribal Arab society sees modesty, which is strongly recommended in Islam, rather differently than a highly urbanized environment in Egypt. Social perception shapes, through beliefs and practices, how reticence is expressed. Islamic modesty, symbolized by the hijab, also raises the question of universality/particularity.

In fact, just wearing it establishes a double particularization: (1) it particularizes the female body from the male body, for Muslim clothing sets boundaries to prevent indecent exposure, and (2) hijab-wearing women practice a Qur'anic obligation in a western society that has a different standard of modesty. A recent sociological study reveals that the hijab allows women to go further than their particular feelings and modesty, for it is related to "a broader system of normative gender relations operating within the community at large and above all a type of practice through which one develops the moral dispositions necessary to carry out such a system."[59]

In the aftermath of the French parliament's outlawing "ostentatious" religious signs, including the hijab, in March 2004 the ECFR issued an important statement. Its legal decision condemned this decision and advised Muslims in France to stand up for their legitimate rights. It stated:

1. Coexistence is an Islamic principle that should regulate societies;
2. Coexistence cannot be applied without respect for individual and collective freedoms and the preservation of human rights;
3. There is no real incompatibility between the demands of pluralism and diversity on the one hand and national unity on the other;
4. The hijab is an act of worship and a divine prescription; it is not a simple religious act and certainly not a political symbol;
5. Compelling the Muslim to remove her hijab is an act of persecution of Muslim women, which is not in accord with the French values;
6. Banning the hijab constitutes religious discrimination against Muslims and is contrary to all western constitutions;
7. The board recommends that Muslims in France demand their legitimate rights and oppose this unjust law through peaceful and legitimate means, in words and acts, in accordance with the law;
8. The board invites government officials at all levels in France to reconsider this bill in accordance with the principles of national unity, social peace, and solidarity
9. To monitor this case, the board established a committee to present its views to the relevant departments in France, including Muslims, and to open the door for dialogue.[60]

Here, the ECFR clearly displays a sense of awareness that the hijab is not only a matter for jurists, but also a subject of concern to many voices within a multifaceted public space. The board of jurists also reveals its full understanding of the cultural code of the French public space by defending the hijab against the accusation of disrupting French values. Besides, the ECFR is conscious of the fact that Muslim minorities have divergent understanding of texts and customs. Hence, it pinpoints that "it is not right either to take into account the outrageous behaviour of some Muslims to justify the deprivation of five million Muslims in France of their rights."[61] On the other hand, one has to be sensitive to the fact that even if many families can be identified as Muslims, this does not necessarily imply that the third-generation of Muslim immigrants is respecting Islamic ethics and law. On the ground, the majority of these individuals in France, as shown by sociological studies, do not practice Islam. A recent study shows that only 33 percent declare that they believe in and practice Islam.[62]

Interestingly enough, the ECFR used the argument of freedom vs. secularism, both of which express western values, to claim state neutrality with regard to their attire: "Secularism should not be either a justification to launch 'exclusion laws' that would result in destroying the most fundamental rights of man and his freedom: individual liberty and religious."[63] Regardless of the outcome, Muslim minorities came to discuss a legal matter (in Islamic law) with non-Islamic opponents in a non-Islamic public space with arguments borrowed from that same space. Be that as it may, this ongoing debate allowed them, and especially Muslim women, to be included in the public deliberation.

Further, the ECFR drew attention to the fact that this particular French law isolates those who wear the hijab: "National unity must not at any rate constitute a pretext to trample on individual and religious freedom, or threaten the opportunities of French Muslims and others in education, and to marginalize their role as citizens. Such behavior would push Muslims in isolation instead of making contacts with other French citizens."[64] Here, the council rejects the law by virtue of national unity, inclusiveness, and social equity. In other words the ambiguity of the French law, motivated by sociopolitical concerns, is deconstructed by the same claims to which it refers.

For the most part, the statement's last three points emphasize its deliberative character. First, it recommends that Muslims in France "demand their legitimate rights, and oppose this unjust law, using peaceful and legitimate means, in words and acts, in accordance with the law."[65] Further, it encourages them to seek the support of other Muslims despite the disagreement on wearing the hijab. If we take public deliberation in the sense of voting, campaigning, letter writing, and pamphleteering,[66] then Muslim women largely responded to the conditions of political deliberation. As for the outcomes, one must admit that deliberation did not achieve consensus.

Subsequently, it invites the French authorities "to reconsider this bill in accordance with the principles of national unity, social peace and solidarity."[67] In this regard, the statement calls upon Muslims to cooperate with non-Muslims who are willing to defend this right on the "principles of individual freedoms, religious and human rights, even if they do not share the same beliefs and religious practices."[68] Al-Qaradawi himself had a dialogue with the French prime minister and expressed "his annoyance with the law banning the hijab."[69] Thus one can say that Anver Emon is not wide of the mark when he sees in the immigrant Muslim woman "the challenge of accommodating minorities amidst a universal, albeit ambiguous, claim of French core values."[70]

Finally, the statement encourages Muslim jurists to continue their deliberations by announcing the formation of a "committee from among its members, to present its views to the relevant departments in France, including Muslims, to open the door for dialogue."[71] These three points plainly illustrate the council's readiness for collective action with the French Muslim community and western societies.

Conclusion

Overall, the ECFR has shown a constant interest in deliberating within the *fiqh* council, with other voices in the French Muslim community, with French civil society, and with political actors. Within the Muslim milieu, deliberative *ijtihād* carried out via minority *fiqh* has led to affirmative action. The ECFR handled the case of the hijab in a way that allowed it to keep up an ongoing deliberation between the jurists and the public. Thus, minority *fiqh* jurists showed their commitment to preserving Muslim identity, being religious authorities after all, while displaying their awareness of the complex realities faced by Muslims in the West.

Relying on the public interest (*maṣlaḥah*) as being the core intent of Islamic law, minority fiqh develops a stronger concern for maintaining social ties in the West between Muslims and non-Muslims. At this point, it clearly promotes integration and, accordingly, any principle that could enable these Muslims, while safeguarding the Islamic way of life, to interact with their non-Muslim counterparts.

Furthermore, minority *fiqh* jurists perceive their task as providing a local western form of a universal deliberative *ijithād*. Thus they consider the latter a necessity for any renewal of Islamic law. This being the case, reform should not be achieved only within juristic councils or via jurisprudence. On the contrary, minority *fiqh* jurists insist that these councils be open to scholars of the natural and social sciences and call upon them to establish an effective link with Muslim societies. In other words they uphold, in deliberative terms, the concepts of community, consultation, and pluralism.

Endnotes

1. Irshad Abdal-Haqq, "Islamic Law: An Overview of Its Origin and Elements," in *Understanding Islamic Law: From Classical to Contemporary*, ed. Hisham M. Ramadan (Lanham, MD: AltaMira Press, 2006), 18.
2. Abd Allah Salih Hammu Babhun, *Al-Ijtihād al-Jamā'ī wa-Atharuhu fī al-Fiqh al-Islāmī* (Amman: Jordan University, 2006), 82-84.
3. Abd al-Rahim Ali Muhammad Ibrahim, "Al-Ijtihād al-Jamā'ī wa Majāmi' al-Fiqh al-Islāmī," *Risālat al-Taqrīb* 34, no. 35 (2002): 367.
4. Muhammad Khalid Masud et al., "Muftis, Fatwas, and Islamic Legal Interpretation," in *Islamic Legal Interpretation: Muftis and Their Fatwas*, ed. Muhammad Khalid Masud et al. (Cambridge, MA: Harvard University Press, 1996), 30.
5. Ibrahim, "Al-Ijtihād al-Jamā'ī," 367.
6. Muhammad Qasim Zaman, "The Ulama and Contestations on Religious Authority," in *Islam and Modernity: Key Issues and Debates*, ed. Muhammad Khalid Masud, Armando Salvatore, and Martin van Bruinessen (Edinburgh, UK: Edinburgh University Press, 2009), 227. Abdallah Ahmad an-Na'im, *Toward an Islamic Reformation: Civil Liberties, Human Rights, and International Law* (Syracuse: Syracuse University Press, 1990), 51. For a review of other Muslim scholars' views of collective *ijtihād*, see Aznan Hasan, "An Introduction to Collective *Ijtihād* (*Ijtihād Jamā'ī*): Concept and Applications," *The American Journal of Islamic Social Sciences* 20 (2003): 26-36; Nadirsyah Hosen, "Nahdatul Ulama and Collective *Ijtihād*," *New Zealand Journal of Asian Studies* 6 (2004): 5-9.
7. Taha Jabir al-Alwani, *Ab'ād Ghā'ibah 'an Fikr wa Mumārasāt al-Ḥarakāt al-Islāmiyyah al-Mu'āṣirah* (Cairo: Dar al-Salam, 2004), 100.
8. Ibid., 98.
9. Al-Alwani, *Ab'ād Ghā'ibah*, 96.
10. Ibid., 97.
11. Ibid.
12. Taha Jabir al-Alwani, *Towards a Fiqh for Minorities: Some Basic Reflections* (London: International Institute of Islamic Thought, 2003), ix.
13. Ibid., 254.
14. Ibid., 133.
15. Hasan Ali Daba, *Al-Qaraḍāwī wa Dhākirat al-Ayyām* (Cairo: Maktabat Wahba, 2004), 86.
16. Ibid., 87.

17. *The Qur'an*, tr. M. A. S. Abdel Haleem (Oxford: Oxford University Press, 2005), 67.
18. Daba, *Al-Qaraḍāwī*, 86.
19. Ibid.
20. Abd Allah ibn al-Shaykh al-Mahfudh ibn Bayyah, *Ṣinā'at al-Fatwā wa Fiqh al-Aqalliyyāt* (Jeddah: Dar al-Minhaj, 2007), 148-49.
21. Ibid.
22. Ibid.
23. Ibid., 149.
24. Ibid.
25. Ibid.
26. Ibid.
27. Ibid., 150.
28. Muhammad Khalid Masud, "Islamic Law and Muslim Minorities," *ISIM Newsletter* 11 (2002): 17.
29. Yusuf al-Qaradawi, *Fiqh of Muslim Minorities* (Cairo: al-Falah Foundation for Translation, 2003), 8-12.
30. Al-Alwani, *Towards a Fiqh for Minorities*, 3.
31. For a comprehensive study of al-Qaradawi's minority *fiqh*, see Sarah Albrecht, *Islamisches Minderheitenrecht Yūsuf al-Qaraḍāwī Konzept des fiqh al-aqalliyyāt* (Würzburg: Ergon-Verl, 2010).
32. "Al-Bayān al-Khitāmī li al-Dawrah al-'Ādiyah al-Thāniyah 'Ashrah li al-Majlis al-Urūbī li al-Iftā' wa al-Buḥūth," Dublin, December 31, 2003-January 4, 2004, http://www.e-cfr.org/ar/index.php?ArticleID=280.
33. Abd al-Majid al-Najjar, "Fiqh al-Aqalliyyāt bayna Fiqh al-Tarkhīṣ wa Fiqh al-Ta'sīs: Al-Majlis al-Urūbī li al-Iftā' unmūdhajan," *Al-Nadwah al-'Ālamīyah ḥawla Fiqh al-Aqallīyāt* (Kuala Lumpur: 2009): 13-14.
34. Ibid., 20-22.
35. Ibid., 23.
36. Ibid.
37. The ECFR's functioning has been thoroughly investigated in Alexandre Caeiro, "The Social Construction of Shari'ah: Bank Interest, Home Purchase, and Islamic Norms in the West," *Die Welt des Islams* 44 (2004): 351-75. Alexandre Caeiro, "The Power of European Fatwas: The Minority *Fiqh* Project and the Making of an Islamic Counterpublic," *International Journal of Middle East Studies* 42 (2010): 435-49.
38. Muhammad Qasim Zaman, "Consensus and Religious Authority in Modern Islam: The Discourses of the 'Ulamā'," in *Speaking for Islam: Religious Authorities in Muslim Societies*, ed. Gudrun Krämer and Sabine Schmidtke (Leiden and Boston: Brill, 2006), 176.
39. Jean-Paul Charnay has described this pluralistic Muslim legal process as being "une recherche entre diverses solutions pour découvrir la plus adéquate au cas concret envisagé. Elle permet aussi la lutte dialectique des prétentions opposées

qui s'affrontent au cours du litige." See Jean-Paul Charnay, "Pluralisme normatif et ambigüité dans le Fiqh," *Studia Islamica* 19 (1963): 78.

40. Robert Justin Lipkin, "Reconstructing the Public Square," *Cardozo Law Review* 24 (2003): 2082-86.
41. Sherman A. Jackson, "Muslims, Islamic Law, and the Sociopolitical Reality in the United States," *The American Journal of Islamic Social Sciences* 17 (2000): 10.
42. Ibid., 11.
43. Kirsten M. Yoder Wesselhoeft, "Making Muslim Minds: Question and Answer as a Genre of Moral Reasoning in an Urban French Mosque," *Journal of the American Academy of Religion* 78 (2010): 795.
44. Ibid., 795.
45. Ibid., 799.
46. J.-N. Ferrié, B. Dupret, and V. Legrand, "Comprendre la délibération parlementaire: une approche praxéologique de la politique en action," *Revue française de science politique* 58 (2008): 810.
47. Ibid., 98.
48. Ibid., 105.
49. Mostapha Benhada, "For Muslim Minorities, it Is Possible to Endorse Political Liberalism, But This Is Not Enough," *Journal of Islamic Law and Culture* 11 (2009): 79.
50. Ibid., 86.
51. Ibid., 84.
52. Andrew F. March, *Islam and Liberal Citizenship: The Search for an Overlapping Consensus* (Oxford, NY: Oxford University Press, 2009), 225.
53. Caeiro, "The Power of European Fatwas," 435.
54. Ibid., 437.
55. Asif K. Khan, *The* Fiqh *of Minorities: The New* Fiqh *to Subvert Islam* (London: Khilafah Publications, 2004), 17.
56. Mathias Rohe, "Application of Sharī'a Rules in Europe: Scope and Limits," *Die Welt des Islams* 44 (2004): 330-31.
57. Ibid., 332.
58. Ibid.
59. Daniel Winchester, "Embodying the Faith: Religious Practice and the Making of a Muslim Moral Habitus," *Social Forces* 86 (2008): 1770-1171.
60. "Bayān al-Majlis al-Urūbī li al-Iftā' wa al-Buḥūth ḥawla Mas'alat al-Ḥijāb fī Faransā," http://www.e-cfr.org/ar/index.php?ArticleID=280.
61. Ibid.
62. Jérôme Fourquet, *Enquête sur l'implantation et l'évolution de l'Islam de France 1989-2009* (Paris: IFOP, August 2009), 7.
63. "Bayān al-Majlis al-Urūbī."
64. Ibid.
65. Ibid.

66. Lucas Swaine, "Demanding Deliberation: Political Liberalism and the Inclusion of Islam," *Journal of Islamic Law and Culture* 11 (2009): 94.
67. "Bayān al-Majlis al-Urūbī."
68. Ibid.
69. "Al-Bayān al-Khitāmī li al-Dawrah al-'Ādīyah al-Thālithah 'Ashrah li al-Majlis al-Urūbī li al-Iftā' wa al-Buḥūth," Dublin, July 7, 2004-October 7, 2004, http://www.e-cfr.org/ar/index.php?ArticleID=281.
70. Anver M. Emon, "Pluralizing Religion: Islamic Law and the Anxiety of Reasoned Deliberation," in *After Pluralism: Reimagining Religious Engagement*, ed. Courtney Bender and Pamela E. Klassen (New York: Columbia University Press, 2010), 75.
71. "Bayān al-Majlis al-Urūbī."

Bibliography

Abdal-Haqq, Irshad. "Islamic Law: An Overview of its Origin and Elements." In *Understanding Islamic Law: From Classical to Contemporary*. Edited by Hisham M. Ramadan. Lanham: AltaMira Press, 2006.

Albrecht, Sarah. *Islamisches Minderheitenrecht Yūsuf al-Qaraḍāwī Konzept des Fiqh al-Aqalliyyāt*. Würzburg : Ergon-Verl, 2010.

Alwani, Taha Jabir al-. *Fī Fiqh al-Aqallīyāt al-Muslimah* (*Towards a* Fiqh *for Minorities*). Cairo: Dar Nahdat Misr, 2000.

———. *Towards a* Fiqh *for Minorities: Some Basic Reflections*. London: International Institute of Islamic Thought, 2003.

———. *Ab'ād Ghā'ibah 'an Fikr wa Mumārasāt al-Ḥarakāt al-Islāmīyyah al-Mu'āṣirah* (Absent Dimensions in the Action of Contemporary Islamic Movements). Cairo: Dar al-Salam, 2004.

An-Na'im, Abdallah Ahmad. *Toward an Islamic Reformation: Civil Liberties, Human Rights, and International Law*. Syracuse: Syracuse University Press, 1990.

Asad, Talal. "Muslims as a 'Religious Minority' in Europe." In *Formations of the Secular: Christianity, Islam, Modernity*. Edited by Talal Asad. Stanford: Stanford University Press, 2003.

Babhun, Abd Allah Salih Hammu. *Al-Ijtihād al-Jamā'ī wa Atharuhu fī al-Fiqh al-Islāmī*. Amman: Jordan University, 2006.

Benhada, Mostapha. "For Muslim Minorities, It Is Possible to Endorse Political Liberalism, But This is Not Enough." *Journal of Islamic Law and Culture* 11 (2009).

Bowen, John Richard. *Why the French Don't Like Headscarves: Islam, the State, and Public Space*. Princeton: Princeton University Press, 2007.

Bruinessen, Martin van, and Stefano Allievi, eds. *Producing Islamic Knowledge: Transmission and Dissemination in Western Europe*. London: Routledge, 2011.

Caeiro, Alexandre. "The Social Construction of Sharī'a: Bank Interest, Home Purchase, and Islamic Norms in the West." *Die Welt des Islams* 44 (2004).

———. "The Power of European Fatwas: the Minority *Fiqh* Project and the Making of an Islamic Counterpublic." *International Journal of Middle Eastern Studies* 42 (2010).

Cesari, Jocelyne. *When Islam and Democracy Meet: Muslims in Europe and in the United States*. New York: Palgrave Macmillan, 2006.

Charnay, Jean-Paul. "Pluralisme normatif et ambigüité dans le Fiqh." *Studia Islamica* 19 (1963).

Daba, Hasan Ali. *Al-Qaraḍāwī wa Dhākirat al-Ayyām*. Cairo: Maktabah Wahba, 2004.

Emon, Anver M. "Pluralizing Religion: Islamic Law and the Anxiety of Reasoned Deliberation." In *After Pluralism: Reimagining Religious Engagement.* Edited by Courtney Bender and Pamela E. Klassen. New York: Columbia University Press, 2010.

Ferrié, J.-N., B. Dupret, and V. Legrand,. "Comprendre la délibération parlementaire: une approche praxéologique de la politique en action." *Revue française de science politique*, 58 (2008).

Fourquet, Jérôme, *Enquête sur l'implantation et l'évolution de l'Islam de France1989-2009*. Paris : IFOP, 2009.

Gräf, Bettina and Jakob Skovgaard-Petersen, eds. *Global Mufti: The Phenomenon of Yūsuf al-Qaraḍāwī*. New York: Columbia University Press, 2009.

Hasan, Aznan. "An Introduction to Collective *Ijtihād* (*Ijtihād Jamā'ī*): Concept and Applications." *The American Journal of Islamic Social Sciences* 20 (2003).

Hosen, Nadirsyah. "Nahdatul Ulama and Collective Ijtihad." *New Zealand Journal of Asian Studies* 6 (2004).

Ibn Bayyah, Abd Allah ibn al-Shaykh al-Mahfuz. *Ṣinā'at al-Fatwā wa Fiqh al-Aqallīyāt* (The Art of Fatwa and Minority Fiqh). Jeddah: Dar al-Minhaj, 2007.

Ibrahim, Abd al-Rahim Ali Muhammad. "Al-Ijtihād al-Jamā'ī wa Majāmi' al-Fiqh al-Islāmī." *Risālat al-Taqrīb* 34/35 (2002).

Jackson, Sherman A. "Muslims, Islamic Law, and the Sociopolitical Reality in the United States." *The American Journal of Islamic Social Sciences* 17 (2000).

Khan, Asif K. *The* Fiqh *of Minorities:The New* Fiqh *to Subvert Islam*. London: Khilafah Publications, 2004.

Lipkin, Robert Justin. "Reconstructing the Public Square." *Cardozo Law Review* 24, (2003).

March, Andrew. "Sources of Moral Obligation to non-Muslims in the 'Jurisprudence of Muslim Minorities' Discourse." *Islamic Law and Society* 16 (2009).

———. *Islam and Liberal Citizenship: The Search for an Overlapping Consensus*. Oxford and New York: Oxford University Press, 2009.

Masud, Muhammad Khalid, Brinkley Messick, and David S. Powers. "Muftis, Fatwas and Islamic Legal Interpretation." In *Islamic Legal Interpretation: Muftis and their Fatwas.* Edited by Muhammad Khalid Masud, Brinkley Messick, and David S. Powers. Cambridge: Harvard University Press, 1996.

———. "Islamic Law and Muslim Minorities." *ISIM Newsletter* 11 (2002).

Najjar, Abd al-Majid al-. *Fiqh al-Aqallīyāt bayna Fiqh al-Tarkhīṣ wa Fiqh al Ta'sīs: Al-Majlis al-Urūbbī li al-Iftā' Numūdhajan.* Kuala Lumpur: Al-Nadwa al-Alamiyyah hawla Fiqh al-Aqalliyyat, 2009.

Qaradawi, Yusuf al-. *Fiqh al-Aqallīyāt al-Muslimah: Ḥayat al-Muslimīn wasaṭ al-Mujtama'āt al-Ukhrā* (Fiqh of Muslim Minorities: Muslims Living in the Non-Muslim Societies). Cairo: Dar al-Shuruq, 2001.

The Qur'an. Translated by M. A. S. Abdel Haleem. Oxford: Oxford University Press, 2005.

Rohe, Mathias. "Application of Sharī'a Rules in Europe: Scope and Limits." *Die Welt des Islams* 44 (2004).

Salvatore, Armando. "Authority in Question: Secularity, Republicanism and 'Communitarianism' in the Emerging Euro-Islamic Public Sphere." *Theory, Culture & Society* 24 (2007).

Swaine, Lucas. "Demanding Deliberation: Political Liberalism and the Inclusion of Islam." *Journal of Islamic Law and Culture* 11 (2009).

Wesselhoeft, Kirsten M. Yoder. "Making Muslim Minds: Question and Answer as a Genre of Moral Reasoning in an Urban French Mosque." *Journal of the American Academy of Religion* 78 (2010).

Winchester, Daniel. "Embodying the Faith: Religious Practice and the Making of a Muslim Moral Habitus." *Social Forces* 86 (2008).

Zaman, Muhammad Qasim. "Consensus and Religious Authority in Modern Islam: The Discourses of the 'Ulamā'." In *Speaking for Islam: Religious Authorities in Muslim Societies*. Edited by Gudrun Krämer and Sabine Schmidtke. Leiden-Boston: Brill, 2006.

———. "The Ulama and Contestations on Religious Authority." In *Islam and Modernity: Key Issues and Debates*, eds. Muhammad Khalid Masud, Armando Salvatore, and Martin van Bruinessen. Edinburgh: Edinburgh University Press.

The deliberative *ijtihād* practiced by minority *fiqh* is a symbolic form of collective action. He first says that deliberation has a historical role in *fiqh*. He compares three modern views, those of Taha Jabir al-Alwani (collective hermeneutics [epistemological complementarity]), Yusuf al-Qaradawi (collective action), and Abdullah Mahfudh ibn Bayyah (uses *deliberative fatwa*, because *ijtihād* is by nature individual rather than deliberative). These views are complementary rather than competitive. Deliberative *ijtihād* does not compete with traditional *fiqh*, but derives references from it and focuses on reaching decisions for Muslims in a minority situation. The goal is simplicity and pro-activeness.

The capacity of western societies to accommodate Muslim practices requires Muslims to access the western cultural code to negotiate their position. Any development of minority *fiqh* must accept and work within the western public space. He illustrates this by the European Council for Fatwa and Research's (ECFR) approach to the hijab controversy in France. Its fatwa calls upon Muslims to demand their legitimate rights and oppose unjust law through peaceful, legitimate, and legal means; appeals to the government to stand by its own goals of national unity, social peace, and solidarity; and urges Muslims to engage in dialogue with the appropriate government bodies. Belhaj says that these points show that discussing the hijab is not reserved only for Islamic jurists, but must include many voices in the public space. Public deliberation includes voting, campaigning, letter writing, and personal engagement with a variety of civil and political actors.

Ordering Religion, Organizing Politics: The Regulation of the Fatwa in Contemporary Islam

Alexandre Caeiro

Abstract

There has recently been a proliferation of voices calling for urgently regulating the production of fatwas (*ḍawābiṭ al-fatwā, tanẓīm al-iftā'*) in the Muslim world. A specific diagnosis of the situation seems to be widely shared, one that cuts across the usual lines of religious and political orientation: For state and non-state actors, be they traditional ulama, Islamists, or secularists, the production of fatwas is now deregulated beyond control. Contradictory religious opinions have been a feature of the Islamic tradition since the very beginning and have not always been perceived as an embarrassment. The phenomenon of competing fatwas thus represents a larger "crisis" within religious institutions. The proliferation of contradictory religious opinions has become a central issue of debate in both Muslim-majority societies and Muslim-minority communities.

Introduction

There has recently been a proliferation of voices urgently calling for regulating the production of fatwas (*ḍawābiṭ al-fatwā, tanẓīm al-iftā'*) in the Muslim world. Perhaps the most prominent call was articulated in The Amman Message of July 2005, when some 200 Muslim scholars outlined, at the request of King Abdallah II of Jordan, the conditions necessary for issuing legitimate fatwas.[1] Several high-profile international conferences devoted to this subject have been held in quick succession since that famous declaration. Religious scholars and public intellectuals have published books about the spread of abnormal fatwas (*fatāwā shādhdhah*) and attempted to solve this current phenomenon (Ashqar 2009; Bin Bayyah 2007; Jumu'a 2008; Matar 2009; Qaradawi 2008, 2010).

Many media muftis have reflexively engaged in reflecting upon the dilemmas of issuing fatwas on satellite TV and the Internet. Newspapers and magazines across the Muslim world frequently carry articles and op-eds on the need to organize *iftā'*. A specific diagnosis of the situation seems to be widely shared, one that cuts across the usual lines of religious and political orientation: For state and non-state actors, be they traditional ulama, Islamists, or secularists, the production of fatwas is now deregulated beyond control. The resulting proliferation has led to "chaos" (*fawḍā*), which causes "perplexity" (*ḥīrat*) among Muslims and is considered a major quandary of the contemporary Muslim community.

In this article I suggest that this diagnosis of chaos is less self-evident than is often assumed. While acknowledging that the existing situation poses various challenges to religious authority, I argue that the urgency underlying these calls for regulation is shaped by a specific understanding of the fatwa's functions. I start from a simple observation: Contradictory religious opinions have been a feature of the Islamic tradition since the very beginning and have not always been perceived as constituting an embarrassment. Although the issue cannot be dealt with in all its complexity here, I posit that the plurality of religious opinions posed mainly theological and legal problems to premodern Muslim jurists. Theologically, this plurality raised a question about the nature of the Divine Will. Legally, it raised the prospect of uncertainty in adjudication.

Both questions received what were, for many jurists, probably rather satisfying answers. On the one hand, the necessary differentiation between divine source and human fallibility was emphasized (Weiss 1998; Zysow 1984) and, on the other hand, a legal pluralist system was institutionalized under the authority of multiple juristic schools (Hallaq 2001; Rapoport 2003).[2] Premodern jurists apparently dealt with such divergence smoothly; many times they were even willing to valorize this internal pluralism as a strength, a divine mercy. There are undoubtedly many reasons for the current recasting of this proliferation as a "chaos." In this article, I hypothesize that a transformation of the kind of problem engendered by the plurality of religious opinions is also at stake. I argue that today's conflicting fatwas no longer primarily pose a theological or legal problem, but rather a political-ideological dilemma. I make a first attempt here to identify this dilemma and show how it might be addressed productively.

After a very brief reconstruction of some features of what I call the "narrative of chaos," I focus on two of its most prominent features. I then detail the approach of Yusuf al-Qaradawi, a prominent contemporary Islamic scholar whose interventions in many ways problematize this narrative's underlying assumptions. I conclude with some remarks that link the discussion's two sides to the concerns outlined above.

The Narrative of Chaos

Chaos or disorder are rather imprecise metaphors. Drawn from the natural sciences, in which these terms suggest unpredictability, the image of chaos is often used in current debates about fatwas to signify a range of different social phenomena. In the discussion below, I focus on two key aspects: the displacing impact of new media and the politicization of fatwas.[3]

The idea of chaos is perhaps most commonly seen in relation to the impact of new media. By 2009 there were an estimated 200 Arabic television channels and some 260 Islamic websites.[4] According to the conventional narrative, satellite TV and the Internet have provided a platform for the ulama to publicly display their differences (Matar 2009). While contradictory fatwas existed in the past, their inaccessibility to most Muslims ensured that they were content with following their local imams. Now that the spread of mass media has made these contradictions immediately visible and accessible to unprecedented audiences, they are charged with leading to confusion and uncertainty.[5]

Furthermore, these new media are not only often seen as more than simple instruments from which good and evil alike can be derived (an instrumentalist conception of the media). Rather, they are understood as having changed the kinds of questions that are asked, as well as the competencies required for speaking in Islam's name (a performative conception of the media). Charisma and fame, rather than knowledge and piety, have thus become for some the main criteria for issuing fatwas in the new media world.[6] To compound the problem, no regulatory bodies exist to control the quality of the fatwas disseminated via the Internet and satellite television.[7]

"Chaos" is also used to speak about the consequences of the perceived intrusion of politics into religion. Commentators speak of the phenomenon of political fatwas (*fatāwā musayyasah*) and the politicization of the fatwa (*tasīyīs al-fatwā*). Analysts often posit the Second Gulf War and the post-9/11 "war on terror" as two pivotal moments.[8] Saddam Hussein's invasion of Kuwait prompted a "war of fatwas" for and against the American-led military operations in the Gulf (Haddad 1996). The rise in the 1990s of violent movements acting in the name of religion and legitimizing their actions through fatwas gave a further impetus to the discussion. The recent events of Arab Spring have added a heightened urgency to these questions.[9]

One interesting formulation of this problem of religion and politics can be found in the introduction to Fu'ad Matar's *Alf Fatwā wa Fatwā* (*One Thousand and One Fatwas*), written by Khalil Ahmad Khalil (Matar 2009: 27-31). Khalil describes how politics has impinged on the production of fatwas in the context of the modern nation-state.[10] One attribute of the modern nation-state's sovereignty is its control over the legal process. Processes of codification have transformed Islamic law from a jurists' law into a state law. Khalil suggests that the modern state's search for legitimacy has created pressures for Muslim scholars to justify its policies, thereby leading to a standoff between the competing powers of the ulama and the state. The rise of political Islamic movements in the wake of the Iranian Revolution has added further impetus to this power struggle. Fatwas have thus become entangled in this standoff, oscillating between support for and contestation of the political regimes and unable to carry out their own metabolism. Matar offers ample examples of the growth of sectarian fatwas (a.k.a. *talwīn al-fatwā*), such as *azharīyah*, *wahhābīyah*, *khumaynīyah*, and *sistanīyah*.

The phenomenon of competing fatwas thus represents a larger "crisis" within religious institutions (al-'Awwa 1998). The media depicts the proliferation of competing religious advice as symptomatic of the "convulsions, contests and inner strife" that result from wider "political, religious, social and ideological factors" in the Muslim world ("Ba'd al-ḥaqīqah ḍabṭ al-fatāwā," *Okaz*, 27/1/2009). Some observers have criticized attempts to abstract the fatwas from the Muslim world's wider sociopolitical contexts. According to Saudi intellectual Issan al-Haliyan, attempts to regulate fatwas that do not fall within the larger context of Islamic discourse are doomed to fail. Secularists in the Arab world see this proliferation as a symptom of the wave of fundamentalism that spread through Muslim countries after 1967. Although they do not share the secularists' critique of fundamentalism, this phenomenon has made religious scholars committed to the Islamic legal tradition ambivalent toward the Islamic revival.

The narrative of chaos in many ways presents a compelling story. Even from a simple historical perspective, it seems to coincide broadly with the proliferation of satellite television channels and Internet sites. It emerged in the politicized contexts of the Rushdie Affair, the Second Gulf War, and the terrorist attacks of 9/11. But this diagnosis is not unanimous. In a recent discussion on Al-Jazeera, Mauritanian scholar 'Abd Allah Bin Bayyah (vice-president, International Union for Muslim Scholars) appeared to relativize the problem by suggesting that the challenges affecting fatwas in a media world are no different from those affecting politics, economics, and other fields.[11] During an interview with a local newspaper, Mufti of Egypt Ali Jumu'a declared that very few contemporary fatwas are actually mistaken.[12] He distinguished clearly between the fatwa and the religious discourse in general. In addition, he downplayed differences among muftis by portraying them as mere differences in how the questions are framed and understood, rather than the result of conflicting modes of interpreting Islamic law. These statements suggest that the diagnosis of fatwa chaos is not as self-evident as it sometimes seems.

Yusuf al-Qaradawi's Alternative Account

In this section I analyze Qaradawi's "alternative" account of the fatwa. His interest in the genre is well-known, given the publication of four volumes of his personal religious opinions, *Fatāwā Mu'aṣirah* (*Contemporary Fatwas*), and his attempts to provide adequate methodological guidelines for issuing fatwas. The latter has now yielded three books: *Al-Fatwā bayna al-Inḍibāṭ wa al-Tasayyub*, initially published in the journal *Al-Muslim al-Mu'āṣir* (and in book format in 1988); *Mūjibāt Taghayyur al-Fatwā fī 'Aṣrinā* (2008); and *Al-Fatāwā al-Shādhdhah* (2010). Moreover, he has often discussed the fatwa's various dimensions and facets during his weekly appearances on "Al-Sharī'ah wa al-Ḥayāt." I draw on the transcripts of some of these episodes as well as the above-mentioned books.

Describing his account as "alternative" perhaps requires some explanation. Qaradawi is very much part of the actors and networks calling for the regulation of fatwas.[13] He has attended and been involved in organizing conferences that seek to counter the proliferation of competing religious opinions. He gave the opening speech at Kuwait's 2007 symposium on "Al-Iftā' fī 'Alam Maftūḥ" (Fatwa-Giving in an Open World) and contributed an article to the proceedings (Qaradawi 2007). Insofar as one of the ulama's responses to the perceived chaos of fatwas has been to institutionalize collective *fiqh* councils, al-Qaradawi has often been at the forefront of such initiatives. In addition to being the founder and chairman of the International Union of Muslim Scholars (IUMS) and the European Council for Fatwa and Research (ECFR), he regularly participates in the sessions of the Saudi-based international *fiqh* councils. He thus clearly shares many of the concerns of those who support regulation.

However, as I try to show, his account differs from the narrative of chaos in some important ways. For example, to my knowledge Qaradawi has never described the current situation as one of "chaos," even when pushed to do so by the presenter of "Al-Sharī'ah wa al-Ḥayāt" in an episode which the producers called "Fawḍā al-Fatāwā." Unlike many of his contemporaries, Qaradawi does not seem to consider this an intractable problem; on the contrary, he recently wrote that its solution is actually very simple.

One must recognize from the outset that Qaradawi's engagement with the problematics of fatwas are framed by his own position as a global media mufti. The use of media has been integral to his activities as a religious scholar and as a moral guide. His books (fatwa collections and theoretical reflections on the fatwa) have already been alluded to. Since 1996, he has also been the primary guest on Al-Jazeera's prime-time "Al-Sharī'ah wa al-Ḥayāt." Setting up a personal website (www.Qaradawi.net) in 1997 was a pioneering move. Qaradawi's reliance upon the mass media to cut across time and space has created a particular set of tensions that is still being worked out. For example, how to reconcile the emphasis on the local context (*fiqh al-wāqi'*) for issuing fatwas with his own position of a global mufti; how to emulate Imam Malik ibn Anas' refusal to answer questions (which Qaradawi and others often cite) during live broadcasts of this particular television program; or the extent to which the repeated emphasis on *ijtihād* and *tajdīd* may help undermine the viability of the very structures capable of maintaining the religious authority that he explicitly seeks to secure.

Traditional Muslim scholars with wide access to the Internet and satellite television are often some of the harshest critics of the new media's impact on the structures of religious authority. Qaradawi, however, is not among them because he operates with a neutral understanding of media technologies. His understanding of the proliferation of conflicting fatwas is therefore to be found elsewhere. His 150-page *Al-Fatāwā al-Shādhdhah*, originally presented in January 2009 at the Makkan conference on "The Fatwa and its Rules," provides a number of alternative explanations for this phenomenon (Qaradawi 2010: 127-43). In this book, Qaradawi starts by placing this issue within its historical context. Stating that abnormal fatwas have always existed, he then identifies six main reasons for this phenomenon: the mufti's lack of proper qualifications, the lack of respect for specialization in *fiqh*, the rush (*al-tasāru'*) to issue a fatwa,[14] the excessive attachment to one's opinion (*al-i'jāb bi al-ra'ī*) with the associated unwillingness to debate, political motives (*al-ahwā' al-siyāsīyah*), and the excessive use of *maṣlaḥah*.

While these explanations are by and large conventional, they characteristically shift our attention from the impact of new media and toward questions of hermeneutics. Although he generally seems to subscribe to the idea that fatwas are (or should be) non-sectarian, Qaradawi does not seek to downplay differences in juristic approaches or to blame them exclusively on a lack of proper qualifications. The fatwas issued by non-qualified scholars (i.e., those who are trained in literature, history, philosophy, Sufism, positive law, or in Islamic sciences other than *fiqh*[15]) elicit less than three largely generic pages of discussion and without any concrete example (Qaradawi 2010: 26-28).[16] He seems to accept the "intrusion" of non-qualified scholars as an inevitable feature of social life, since there are intruders in "all arts, disciplines and crafts" (p. 27).

Most of the contemporary fatwas he identifies as abnormal in this book seem to be the product of qualified scholars, rather than the product of non-qualified scholars. He considers these differences the result of the issuing scholar's individual temperament, sensibility and hermeneutics – between those who favor the letter and those who privilege the spirit of the law, those who emphasize *taysīr* and those who stress conformity, and so on. While Qaradawi clearly considers one approach more adequate than the others (both on principled and on contextual grounds: the *taysīr* approach that reads the texts with a *maqāṣidī* vision is closer to the Prophet's practice, and more appropriate in our contemporary times where piety has become so hard to practice), he does not delegitimize other approaches as un-Islamic or inauthentic.

Qaradawi has also addressed regulation in his weekly talk show.[17] Bearing in mind how the current "chaos" narrative often considers the intrusion of politics into the formulation of fatwas to be a key feature, let's consider his response to the idea that fatwa and politics should be distinguished. In the episode aired on January 10, 2010, "The Fatwa and Politics," Qaradawi was asked to consider the possibility of separating the fatwa from politics.[18] This was prompted by a fatwa issued by Shaykh al-Azhar Muhammad Sayyid Tantawi (d. 2010) on behalf of the Majma' al-Buḥūth al-Islāmīyah allowing the construction of a wall that would separate Egypt from Gaza (thus closing off the tunnels that connected Gaza with the outside world). The episode is unusual insofar as it is the only instance I am aware of in which the presenter (or the producer) repeatedly challenged Qaradawi's views.

Questions were asked successively in an attempt to elicit his acknowledgment of some form of separation between religion and politics – a separation that Qaradawi rejects[19]: "Is it possible for religion to enter into the field of politics?" "If the language and logic of politics differ from those of *fiqh*, how can one trump the other?" "Is it not necessary to distinguish between the fields of religion and politics?" "Should the mufti not understand the science of politics before speaking about politics?" "Should the mufti not refrain from issuing fatwas on participating in elections or the building of the wall?" "What are the religious-legal bases for declaring the building of the wall forbidden?" "Was the war of fatwas during the Iraq invasion of Kuwait not a proof of the political manipulation of religion?" In his answers, al-Qaradawi insisted on the Shari'ah's totalizing nature, for it rules over all the actions of the moral subject (*al-sharī'ah ḥākimah 'alā jamī' af'āl al-mukallafīn*).

The logic of *fiqh* trumps that of politics (*al-fiqh huwa al-ḥākim*). He argues that the term *fatāwā siyāsīyah* is used imprecisely to describe fatwas that conform to the ruler's desires, regardless of whether they are founded or unfounded. Muftis must resist the attempt to limit political discussions to specialized political scientists, just like they resist the attempts to keep debates about running the economy restricted to economists. They must study the issue carefully (*fiqh al-wāqi'*) and may mobilize different types of expertise to grasp what is at stake, but ultimately they must issue a fatwa and decide the case. Qaradawi opines that the idea of the fatwa's politicization has been greatly exaggerated. Even during Iraq's invasion of Kuwait, the fatwas issued by muftis in each Muslim country primarily reflected the regional conflict's local impact, not the policies of each state.

Qaradawi's remarkable unwillingness to cast conflicting fatwas as a problem in this episode seems to be connected to his confidence, reiterated periodically, in the Muslim's ability to distinguish between the opinions of real scholars and those of their inauthentic challengers. He thus challenges the oft-postulated link between conflicting fatwas and confusion of the masses. In addition to perplexity, the standard Muslim responses to the proliferation of fatwas across the Islamic world have been irony, sarcasm, and outright criticism. A particular conception of the fatwa's effects seems to be at play here. Qaradawi sees no direct relation between the mufti's speech act and the Muslims' practices, for fatwas are effective only insofar as Muslims decide to act upon them. He believes that Muslims have sufficient religious awareness to differentiate between conflicting opinions and act responsibly. This, perhaps, underlies his own understanding of regulating fatwas as something simple, as opposed to something intractable, that requires only minimal coordination among religious scholars.

Conclusion

The proliferation of contradictory religious opinions has become a central issue of debate in both Muslim-majority societies and Muslim-minority communities. The assumptions guiding this debate, however, have rarely been seriously examined. In this paper I have been primarily concerned with two key tropes of the chaos narrative: the new media's impact and the fatwa's politicization. By emphasizing the fragmentation of authority induced by new media technologies, as well as appealing to a normative differentiation between the spheres of religion and politics, Muslims seem to have borrowed their terms from mainstream western social scientific categories. A close reading of the writings of Islamic scholars reveals some of the tensions and problems inherent in these categories. The idea that the fatwa should not be politicized presupposes understandings of the proper relation between religion and politics that many Muslims might not be prepared to affirm. The strength of the critique of the political fatwa vanishes when one simply refuses, as does Qaradawi, to accept a principled separation between the two realms.

The impact of new media is also more ambivalent than is sometimes portrayed. While it is clear that under certain conditions new technologies may help displace religious authority, it is also apparent that new media have enabled traditional actors and institutions to extend their influence and reach larger audiences.[20] On the one hand, the idea of "chaos" does not seem to do justice to the remarkable restraint that Muslims have exercised while using media technologies, including their deferral to recognized religious scholars. On the other hand, Muslim scholars have largely managed to maintain religious authority outside the purview of the nation-state, despite tremendous pressures to assimilate into its framework. A degree of disorder may seem to be an inevitable price for continuing to rely upon the Islamic discursive tradition's self-regulatory powers.

I turned to Qaradawi writings to complicate the chaos narrative. Rather than shying away from difficult questions, Muslim scholars like Qaradawi have been willing to recognize the role of temperament and sensibility in shaping differing religious opinions. In turn, this recognition has allowed the ulama to preserve and cultivate a shared space of scholarly debate. Religious scholars nevertheless seem reluctant to address a different set of fatwa-related questions. For them, the fatwa's integrity as an instrument for communicating the Divine Will reposes, understandably, on its construction transcending all sectarian and ideological concern. The idea of the fatwa as somehow being above politics seems, at least in their opinion, to be the key to preserving the Islamic legal tradition.

But this view leads to an impasse, as seen during the discussions on "Al-Sharī'ah wa al-Ḥayāt." The ulama's reluctance to further disclose and reflect on the underlying ideological orientations and political commitments that guide the mufti's search for God's law – in the way that Khaled Abou El Fadl, for example, has done in *Speaking in God's Name* – is now being severely tested due to the complex interweaving of religion and politics.[21] The oft-invoked need to devise a proper understanding of reality (*fiqh al-wāqi'*) is insufficient here, since perceptions of reality are always already mediated by these orientations and commitments. As sociologists have pointed out, reality is a social construction. What actors consider to be phenomena lying outside of their control – in other words, "reality" – varies from individual to individual. *Fiqh al-wāqiʿ* neither examines this construction nor teaches one how to transform existing social conditions and remake the world. The common accusation leveled by muftis against scholars who "fail to take reality into account" in their fatwas often detracts from the fundamental underlying issues.

The idea of the fatwa as standing above politics was perhaps most plausible when it was no more than an instrument concerned primarily with issues of salvation. Today, however, it has increasingly become embedded in *civilizing processes* that seek not only to shape moral selves, but also to create modern citizenries.[22] As the religious scholar Usama Umar al-Ashqar stated in a recent book, fatwas should educate, guide, civilize, and contribute to the political, economic, and social development of Muslim nations (Ashqar 2009). These expectations have extended the fatwa's role far beyond its traditional purview, and yet the transformation they imply is rarely acknowledged.

One way of understanding this transformation is through *functionalization*.[23] Fatwas have been removed from their original contexts and placed strategically into projects of social governance. The process not only renders the idea of the fatwa as somehow standing above politics increasingly fragile, but also recasts the problem of divergent opinions. Under the current configuration, one of the fatwa's functions is to enable forms of collective mobilization for a variety of civilizing projects. It is perhaps the unwillingness of traditionalists, Islamists, and secularists alike to give up on the fatwa for purposes of collective mobilization that underlies their intriguing agreement on the diagnosis of the "chaos" of contemporary *iftā'*. More fundamentally, however, it is arguably a misrecognition of the kind of problem represented by conflicting fatwas that makes the phenomenon often appear so intractable.

Endnotes

1. The Amman Message's main points were subsequently reiterated by the Organization of Islamic Cooperation (OIC) in December 2005, by its International Islamic Fiqh Academy in July 2006 (with slight modification), and by a large gathering of European Muslim scholars (The Topkapi Declaration).
2. I do not wish to imply that there were no conflicts in pre-modern Islam. While the traditional legal pluralism allowed Muslim societies to manage the different understandings of Islamic law, this was not without its own set of tensions. As Sayf al-Din Abd al-Fattah pointed out in an episode of "Al-Sharīʿah wa al-

Hayāt" ("Ṣinā'at al-Fatwā," November 15, 2009), the *Lisān al-'Arab* recognizes and defines *al-tafātī* as "fighting or combating via the fatwa."

3. These two factors do not, of course, tell the whole story. Other oft-mentioned elements include the complexification of knowledge regimes, the rapidity of change, the penetration of market logics, the emergence of Islamist terrorism, intergenerational changes, and others. I cannot do full justice to them here.
4. See Al-Jazeera's "Al-Sharī'ah wa al-Hayāt," episode "Ṣinā'at al-Fatwā" with Shaykh Abd Allah Bin Bayyah, November 15, 2009, http://www.aljazeera.net/NR/exeres/C4A769DB-3B5F-49BF-A0F0-9C5E9EA76F60).
5. For a visual illustration of this perplexity, see Yara Qassem's painting in Omnia El-Desouki's article on the "Chaos of Fatwas?" *Al-Ahram Weekly*, http://weekly.ahram.org.eg/2011/1033/feature.htm).
6. See Usama Umar al-Ashqar, *Fawḍā al-Iftā'* (Beirut: Dār al-Nafa'is, 2009), 113 and "Tashrī' bi Tajrīm al-Fatwā min Ghayr al-Mutakhaṣṣisīn," *Al-Sharq al-Awsaṭ*, June 22, 2006.
7. See Salman al-'Awda, "Muftī al-Faḍā'iyyat Hal min Ḍābiṭ?" IslamOnLine.net; Ali al-Qurah Daghi, "Al-Fatāwā al-Mubāshirah fī Wasā'il al-I'lām," IslamOnLine.
8. For an analysis of how the fatwa became entangled with the "clash of civilizations" discourse and the making of a new global order, see Sayf al-Din Abd al-Fattah Isma'il, "Fatāwā al-Ummah wa Uṣūl al-Fiqh al-Ḥaḍārī," *Al-Iftā' fī 'Ālam Maftūḥ. Al Wāqi' al-Māthil...wa al-Amal al-Murtajā*, vol. 1 (Kuwait: Al-Markaz al-'Alami li al-Wasatiyyah, 2007).
9. In 2011, Al-Jazeera's weekly "Al-Sharī'ah wa al-Hayāt" discussed the relation between *fuqahā al-thawrah* and *fuqahā' al-sulṭah* in several episodes.
10. See also Mu'taz al-Khaṭīb, "Al-Fiqh wa al-Faqīh wa al-Dawlat al-Ḥadīthah: Ishkālīyāt al-Tanāfus bayna Sulṭatay al-Fatwā wa al-Qānūn," (2007), http://www.almultaka.net/ShowMaqal.php?module=30a1924ae9f288e2154f90c83936ac14&cat =3&id=51&m=a801508f366c9a149882ebf6c58c91f3.
11. See Al-Jazeera's "Al-Sharī'ah wa al-Hayāt," episode "Ṣinā'at al-Fatwā."
12. Ethar Shalaby, "Issuing Incorrect Fatwas Is Uncommon, says Grand Mufti Ali Gomaa," *The Daily News Egypt*, September 9, 2007.
13. Qaradawi was among the selected twenty-four senior scholars who enabled The Amman Message by answering the king's questions on the definition of a Muslim, the practice of *takfīr*, and the qualifications required to issue fatwas ("The Amman Message," vi.) Their answers are available at the "Fatwas of the 'Ulama," http://www.ammanmessage.com/.
14. Contrary to many, Qaradawi does not associate quickness with the immediacy of satellite television. Rather, he sees the speed with which some muftis issue fatwas as a psychological and moral problem stemming from their misplaced love for fame. See Yusuf Qaradawi, *Al-Fatāwā al-Shādhdhah* Cairo: Dar al-Shuruq, 2010), 132.

15. This claim is somewhat ironic, given Qaradawi's own training in *uṣūl al-dīn* and the perception in some Muslim circles that he is more of a *dā'īyah* than a *faqīh*.
16. On p. 30 of Qaradawi, *Al-Fatāwā al-Shādhdhah*, Qaradawi discusses the *ijtihād* of the late Tunisian president Habib Bourguiba on dividing inheritance shares equally between brother and sister. He cites this example not as a fatwa from a non-qualified mufti, but as an application of *ijtihād* outside its legitimate field.
17. For studies of Qaradawi in "Al-Shari'ah wa al-Hayāt," see Noah Feldman, "Shari'a and Islamic Democracy in the Age of Al-Jazeera," in *Shari'a: Islamic Law in the Contemporary Context,* ed. Abbas Amanat and Frank Griffel (Stanford: Stanford University Press, 2007); Ehab Galal, "Yusuf al-Qaradawi and the New Islamic TV," in *The Global Mufti: The Phenomenon of Yusuf al-Qaradawi,* ed. Bettina Gräf and Jakob Skovgaard-Petersen (London: Hurst, 2009); Anne-Sofie Roald, "The Wise Men: Democratization and Gender Equalization in the Islamic Message: Yusuf al-Qaradawi and Ahmad al-Kubaisi on the Air," *Encounters* 7, no. 1 (2001); Jakob Skovgaard-Petersen, "The Global Mufti," in *Globalization and the Muslim World: Culture, Religion, and Modernity*, ed. Birgit Schaebler and Leif Stenberg. Syracuse: Syracuse University Press, 2004.
18. The full transcript of this exchange is available at http://www.aljazeera.net/NR/exeres/EEA730DD-B44F-4888-B19F-1668FA6E1444.
19. This principled refusal to accept a separation between religion and politics does not make Qaradawi an advocate of a theocratic state. Indeed, his views on democracy are subtle and seemingly shifting. For his views on Islamic democracy, see Feldman, "Shari'a and Islamic Democracy," 2007.
20. For an instructive discussion of the impact of new media, see Charles Hirschkind, *The Ethical Soundscape* (New York: Columbia University Press, 2006).
21. One might, however, read the current proliferation of scholarly discourses on the *maqāṣid al-Sharī'ah* as an attempt to address the issue.
22. Armando Salvatore made this point in the context of public Islam's emergence in Egypt at the turn of the twentieth century.
23. I borrow the concept of functionalization from anthropologist Gregory Starrett, for whom it denotes "processes of translation in which intellectual objects from one discourse come to serve the strategic or utilitarian ends of another discourse. This translation not only places intellectual objects in new fields of significance, but radically shifts the meaning of their initial context." See Gregory Starrett, *Putting Islam to Work: Education, Politics, and Religious Transformation in Egypt* (Berkeley, Los Angeles, and London: University of California Press, 1998), 9. For an interesting discussion of religion's functions from the perspective of Islamic scholars, see the episode of "Al-Sharī'ah wa al-Hayāt" on "Waẓā'if al-Dīn" with Moroccan scholar Ahmad al-Raysuni, which aired on March 14, 2010 (http://www.aljazeera.net/NR/exeres/59D5A2F8-2A42-4D3A-AF23-96476E422A5F).

Bibliography

Abd al-Fattah Isma'il, Sayf al-Din. "Fatāwā al-Ummah wa Uṣūl al-Fiqh al-Ḥaḍārī." In *Al-Iftā' fī 'Ālam Maftūḥ. Al Wāqi' al-Māthil...wa al-Amal al-Murtajā*. Vol 1. Kuwait: Al-Markaz al-'Alami li al-Wasatiyyah, 2007.

Abou El Fadl, Khaled. *Speaking in God's Name: Islamic Law, Authority and Women*. Oxford: Oneworld, 2002.

The Amman Message (2004), http://www.ammanmessage.com/.

Ashqar, Usama Umar al-. *Fawḍā al-Iftā'*. Beirut: Dār al-Nafa'is, 2009.

Awwa, Muḥammad Salim al-. *Azmat al-Mu'assasat al-Dīnīyah*. Cairo: Dar al-Shuruq, 1998.

Bin Bayyah, Abd Allah. *Ṣinā'at al-Fatwā wa Fiqh al-Aqallīyāt*. Jeddah and Beirut: Dar al-Minhaj, 2007.

Feldman, Noah. "Shari'a and Islamic Democracy in the Age of Al-Jazeera." In *Shari'a: Islamic Law in the Contemporary Context*. Edited by Abbas Amanat and Frank Griffel. Stanford: Stanford University Press, 2007.

Galal, Ehab. "Yusuf al-Qaradawi and the New Islamic TV." In *The Global Mufti: The Phenomenon of Yusuf al-Qaradawi*. Edited by Bettina Gräf and Jakob Skovgaard-Petersen. London: Hurst, 2009.

Haddad, Yvonne Y. "Operation Desert Storm and the War of Fatwas." In *Islamic Legal Interpretation: Muftis and Their Fatwas*. Edited by M. K. Masud, Brinkley Messick, and David Powers. Cambridge, MA: Harvard University Press, 1996.

Hallaq, Wael. *Authority, Continuity and Change in Islamic Law*. Cambridge: Cambridge University Press , 2001.

Hirschkind, Charles. *The Ethical Soundscape*. New York: Columbia University Press, 2006.

Jumu'a, Ali. *Ṣinā'at al-Iftā'*. Cairo: Nahdat Misr, 2008.

Khaṭīb, Mu'taz al-. "Al-Fiqh wa al-Faqīh wa al-Dawlat al-Ḥadīthah: Ishkālīyāt al-Tanāfus bayna Sulṭatay al-Fatwā wa al-Qānūn," http://www.almultaka.net/Show Maqal.php?module=30a1924ae9f288e2154f90c83936ac14&cat=3&id=51&m= a801508f366c9a149882ebf6c58c91f3.

Matar, Fu'ad. *Alf Fatwā wa Fatwā: Muslimūn fī Mahabbi Fawḍā al-Fatāwā*. Beirut: Al-Dar al-Arabiyyah li al-'Ulum Nashirun, 2009.

Qaradawi, Yusuf al-. *Al-Fatwā bayna al-Inḍibāṭ wa al-Tasayyub*. Beirut, Damascus, and Amman: Al-Maktab al-Islami, 1988.

———. "Mūjibāt Taghayyur al-Fatwā." In *Al-Iftā' fī 'Ālam Maftūḥ. Al Wāqi' al-māthil ...wa al-Amal al-Murtajā*. Vol 1. Kuwait: Al-Markaz al-'Alami li al-Wasatiyyah, 2007.

———. *Mūjibāt Taghayyur al-Fatwā fī 'Aṣrinā*. Cairo: Dar al-Shuruq, 2008.

———. *Al-Fatāwā al-Shādhdhah*. Cairo: Dar al-Shuruq, 2010.

Rapoport, Yossef. "Legal Diversity in the Age of *Taqlīd*: The Four Chief *Qāḍī*s under the Mamluks." *Islamic Law and Society* 10, no. 2 (2003).

Roald, Anne-Sofie. "The Wise Men: Democratization and Gender Equalization in the Islamic Message: Yusuf al-Qaradawi and Ahmad al-Kubaisi on the Air." *Encounters* 7, no. 1 (2001).
Skovgaard-Petersen, Jakob. "The Global Mufti." In *Globalization and the Muslim World: Culture, Religion, and Modernity*. Edited by Birgit Schaebler and Leif Stenberg. Syracuse: Syracuse University Press, 2004.
Starrett, Gregory. *Putting Islam to Work: Education, Politics, and Religious Transformation in Egypt*. Berkeley, Los Angeles, and London: University of California Press, 1998.
Weiss, Bernard G. *The Spirit of Islamic Law*. Athens, GA, and London: The University of Georgia Press, 1998.
Zysow, Aron. "The Economy of Certainty: An Introduction to the Typology of Islamic Legal Theory." PhD diss., Harvard University, 1984.

Discussion

Discussant: Jamal Barzinji
I congratulate Alexandre for this quality paper. The chaos in fatwa is only a reflection of the chaos in the ummah itself. As the ummah settles down, I think this will work itself out. The governments and rulers are not trusted by the people and have no right to criminalize *iftā'*. What is missing is a platform in which debate can take place. Until the new regime came into power in Turkey, there was no Muslim country in which a free debate could occur, an approach that could marginalize extreme views and make room for meaningful debate.

I think Shaykh Yusef stopped short of pointing finger at those fatwas issued to please a ruler. In Saudi Arabia there was a real fear that Saddam Hussein would invade and there was honest confusion; but Shaykh Tantawi faced a ruthless regime and had no choice, though only Allah knows what was in his heart. I respect his position that the ummah has always confronted ridiculous fatwas, but this did not concern the ummah until now, given that it is now under pressure from the West about terrorism, or perhaps out of our own greater sensitivity. I think Tantawi was a sincere man trying to honestly address the question without alienating himself from the regime.

I don't think that an invisible hand regulates *iftā'*; rather, it is a very visible hand. Trust in the ummah; be patient for the scholars to regulate one another by their debates.

Discussant: Imad-ad-Dean Ahmad
Both supply and demand, as well as price intermediation, distinguishes the "marketplace of ideas" from ordinary markets. The new media does not cause the problems of chaos, but rather exacerbates them by reducing the costs of seeking and issuing fatwas. Qaradawi is correct that the mufti is effective only as long as his followers are willing to act on his opinion. But to what degree is his own ambiguity political?

Caeiro: I did not want to circulate this paper because it is so chaotic. I wonder to what degree the perception that there is new crisis is due to our idealization of the past and to what degree the people who depict a crisis have an agenda. I wonder to what degree it is the military superiority of the West that is the crisis. Perhaps we pay too much attention to that. People sometimes think that establishing a supreme *iftā'* council will solve the problem; I question that. Maybe it is a good thing that issuing one fatwa prompts a counter-fatwa. The contrary view seems authoritarian. I like Dr. Jamal's notion of the "visible hand" that leads to an eventual consensus over time.

While "market" is a common metaphor in sociology, it is a lazy one. If there is no price intermediation, then is it really a market? Maybe it is the public rather than the market that should be the focus. Qaradawi's motives may be political, but he is aware of the need to create a dis-embedded Islamic thinking. We all operate in a politicized world, but maybe he is more willing to engage in discussion than some others.

General Discussion

- A measure of chaos is necessary and healthy. It might be helpful to have an authority like a supreme council of *iftā'* where one is necessary, but what is really essential is the mufti's character. People are reluctant to give fatwas, fearing they may make a mistake to people or God. The alternative to chaos is something far worse. There are always those eager to replace chaos with dictatorship. Maybe we should look at chaos as a creative force.
- The difference between Tantawi and Qaradawi on the Gaza wall may be an example of differences due to phrasing.
- Without dismissing the suggestion that an alternative metaphor to the market is needed when speaking of the public contestation of ideas, that particular metaphor can also be applied to the blood supply, which also is a market without price intermediation. After disasters when the need for blood rises, so does the supply. When the crisis is over, both the supply and demand drop. The market may be the appropriate metaphor because there is a supply of and demand for fatwas.
- Are we speaking of chaos or diversity? Is there a place in the paper for unity in diversity? Traditional Islamic society was built on diversity. Modernism seems to see diversity as dispersive, as a threat. Seeing the chaos of fatwa as a threat is a little like the communists seeing more than one brand of soap on the shelf as a threat.
- In the huge demonstrations against in the buildup to the Iraq war, not a single sign supported Saddam Hussein. Maybe this diversity is not chaos, but rather a mercy to the ummah. The elephant in the room is engaging in terrorism based on fatwas. Putting the muftis under a single authority may not be in the spirit of Islam.
- Perhaps some fatwas are shocking because they deal with subjects that have not been discussed for a long time.
- Chaos is in the nature of *iftā'*. Crisis comes from the fatwa's substance.
- There seems to be a public ability in the ummah to always take the middle of the way and reject extremist tendencies. For instance, the Shi'a groups that have survived and done well are the most moderate. The others either disappeared or

were pushed to the fringe. In Sufism too, Ibn al-Arabi is Shaykh al-Akbar for a rather small minority of Sufi scholars. There is a level on which *ijmā'* operates and supports the hadith "My community does not agree on error."

- Chaos is not diversity; *fawḍā* is not *tabī'ah*. Chaos is that which cannot be predicted or regulated, like long-term weather. The creative chaos of diversity is positive.
- The opposite of chaos is cosmos, not control, but order. Why should a council be considered an alternative to chaos? Why can't you have both: let the open issuance of fatwas continue, but also have multiple fatwa councils.
- It would be appreciated it if this institutionalization could give Muslims in the United States a role.
- Is chaos the right translation of *fawḍā*, which comes from a root that puts everyone on the same level, anarchistic as opposed to hierarchical?
- Laziness in metaphors is a reference to the term "market logic," which doesn't really say anything since there are multiple markets with multiple logics. I need to look further into the question of social entropy. Chaos means unpredictability; that is in the nature of the social world. Merely having a website doesn't make one equal to everyone else with a website. AMJA (the Association of Muslim Jurists in America) is based all over the world. How do its members incorporate the view that the fatwa should be responsive to local times and places? There is an intergenerational dimension to this perception of chaos. Thanks for the distinction between crisis and chaos; I shall give that thought. There are different concepts of order that need to be historicized, and Muslims should be asked how they conceive order.
- The Bible says the heavens and Earth were in chaos until God imposed the cosmos.
- What is missing from the notion of chaos is relating plurality to the notion of the scholars' lack of qualifications. There is a literal vs. a purposive understanding. When Qaradawi tells people to vote, they ask for whom they should vote. He suggests those who oppose homosexuality, but there are no such parties in France.
- A scholar can be expelled from his own country or killed as an apostate because of his fatwa.

Fatwa in the Era of Globalization

Moustafa Kassem

Abstract

Issuing religious edicts is one of the last tangible forms of influence that traditional Islamic scholars maintain in a post-modern age of increasing secularization. Expanding Muslim communities living as minorities in western society are facing a crisis of identity as they struggle to assimilate and are no longer as receptive to conventional forms of religious authority as former generations were. Likewise, citizens of Muslim-majority countries are challenging sources of temporal and spiritual leadership. As religious authority in different groups is becoming less dependent on ethnic origin, Islamic scholars must adapt to the changing needs of society for their edicts to continue to be relevant. This paper explores the evolving role of the traditional fatwa as it relates to the new paradigm of global interconnectedness in three parts. First, it conducts an examination of the meanings and origins of the fatwa based on Islamic primary sources and interpretations of traditional scholars. Then, it discusses qualifications and characteristics of the traditional and contemporary mufti. Finally, it discusses and recommends for adaptation examples of new methodologies and areas of focus for Islamic religious edicts.

Introduction: Defining the Term *Fatwa*

The general meaning of the term *fatwa* is related to the verbal noun *al-iftā'*, which means a response that makes something clear.[1] The verbal form appears in the Qur'an with this meaning: "O notables, explain to me my dream, if it be that you can interpret dreams" (Q. 12:43).

Pharaoh had a dream that he thought was of some significance, but did not understand what it was. So he asked the members of his advisory council to clarify its meaning and explain its significance, provided that they could interpret dreams. Since they could not, they deferred their response. Eventually the matter was brought to Prophet Yusuf's attention, who at that time was in prison, saying: "O Yusuf, man of truth. Explain to us (the dream) of seven fat cows whom seven lean ones were devouring, and of seven green ears of corn, and (seven) others dry" (Q. 12:46).

An alternate meaning of fatwa involves giving suggestion and guidance, as in the case of the Queen of Sheba who asked the members of her council to advise her upon receiving King Solomon's ultimatum: "O chiefs, advise me in (this) case of mine" (Q. 27:32). As they suggested, she sent a delegation to him and eventually embraced Islam.

When used in religious terms, fatwa means to answer a question pertaining to the religious ruling of a particular action.[2] This usage appears in the recorded sayings of Prophet Muhammad: "Sin is that which causes doubts and perturbs the heart, even if people give a fatwa that it is lawful or you seek your own fatwa on the matter."[3]

In its commonly understood application, well-informed Islamic scholars issue a fatwa to inform an individual or the general public about the status of a particular action with regards to its permissibility, prohibition, rewards, and punishment. Like any other field of expertise, those who need consultation or knowledge should seek the most qualified scholar. In fact, Allah the Most High commands us: "Ask the followers of the Remembrance if you know not" (Q. 16:43), even though the actual verse refers to the Jewish scholars' knowledge of previous prophets.

Traditional Applications

Scholars of the sciences of Islamic jurisprudence have divided all possible religious or non-religious actions into five major categories based upon evidence from the primary and secondary sources of Islamic knowledge, namely, the Qur'an, Sunnah (the prophetic traditions), scholarly consensus, and analogy:

1. *Wājib* (Mandatory): Actions that are rewarded if done and punished if not done.
2. *Mustaḥab* (Preferable): Actions that are rewarded if done and not punished if not done.
3. *Mubāḥ* (Permissible): Actions that carry no reward or punishment.
4. *Makrūh* (Not preferable): Actions that are not punished if done but are rewarded if they are not done.
5. *Ḥarām* (Forbidden): Actions that are punished if done but are rewarded if they are not done.

The general public always needs Islamic scholars to clarify the Islamic position on various issues by determining their proper categorization. These scholars, in turn, have a unique responsibility due to their awareness of the sources of Islamic jurisprudence as well as their wisdom and experience in relating this knowledge to reality.[4] Therefore, they and the jurists hold a special position and status because they report to people how Allah, the Creator, views a particular issue.[5] Prophet Muhammad has stated: "Indeed, the [Islamic] scholars are inheritors of the prophets and, verily, the prophets have not left behind gold or silver. Verily, they have left behind knowledge."[6]

The Basis for Religious Edicts

Islamic scholars may issue a fatwa only if they are certain about the basis on which it can be made. To determine the answer, they must follow a certain methodology that includes, in general order of importance, the Qur'an, the Sunnah, scholarly consensus (*ijmā'*), analogy of an unknown ruling to a known ruling (*qiyās*), public benefit (*al-maṣāliḥ al-mursalah*), the prevention of harm (*sadd al-ḍarrā'*), the Companions' position, and cultural significance (*'urf*). They are strongly warned against pronouncing any type of verdict based on insufficient information or personal inclinations. Prophet Muhammad said:

> There are three types of judges, two of whom are in hell and one who is in heaven. The first two are those who judge and intentionally give an unjust ruling, and those who rule without knowledge and impinge on people's rights. They are in hell. The judge who rules according to the truth is in heaven.[7]

Distinguishing Characteristics of the Fatwa

The main difference between the positions of Islamic scholars and those of other religions is that an Islamic ruling can only be given on the basis of evidence derived from the sources of revelation in the form of general principles or specific rules.[8] This frame of reference, the Qur'an and Sunnah, has been preserved in order to guide humanity: "Verily We: It is We Who have sent down the remembrance and, surely, We will preserve it" (Q. 15:9).

The principles, information, and laws proclaimed in the Qur'an have been preserved via the uncorrupted Qur'anic text as well as the prophetic traditions. The authenticity of these primary sources is verifiable, thanks to Allah's Mercy and centuries of diligent memorization and Islamic scholarship. Every Qur'anic verse and much of the Prophet's life and speech have been preserved with verifiable chains of narration.

Al-Hafidh Abu Ali al-Ghasaani, an eminent Andalusian hadith scholar, identified the detailed sciences of preserving the authenticity of religious information, its narrators' identities, and the linguistic means by which we can understand its exact meanings: "Allah has given this nation three things that He never gave to any nation before: *al-isnād* (verifiable chains of narration), *al-ansāb* (genealogical knowledge), and *al-'irāb* (precise linguistic vowel-markers)."[9]

The Mufti: Qualifications and Characteristics

The term for someone who holds an official position of giving *iftā'* or is requested to give a fatwa is *mufti*. Imam al-Nawawi detailed the characteristics that such a figure should have.

> The mufti should be responsible for his actions (mature, sane, etc...), Muslim, reliable, safe and free from traces of corruption and inappropriate behavior, wise at heart, mentally capable, able to think clearly, conduct himself well and make correct deductions, and fully conscious. These are the conditions and they are applicable to free people as well as slaves, women, blind people, and mutes, as long as they are able to communicate through writing or understandable gestures.[10]

The responsibility of this position, as with any other position, should be granted based on one's qualifications as opposed to one's social status, race, personal connections, or gender. Although in Islamic civilization women have not traditionally held positions of political leadership or judicial authority, they have played major roles as influential scholars and teachers. The first and best example of this is Aisha, the Prophet's wife who became an influential scholar. The Companions sought her opinions on important matters after her husband's death (632) until her own death almost fifty years later in Madinah.[11]

The muftis' most important qualification is the ability to perform *ijtihād* (interpreting Islamic law so that it can be applied to new situations and issues). The scholars of the sciences of Islamic jurisprudence (*uṣūl al-fiqh*) agree that those who undertake this task (viz., a *mujtahid*) must have mastered five realms of Arabic-language knowledge: the sacred texts of the Qur'an and the Hadith, instances of *ijmā'*, abrogated and abrogating texts (*al-nāsikh wa al-mansūkh*), and *uṣūl al-fiqh*.

The second aspect of the muftis' qualification, after their Islamic knowledge and upright character, is their awareness and understanding of current events and issues upon which they are requested to rule.[12] For example, qualified scholars in Islamic finance should not only be aware of classical writings on trade transactions, but also educated about the intricacies of modern banking and the current economic situation. Only combining classical and contemporary understandings can equip them to issue rulings that will truly reflect and uphold the Shari'ah's deeper goals and objectives (*maqāṣid al-Sharī'ah*), namely, preserving life, religion, property, familial bonds, and honor. According to Abu Aminah Bilal Phillips, "A scholar should be open-minded in his search for knowledge. Otherwise, his rulings are likely to be biased and sectarian."[13]

In addition to acquiring knowledge and information from a variety of sources, scholars should consider the situation and expected outcomes and effects of their religious rulings. An example of wisdom used while considering the questioner's (*mustaftī*) situation is the story of the one who asked Ibn Abbas, the eminent Companion and scholar, about the punishment for murder:

> A man asked Ibn Abbas: "Is there a repentance for one who purposely kills a Muslim?" He replied: "No, there is only hellfire." When (the questioner) left, we (Ibn Abbas' students) said to him (Ibn Abbas): "This is not how you used to give us verdicts. You used to say that was possible for someone who killed a Muslim to have his repentance accepted. So what happened today?" Ibn Abbas said: "I perceived him to be in a state of anger, wanting to kill a Muslim." After that, they followed the man and found him to be as Ibn Abbas had described him.[14]

Islamic scholars in general, and muftis in particular, may build their qualifications using a variety of means. In general, they are expected to begin their education by memorizing the Qur'an and a large number of hadith. This memorization can be certified by a school diploma, an *ijāzah* (a personal certification given by a shaykh), or a certificate issued by an institute of Qur'anic memorization. Muftis may complete their higher education in Islamic law at a specialized institute, such as the Mahad al-Haram in Makkah or the Dar al-Hadith. However, as more universities now offer programs in Islamic studies, *fiqh*, Shar'iah, and *uṣūl al-fiqh*, the increasing trend is to give preference to those who have attained the highest degree from such institutions in addition to their specified religious training.[15]

As is true with all scholarly disciplines, the primary barrier to entry is the consensus of well-established scholars regarding the prospective mufti's qualifications.[16] The form and level of consensus, however, may vary greatly from place to place. Recent times have witnessed a partial formalization of the consensus process. In countries with a government-supervised religious establishment, such as Saudi Arabia and Egypt, the king or executive authority may require some type of license or permission before a scholar may issue a fatwa. In 2010, King Abdullah Al Saud issued a royal decree instructing General Mufti Abdul-Aziz Al Sheikh to report to him regarding those individuals qualified to give fatwas. This decree also prohibited anyone who is not a Council of Senior Scholars member from issuing a fatwa. The order excluded fatwa on simple matters of worship considered a necessity for education.[17] However, government regulation of the fatwa process remains controversial: supporters cite a need for regulation and opponents draw attention to the possible censorship of qualified individuals who can contribute to the body of Islamic knowledge and understanding.[18]

In nations where there is no definitive authority on matters of religion and Shari'ah, the situation is often different. As the Muslim population of many developed nations continues to grow rapidly, the founding and development of scholarly institutions, think tanks, and councils has seldom been sufficient to meet existing needs. This, in turn, has led to many unqualified, uneducated, and previously unknown individuals giving lessons, advice, and rulings on issues that have mislead and misinformed many people. According to King Abdullah: "We have observed the fallout from unqualified people issuing fatwas. It is our duty to stop them in order to preserve our religion."[19]

The Role of Technology and Social Media

In particular, the Internet has been a forum for the rampant distribution of Islamic information and a multitude of opinions without any established standards for credibility or accountability. Abdallah El-Tahawi states, in his article "The Internet is the New Mosque":

> Specifically, the internet has become not only a clearinghouse for Koranic text, but also for religious guidance and even fatwas (religious edicts). The new, global online Islam has been propagated by countless websites maintained by sheikhs, religious scholars, and even laymen. Today, any person can look up a fatwa on any subject, checking whether a particular action is *ḥarām* (forbidden) or *ḥalāl* (permissible), sometimes within minutes, with just a few clicks of the mouse.[20]

On the other hand, if the scholars' credibility and qualification has been sufficiently established, the Internet can be used to enhance accessibility for those who do not live close to a mufti or *mujtahid* and do not possess their personal contact information. El-Tahawy, later in his article, states:

> [O]nline fatwas are the new, widely available alternative for the Muslim masses. Regardless of one's stance toward online fatwas, the established fact is that they have become a means for Internet users to present their problems and receive detailed religious advice. Moreover, this impersonal means of communication allows users to ask more frank questions than social norms in their country permit.[21]

We should view the Internet as a tool and means of communication that can be used to benefit and educate or abused for personal gain, as is the case with any other tool. Its future usage as regards issuing fatwas and religious advice will reflect the state of organization as regards the global community of scholars. The degree to which they are united and accredited will be the measurement by which questioners can determine if they are approaching a reliable source for a religious ruling.

The Possibility of Regulation

As scholars have noted, one of the Shari'ah's special qualities is its applicability to every region and age from its revelation to the end of times. As Robert Crane elucidated during his presentation at the Eighteenth Anniversary of the founding of the Institute for Islamic Thought, "Islamic jurisprudence is absolute in principles but relative in application according to time and place."[22] We should hope for the scholarly discipline of interpreting the Shari'ah to adapt to the global environment so that it can once again become a key factor in world affairs.

First of all, some type of standardization of the educational requirements must be devised in order to provide an objective measure of credibility for those claiming to be Islamic scholars and jurists. Implementing standardized tests for those who have completed their higher education as well as memorization requirements may reliably measure what the scholars know, can do with their knowledge, and serve as a performance goal that would be a final barrier of entry to the field, much like the MCAT (medicine), bar (law), and CPA (accounting) exams. A major challenge would entail designing a testing system that adheres to the major principles of standardized testing:

1. Reliability: The exam should produce consistent results.
2. Validity: The exam should measure what it is intended to measure.
3. Fairness: The exam should not place scholars at a disadvantage because of gender, nationality, school of thought, or disability.[23]

Implementing this would require the efforts of scholars who are both knowledgeable and experienced in the Shari'ah, the various methodologies of jurisprudence, as well as the fields of industrial/organizational psychology and standardized testing.

Fatwas in the Private Sector

As the importance of the fatwa and Shari'ah advisory boards continues to grow in the private sector, we should also expect to see the corresponding growth and development of its institutions. Until now, the role of Islamic scholars of finance, for example, has been largely individualistic, unsupervised, and unregulated. In addition to the lack of defined standards for establishing their qualifications, it has been common for a single scholar to sit on dozens of Shari'ah advisory boards. This situation not only necessitates a conflict of interest, but also prevents the scholar from fully committing his resources and capacities to any particular project. The most active Shari'ah scholar in the Islamic banking world, Dr. Nizam Yaqubi currently is a member of seventy-eight Shari'ah advisory boards and the chairman of ten of them.[24]

The first of two apparent solutions to this dilemma is for a governmental or private accreditation agency to limit the number of boards upon which a Shari'ah advisor can sit. The Bahrain-based Accounting and Auditing Organization for Islamic Financial Institutions (AAOIFI) has already adopted some initiatives related to this practice. However, as they are not really enforced, they are unlikely to have much impact in the near future. A more effective and influential example is the Malaysian government's requirement that each Shari'ah scholar be registered and that each scholar sit on only one advisory board in each sector at any particular time. Perhaps this can serve as a model for future efforts to incorporate scholars as consultants, advisors, and employees in international business and banking ventures.[25] Another alternative to prevent qualified scholars from spreading their talents and services too thinly is to shift the fatwa paradigm from its current focus on the individual to a more collective effort by creating consultative bodies, foundations, and firms that are supervised by senior scholars.[26]

Conclusion

Perhaps the greatest benefit derived from the people's changing demands and needs for relevant interpretations of Islamic law is how scholars and their methodologies will adapt to those needs. The older models based upon the reliance on single schools of thought (*madhāhib*), and the exclusion of others, no longer suit the needs of cooperating international councils, companies, educational institutions, and policymakers. Instead, decisions will be made after interdisciplinary research and new examinations of established judicial precedents, both of which will take into account the strongest arguments and evidence from all of the classical schools of thought and scholarly deliberations.[27]

Indeed, the increasing global need for competent, capable, and wise Islamic scholars, researchers, and muftis will continue to challenge students to develop themselves as carriers of knowledge who are in touch with the realities of a fast-changing world. Educators and academic institutions need to constantly reexamine and update their curricula to reflect these emerging needs. They should use case studies and recent examples to illustrate the complex situations that are unique to the modern era and encourage a balanced approach to Islam that considers an issue's various aspects as well as the merits and methodologies of different opinions regarding their rulings and solutions. Most importantly, the increasing Muslim population will prove to be the most important factor influencing the fatwa's role and future impact. The degree to which they adhere to Islam and search for solutions within an Islamic framework will be the degree to which fatwa will play a decisive role in this era of globalization.

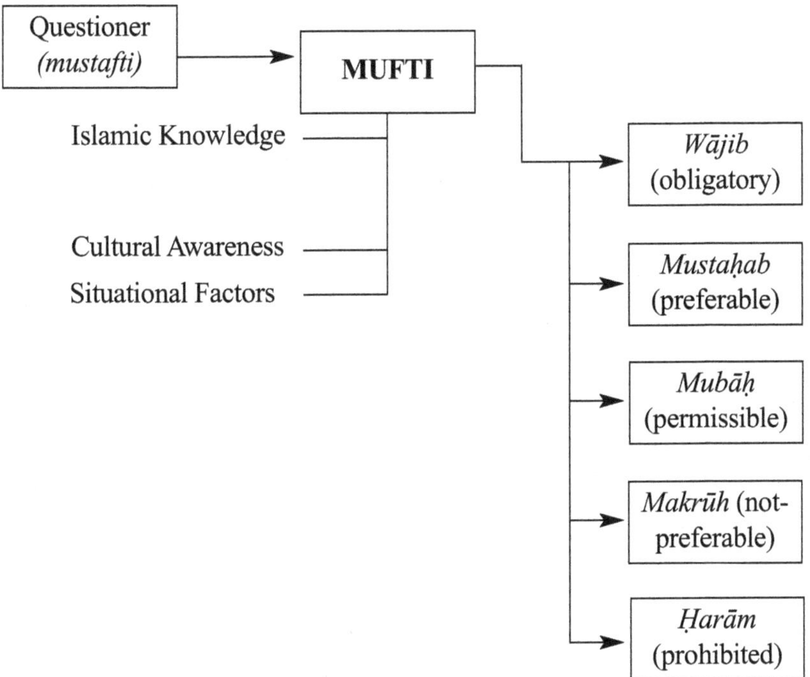

Endnotes

1. M. Ibn Manthur, *Lisān al-Arab* (Bulaq: al-Matba'ah al-Kubra al-Amiriyyah, 1890), 5:3348.
2. U. U. Al-Ashqar, *Fawḍā al-Iftā'* (Jerusalem: Dar al-Nafa'is, 2008), 9.
3. Ibn Hanbal, *Musnad al-Imām Aḥmad* (Cairo: Mu'assasat Qurtubah, 2001), 4:243.
4. A. K. Zaydaan, *An Introduction to Shar'iah Studies* (Baghdad: Mu'assasat al-Risalah, 1969), 29.
5. Al-Ashqar, *Fawḍā,* 11.
6. M. I. al-Tirmithi, *Al-Jāmi' al-Ṣaḥīḥ* (Riyadh: Dar al-Salam, 2008) 3:123.
7. Ibid.
8. Zaydaan, *Introduction,* 38.
9. J. Al-Suyuti, *Tadrīb Al-Rāwī fī Sharḥ Taqrīb al-Nawawī* (Cairo: al-Kawthar Library, 1994), 1:112
10. Y. I. al-Nawawi, *Adab al-Fatwā wa al-Muftī wa al-Mustaftī* (Cairo: Mu'assasat allhram, 1998), 47.
11. S. R. Al-Mubarakpuri, *The Sealed Nectar* (Riyadh: Dar al-Salam, 2002), 234.
12. Ibid.
13. B. Philips, *The Evolution of Fiqh* (Raleigh, NC: International Islamic Pubilishing House, 1983), 132.
14. A. B. Ibn Abi Shaybah, *Musanaf Ibn Abī Shaybah* (Riyadh: Maktabat Alrushd, 2004), 4:92.
15. M. M. Scott-Baumann, *The Training and Development of Muslim Faith Leaders: Current Practice and Future Possibilities* (London: Communities and Local Government Publications, Crown 2010), 44.
16. Al-Nawawi, *Adab al-Fatwā*, 23.
17. F. Sidya, "Fatwas Only by Senior Scholars: King," *Arab News*, 2010.
18. Al-Ashqar, *Fawḍā al-Iftā',* 32.
19. Ibid.
20. A. El-Tahawy, "The Internet is the New Mosque: Fatwa at the Click of a Mouse," arabinsight.org, arabinsight.orgaiarticles188.pdf., 11, accessed March 2011.
21. Ibid., 13.
22. R. D. Crane, "*Maqāṣid al-Shari'ah*: A Strategy to Rehabilitate Religion in America. Eighteenth Birthday Celebration," 1999, 7.
23. S. Zucker, *Fundamentals of Standardized Testing*, 3.
24. M. Parker, "Are Shari'ah Advisories Becoming an Endangered Species?" *Arab News,* 2010.
25. Ibid.
26. Ibid.
27. S. Tahir, *The Future of Islamic Banking* (Tehran: 2003).

Bibliography

Al-Ashqar, U. U. *Fawḍā al-Iftā'*. Jerusalem: Dar al-Nafa'is, 2008.

al-Mubarakpuri, S. R. *The Sealed Nectar.* Riyadh: Dar al-Salam, 2002.

Al-Nawawi, Y. I. (d. 1380). *Adab al-Fatwā wa al-Muftī wa al-Mustaftī.* Cairo: Mu'assasat al-Ihram, 1998.

Assulami, A. *Uṣūl al-Fiqh* (Matters that the Judicial Scholar Must Not Be Ignorant of). Riyadh: Dar al-Tadmuriyyah, 2005.

Al-Suyuti, J. (d. 1505). *Tadrīb al-Rāwī fī Sharḥ Taqrīb al-Nawawī.* Cairo: al-Kawthar Library.

Al-Tirmidhi, M. I. (d. 892). *Al-Jāmi' al- Ṣaḥīḥ*. Riyadh: Dar al-Salam, 2008.

Crane, R. D. "Maqāṣid al-Sharī'ah: A Strategy to Rehabilitate Religion in America. Eighteenth Birthday Celebration." Herndon, VA: IIIT, 1999.

El-Tahawy, A. (d. 933). "The Internet Is the New Mosque: Fatwa at the Click of a Mouse." Retrieved March 2011 from arabinsight.org.arabinsight.orgaiarticles 188.pdf.

Farooq, M. O. "The Riba-Interest Equation and Islam: Reeaxamination of Traditional Arguments." Fayette: Upper Iowa University, 2005.

Goolam, N. "*Ijtihād* and its Significance for Islamic Legal Interpretation." *Michigan State Law Review* (2006).

Hilal, I. "Studies in Uṣūl al-Fiqh," 1999. Retrieved from Islamic Truth: www.islamic-truth.fsnet.co.uk

Ibn Abi Shaybah, A. B. (d. 235 AH). *Musanaf Ibn Abī Shaybah*. Riyadh: Maktabat al-Rushd, 2004.

Ibn Hanbal, I. A. (d. 855). *Musnad Imam Ahmad ibn Hanbal.* Bierut: Mu'assasat al-Risalah, 2001.

Ibn Manzur, M. (d. 1311). *Lisān al-Arab.* Bulaq: al-Matba'ah al-Kubra al-Amiriyyah, 1890.

Parker, M. "Are Shari'ah Advisories Becoming an Endangered Species?" *Arab News*, December 12, 2010.

Philips, B. *The Evolution of Fiqh.* Raleigh, NC: International Islamic Publishing House, 1983.

Ramadan, H. M. "The Future of Islamic Law Scholarship." *Michigan State Law Review* (2006).

Scott-Baumann, M. M. *The Training and Development of Muslim Faith Leaders: Current Practice and Future Possibilities.* London: Communities and Local Government Publications, 2010.

Sidya, F. "Fatwas only by Senior Scholars: King." *Arab News*, August 12, 2010.

Tahir, S. *The Future of Islamic Banking.* Jeddah: Central Bank of the Islamic Republic of Iran and the Islamic Research & Training Institute of the IDB, 2003.

Y-Sing, L. "Islamic Finance Taps Women Scholars." Reuters. 2010.

Zaydaan, A. K. *An Introduction to Islamic Shariah.* Baghdad: Mu'assasat al-Risalah, 1969.

Zucker, S. *Fundamentals of Standardized Testing.* San Antonio: Pearson, 2003.

Discussion

Discussant: Mahmoud Ayoub

The Internet is creating confusion in many fields, including this one, but we cannot deny its importance. You can write a question to someone like Yusuf al-Qaradawi and get an answer within three days. You should be careful of your high bar for a mufti's qualification. The mufti is also usually a *faqīh*, and usually those who issue fatwas about medical or scientific matters ask experts in those areas. The *marāji'* in the Shi'a system, due to the zakat system, often control a great deal of wealth. I think we should institutionalize *iftā'* rather than limit it to individuals. Asked about a conventional mortgage, an *'ālim* who does not know enough about finance or the American environment may issue a peculiar fatwa. For example, one *'ālim* said one could have a car loan but not a home loan, even though the latter is more important. Many fatwas today require more research that an institution can facilitate and then store in a fatwa bank.

Including women in *iftā'* is neither simple nor easy, given the *fiqh* limitations on them. You know the famous, or infamous, hadith related on the authority of Ibn Mas'ud that a woman is deficient in reason and religion. The idea that her testimony is half that of a man has prevented women from being judges. We must deal with these issues before saying that they should be included in *iftā'*. We have a lot of work to do before we can entertain this particular possibility. But I admire your ideals and hope that we can rise to the standard you have set.

Discussant: Alexandre Caeiro

I think the paper provides a largely normative account of the fatwa that draws on the traditional genre. At first sight it looks like a mere repetition of previous accounts with a striking sense of continuity that allows Mustafa to draw legitimately and eclectically from a thirteenth-century Shafi'i jurist, al-Nawawi, and a contemporary Jordanian Usama Sulayman al-Ashqar. The genre is also reflexive with a certain contemporary naivety that provides interesting material on the Muslim understanding of religious authority. In the future, Mustafa might wish to explore the differences between these two scholars' accounts. There is a familiar narrative of the fatwa's decline both in terms of the mufti's quality and piety. There is also the idea that the mufti has the right to paint a negative picture of society if it will prompt people to greater piety.

I would raise three questions on these lines: standardization, the Internet, and the shifting fatwa: (1) Do you agree that the suggestion of standardization implies that the problem of strange fatwas today is due to the lack of qualified ulama? (2) You have a nuanced analysis of the Internet's impact. The social sciences never see the media as neutral (viz., the medium is the message). Don't you think that websites with known scholars are privileged over other websites? 3) The paper ends with a call for a shift in the fatwa paradigm from an individual to a collective process, which is already taking place within fiqh councils. How would you respond to the claim that such a shift would take us to a framework that is very different from the traditional Islamic legal tradition with which you open your paper?

Kassem: The Internet can educate and benefit or be used for personal gain like any other tool. It will ultimately reflect the international community of scholars. I was concerned with those people who do not know who is and who is not a scholar. My understanding of the hadith about women is that the Prophet said: "I have never seen a people so deficient in thinking and religion." I took it as a response to a particular situation as opposed to a general comment pronouncement on their qualities or deficiencies.

General Discussion

- When you analyze it, the hadith is not a proper hadith; rather, it is *mudraj*, because it is Ibn Mas'ud's words and not those of the Prophet. But that is not the issue. The hadith "A people led by a woman will not prosper" is the problem.
- The actual text of the other hadith calls upon women to do more good deeds because no one takes away the common sense of a man more than a woman.
- Neither hadith is acceptable because we know that the Prophet loved women. After all, he said that three things were made lovable in this world: women and perfume (which are related) and then prayer.
- We should consider including women on consultative bodies, beginning with research. We shall never be finished with *iftā'* because we will always have new questions. Including young people is important. Islamic finance prompts a resurgence in fatwas as the science of economics becomes more familiar to people. We cannot test *taqwā* on a bubble sheet, but we can test critical thinking and knowledge. We need some tools for investigation, and this might be one of them. As for the shift in the fatwa paradigm, the instruction "consult your heart" is very important, for it does not deal with issues that are completely clear, like whether to pray or drink wine. There are cases where you should ask the scholars about their methodology and proofs so you can make the decision yourself. We need to remember "consult your heart" and treat scholars as servants of the *dīn* who exist to serve the people and increase their knowledge.
- A clear distinction is needed between fatwas relating to *'ibādāt* and *mu'āmalāt*. The paper's shift of paradigm was from the individual to the collective; perhaps it should be from being a reactive mufti to a proactive mufti. Then instead of deliberative bodies, we should be promoting think tanks that deal with technology and globalization in an attempt to influence policy rather than just answering questions. As a process of question and answer *iftā'* has always had a small audience; in reality, it has never been used as an educational tool to expose the ummah to larger questions.
- A fatwa is a response to a question or a need. Perhaps the need is the more important focus now. Some people may be qualified to answer a question in a limited area only. This duty could be extended to specialized think tanks. Having Islamic scholars on board with other experts is another way to address that problem.

- The paper paints a bleak picture of both the muftis and those who are asking questions. The further people move away from the *qalb* (heart), the more they need to ask questions. A different kind of educational process would reduce the need for people to call an expert in Saudi Arabia for a fatwa. The mufti doesn't do that kind of education. Peer review bodies like to mirror themselves. Islam has offered other solutions to these issues.
- The standards mentioned in the paper for a mufti are those of a *mujtahid*. People follow popular religious leaders rather than apply standards. People are driven by the answers they desire.
- There is a difference between fatwa and *irshād* (religious guidance) Also, we need social scientists to participate in the *iftā'* process.
- Can't we ask the society, instead of the mufti, and have a fatwa by the nation? Despite globalization, we have a multiplicity of cultures.
- In the past, the qualifications have always been the traditional ones; now, however, we are seeing a synthesis between academic and traditional qualifications. This can have a balancing effect and address other issues, such as cultural sensitivity. Cultural awareness should be required for all muftis.
- We are broadening the definition of a fatwa too much for it to remain a fatwa. *Irshād* may involve a fatwa, but not necessarily. Fatwa is a matter of clarification, while *irshād* may be helping people.
- A fatwa is good council, whether it is done individually or collectively. Even when a fatwa comes out of a research institution, the head of the institution could still sign it. Perhaps we need a mechanism to make fatwas international.
- Where does this idea that women are not supposed to be heard come from? Women issued fatwas, or were at least respected scholars, during the Prophet's lifetime. We are less liberal on this issue now than were the Prophet and his contemporaries.
- Perhaps the reason *iftā'* has become an issue is because of the atrocities that have taken place in the Muslim world. We need a clear definition for fatwa and mufti. One condition for a mufti is that he must know the questioner, a condition that cannot be met over the Internet. We need to distinguish between the imam, who is also a counselor, the mufti, and the *faqīh*. Even in face-to-face situations there is incomplete familiarity between the mufti and the questioner, so we should not discount the Internet too quickly. The Shi'a on the Internet will only give general answers and then refer the questioner to their local mufti for a more specific answer.
- We have gone past the point described above as regards women. Their role in these issues is a matter of qualification. The earliest Muslims consulted with women even on the *khalīfah*'s succession. The politicization of fatwas deserves a paper of its own. In the Shari'ah Council in Pakistan, the politicization was painful. We have no *marāji'* among the Sunnis, for it is the ummah that gives credibility to the muftis, not the political leadership. What we have arrived at in the last ten-fifteen years is that the role of Shari'ah has become the re-articulation

of the *maqāṣid*, regardless of the issue. With millions of Muslims living under non-Muslim rule, we have to articulate a *fiqh al-aqallīyāt*. A number of PhD dissertations have been written on *fiqh al-jam'īyah* (collective jurisprudence). With all of our reservations about Egypt, its grand mufti does have thirty paid researchers. We have a golden opportunity to bring Sunni and Shi'a together in *madāris al-fatwā*. Not a single Sunni *iftā'* body has a single Shi'i scholar and vice versa. Commercialization has been a disgrace on scholarship (see Bin Bayyah's recent book on fatwas). On the issue of incorporating education, we note the following: Out of thirty-five applicants from al-Azhar for a position on the Fiqh Council of North America, only one survived on the basis of showing common sense during the interview. But the other thirty-four are serving somewhere in the world today. If first-generation scholars could consult with merchants and women, why can't we?

- Twenty years ago Shaykh Taha commented on this non-hadith that women are deficient in intellect and religion. How could the Prophet possibly, on the occasion of Eid, disgrace a group of women in such a fashion?
- Suggesting that governments should appoint the fatwa boards is an invitation to oppression.
- The issues we discussed today come down to the question of authority. In many comments, authority was reduced to knowledge. Does this apply now, when other things have more impact than knowledge? If we want to speak of women in the *iftā'* process, we should recognize that institutional authority, rather than any hadith, determines their absence.

Al-Qushayri's Fatwa and His *Risālah*: Their Relevance to Intra-Islamic Dialog Today

Kenneth L. Honerkamp

This is an epistle that the indigent one in need of God Most High, Abd al-Karim b. al-Qushayri, has addressed to all the Sufi community in the lands of Islam in the year 437/1045.

— *Al-Risālah al-Qusharīyah*

Abstract

At a time when suicide bombers are targeting Sufi shrines in India and Pakistan and, as stated by Hamid Algar, "some Western scholars and numerous present-day Muslims see Sufism as an extraneous growth owing little to the authoritative sources of Islam or as a sectarian development that occurred at a given point in Islamic history,"[1] the relevance of the fatwa issued in 436/1044 by Abu al-Qasim Abd al-Karim b. Hawazin al-Qushayri (d. 465/1072)[2]; his famous "Complaint of the People of the Sunna Recounting the Persecution that has Befallen them" = "Complaint," (*Shikāyat Ahl al-Sunnah bimā Nālahum min al-Miḥna*),[3] written in 446/1054; and his Epistle on Sufism (*Al-Risālah al-Qushayrīyah fī 'Ilm al-Taṣawwuf* = *Risālah*) composed in 437/1045 cannot be stressed enough. His fatwa and subsequent imprisonment and exile from his native city of Nishapur exemplifies the sociopolitical ramifications of what is most commonly assumed to be a pronouncement of a juridical or legal nature. The *Risālah* itself historically demonstrates the existence of a virtue-based ethical discourse of formative Sufism that delineates a strategy for attaining wisdom and an intimate knowledge of God. I will refer to this discourse as being a facet of fatwa founded upon correct comportment (*fatwā akhlāqī*).

Introduction

Al-Qushayri, a pillar of Islamic orthodoxy, was known for his mastery of the multiple fields of hadith narration, Arabic grammar, Shafi'i jurisprudence, speculative theology (*'ilm al-kalām*) and the science of Islamic mystical thought (Sufism). He issued his fatwa at a time when Abu al-Hasan al-Ash'ari (d. 324/935), founder of the Ash'ari school, was being cursed as an unbeliever from the pulpit.[4] His fatwa affirmed that the theological precepts being taught by this man accorded with the Sunni creed of the Ahl al-Hadith scholars of al-Qushayri's day. His *Risālah* is a lengthy essay composed both for the Sufis of his time as a reminder of Sufism's inherently ethical nature and as a vindication of its authentic Islamic roots (i.e., its foundational principles were drawn from the Qur'an and the Sunnah) for those who doubted its legitimacy.

His fatwa and *Risālah* compliment each other and today offer anyone, both Muslim and non-Muslim seekers of an understanding of the human spirit, a testimony of humanity's timeless spiritual quest and the textual sources and interpretive and analytic methodologies from which it is drawn. They also provide for the scholar of Islam a wealth of biographical information on early Sufis and their teachings, an in-depth analysis of terminology, and intimate discourse on its practices and ethical character. These latter elements played a central role in Islamic society, for they served as the vehicle by which Islam's essential ideals and values were integrated into the cloth of the community's spiritual, intellectual, social, and even political life.

The *Risālah* represents the confluence of two seminal Islamic traditions: (1) the intellectual textual discourse derived from the foundational elements of Islamic spirituality (viz., the Qur'an and the Sunnah) in conjunction with the texts transmitted down the generations by the scholarly elite that was dedicated to preserving and transmitting the Prophetic example within the ummah; and (2) with an oral tradition that was an integral facet of the textual tradition. The *Risālah* includes this oral tradition along with all of the relevant individual chains of transmission (*asnād*). This oral tradition established itself in the early works of Sufism, such as Abu Talib al-Makki's (d. 386/996) *Qūṭ al-Qulūb*, the works of Abu Abd al-Rahman al-Sulami (d. 412/1021), and the manuals of the formative period of Sufi development such as the works of al-Kalabadhi (d. 380/990) and Abu Nasr Abd Allah al-Sarraj (d. 378/988).

This paper will treat the relevance of this confluence and the need to reintroduce the importance of its role in affirming the legitimacy of both perspectives within the context of intra-Islamic discourse today. Toward realizing this goal, I will present and critique the newly translated *Al-Risālah al-Qushayrīyah fī 'Ilm al-Taṣawwuf*) by Alexander D. Knysh and The Center for Muslim Contribution to Civilization (London: Garnet Publishers, 2007).[5] I do so in the hope that it might play a central role in initiating a new dialog for those less familiar with the major personalities and mentors of formative Sufism as well as its essential teachings and doctrines.

The Fatwa

In 436/1044, al-Qushayri, the renowned scholar and author of *The Epistle on Sufism* (*Al-Risālah al-Qushayrīyah fī 'Ilm al-Taṣawwuf* = *Risālah*), issued a fatwa affirming that the Ahl al-Hadith community of Qushayri's day shared al-Ash'ari's theological perspectives and that they were therefore in complete accordance with Orthodox Sunni Islam. His fatwa, signed by Nishapur's most renowned Shafi'i scholars, stated:

> In the name of God the most merciful the Compassionate – The companions of hadith [narration] (*aṣḥāb al-ḥadīth*) agree that Abu al-Hasan Ali b. Isma'il al-Ash'ari was an imam among the imams of the *aṣḥāb al-ḥadīth* and his school (*madhhab*) is the *madhhab* of the *aṣḥāb al-hadith*. He spoke on the foundational precepts of religious thought (*uṣūl al-diyānāt*) following the path of the Ahl al-Sunnah criticizing and responding to those who differed from them among the people of deviation and innovation. He was a drawn sword against the Mu'tazilites and Rafidites (Shi'is in the terminology of the time) and the innovators among the People of the Qiblah as well as against those who have left the community (*al-millat*) [all together]. Whoever defames [his character] (*ṭa'ana*) or maligns him or curses or reviles him has indeed vilified all the Ahl al-Sunnah. We have written these lines in obedience to this [perspective] on this topic in *Dhu al-Qa'dah* in the year 436. The [truth of the] matter is as stated here (*wa al-amr 'alā hādhihi al-jumlat al-madhkūrat fī hādha al-dhikr*). Written by Abu al-Qasim Abd al-Karim b. Hawazin al-Qushayri.[6]

This fatwa was the result of a controversy that had arisen in Khurasan after the Saljuqs replaced the Ghaznavids in 432/1040. The first Saljuq ruler, Tughril (r. 429/1038-455/1063) at first had good relations with al-Qushayri and the Shafi'i scholars of Nishapur. This state of affairs did not last, however, for, in the words of Algar, "Tughril's minister, Amid al-Mulk al-Kunduri, an adherent of the Hanafi legal school and possibly a Mu'tazilite in theological persuasion gained permission from Tughril to initiate a campaign against the Shi'is (al-Rawafid, in the polemical language of the day) and against "innovators" (Ahl al-Bid'ah). The latter is an imprecise term that seems to have indicated primarily, in this case, the followers of the Ash'ari school of theology."[7] In Nishapur the Ash'arī school had come to be identified with the Shaf'i school of jurisprudence. This turned the anti-Ash'ari rhetoric into an equally vehement anti-Shafi'i rhetoric, with the result that the city's Shafi'i scholars lost privileges to teach and preach in the city's principle mosque. This animosity led to Abu al-Hasan al-Ash'ari being reviled as an unbeliever from the city's pulpits. All of the above led al-Qushayri to issue the above fatwa. Note the year was 436/1044, only a year before he penned his *Risālah*, to which we shall soon return.

Despite his outspoken position against this anti-Ash'ari campaign, al-Qushayri continued to teach and give public lectures in Nishapur. This tense state of affairs continued for ten years, until in 446/1054 he composed an open letter to the scholarly community of the Islamic world, complaining of how the Ash'ari-Shafi'i scholars were being harassed in Nishapur: *The Complaint of the People of Sunnah Relating the Persecution that Has Befallen Them* (*Shikāyat Ahl al-Sunnah bimā Nālahum min al-Miḥna*). This epistle raised the issue to a broader audience. In the *Shikāyat* he enumerates and then categorically refutes the main accusations lodged against al-Ash'ari and affirms that the foundation of Ash'ari theology is based upon the Qur'an and Sunnah.

This long delineation of the spurious nature of the anti-Ash'ari arguments brought matters to a head; al-Kuduri ordered al-Qushayri's arrest and imprisonment in the city's citadel. He was soon released, however, when the local Shafi'is stormed the citadel and freed him. After this he made his way to Baghdad, where he was well received by the Abbasid caliph al-Qa'im bi Amir'illah and the scholars of the city. Tughril died in 455/1063, and Alp Arslan ascended to the Saljuq throne. Al-Kunduri was killed and replaced by Nizam al-Mulk, the renowned founder of the Nizāmīya institutions of higher education, perhaps the first university of the medieval world. Nizam al-Mulk was a Shafi'i and, in Algar's words, "sympathetic to Ash'ari theology." Under the new sultan and his minister, the Shafi'is regained their privileges as Nishapur's scholarly elite and al-Qushayri returned and spent the remainder of his life there. He died on Rabī' al-Awwal 16, 465/December 31, 1072 and was buried next to his master Abu Ali al-Daqqaq (d. 412/1021). In a citation attributed to al-Imam Abd al-Ghafir, al-Qushayri was

> the absolute Imam (*al-imām muṭlaq*); ... the spokesperson of his era and the authority of his time; God's secret among his creation (*sirru Allāh fī khalqhi*)... one who had combined [knowledge of] the Law (*sharī'ah*) and [knowledge of] Divine reality (*ḥaqīqah*). He was knowledgeable of the foundational principles of religion (*uṣūl*) according the school of al-Ash'ari as he was of the branches (*furū'*) of the religious sciences according to the school of al-Shā'fī.[8]

Al-Qushayri: His Life and Social Context

The above events and the textual record we have of them contextualize the sociopolitical and intellectual environment that both nurtured and defined al-Qushayri and the city in which he lived, studied, taught, and preached. Al-Qushayri himself and his *Risālah* reflect an environment, established well before his own time, that resonated with what Laury Silvers has termed Ahl al-Hadith culture, a culture known

> for taking the position that one should settle ethical, legal, or theological matters by referring to already established principles transmitted from the Prophet through his companions and their followers ... and thus [establishing] a common culture of authority grounded in a perceived continuity between the Prophet's community and their own.[9]

This continuity was a measure of the authenticity of all the fields of intellectual discourse of those times. We thus find al-Qushayri, who addressed his *Risālah* to "all the Sufi community of the lands of Islam," was himself a pillar of Islamic orthodoxy, known for his mastery of the multiple fields of hadith narration, Shafi'i jurisprudence (*fiqh*) and speculative theology (*'ilm al-kalām*), and as an initiate to the science of Islamic mystical thought, or Sufism. In al-Qushayri's times, as we have seen, theological discourses directly impacted the sociopolitical atmosphere, legal schools were vying for adherents, and, as Ahmet Karamustafa has stated, "the temptation to process Sufi thought with the new tools of *kalām* and *fiqh* in order to develop a theologically and legally savvy form of Sufism was too irresistible."[10] These tools are evident in the *Risālah* and we find that al-Qushayri, just a generation after al-Sulami (one of his mentors), employed them eloquently and in a masterful fashion to compose the work that would come to assume, as Karamustafa puts it, "canonical status for most later Sufis and observers of Sufism alike."[11]

There is a tendency today to compartmentalize Islamic discourse into the realms of jurisprudence, theology, and mystical ethics (Sufism). Those who study jurisprudence and theology often neglect seminal Sufi works on the grounds that its roots are often derived from their authors' personal experience or as being contextualized within a dated historical ambience. Yet the training and expertise that al-Qushayri brought to bear in his works and the legacy he left testify to his roots in hadith narration and collection, Shafi'i jurisprudence, and Ash'ari *kalām*. Three of the builders of Ash'ari *kalām* served as his mentors[12]: Abu Bakr Muhammad ibn al-Hasan ibn Furak (d. 406/1015), Abu Ishaq al-Isfarayni (d. 418/1027), and the Maliki Abu Bakr al-Baqillani (d. 403/1013).

Under them, al-Qushayri became one of the best known among the Shafi'i-Ash'ari faction of Nishapur, which explains why, along with Abu al-Ma'ali al-Juwayni (d. 478/1085-6), he was persecuted during 445/1053 and 456/1064.

Another key aspect of comprehending the person of al-Qushayri and his participation in the full intellectual discourse of his day is his legacy, namely, his writings. Algar orients these works within his lifetime: "He seems to have been conscious of their value himself, for he employed a number of scribes to copy them under his supervision and used them as texts in many of the classes he taught." Not all his works have reached us today; however, the majority of what has survived is available in print. Along with the *Risālah*, these are:

- *Laṭā'if al-Ishārāt bi Tafsīr al-Qur'ān*, a multi-volume commentary of Sufi exegesis begun in 437/1045.[13]
- *Sharḥ li Asmā' Allāh al-Ḥusnā*, an elucidationg of the 99 names of God and the mystical-ethical facet of each name as it impacts personal piety and practice.[14]
- *Al-Taḥbīr fī al-Tadhkīr Sharḥ Asmā' Allāh al-Ḥusnā*, a similar work.
- *Kitāb al-Mi'rāj*, a work on the hadith and meaning of the Prophet's ascension and its relationship to the nature of sanctity in Islam.[15]
- *Al-Rasā'il al-Qushayrīyah*, including threes short treatises: *Shikāyat Ahl al-Sunnah bimā Nālahum min al-Miḥna* (already mentioned), *Tarṭīb al-Sulūk* (al-Qushayri's own guide to the traveler on the Sufi path), and *Kitāb al-Samā'* (on the Sufi practice of audition).
- *Al-Fuṣūl fī al-Uṣūl* and *Luma' fī al-I'tiqād*, two short dogmatic works of Ash'ari *kalām* edited by Richard Frank in *Mélanges* (1982), 15:53-74 and (1983) 16:59-75.
- *Naḥwa al-Qulūb*, which exists in two editions, the major (*al-Kabīr*) and the minor (*al-Ṣaghīr*), is a Sufi commentary on the rules of Arabic grammar.

Another facet to our understanding of al-Qushayri and his *Risālah* was the existence in Nishapur of jurist-Sufis like Abu Sahl al-Su'luki and traditionalist-Sufis like Abu Abd al-Rahman al-Sulami, who had already contributed to the understanding of Sufism within the aforementioned ambience of Ahl al-Hadith culture. Nishapur, the capital of Khurasan, was known from early times to be the home of such training masters as Hamdun al-Qassar (d. 271/884-85) and Abu Hafs al-Haddad (d. c. 265/878-79) and his disciple Abu Uthman al-Hiri of the Malamatiyah.[16] The Malamatis represented the city's major mystical-ethical school and held the lower soul (*nafs*) in constant suspicion. According to Karamustafa, "unless the *nafs* was controlled it would inevitably waylay the pious believer through self-conceit (*'ujb*), pretense (*iddi'a'*), and hypocrisy (*riyā'*) and would thus prevent the believer from reaching his true goal, which was the achievement of sincere, selfless devotion to God (*ikhlāṣ*)."[17] They therefore avoided any public display of pious or praiseworthy works. This orientation of the early Malamatiyah teaching masters imparted to Khurasan and Nishapur a reputation for sincerity. Al-Junayd (d. 297/910), known as the "Leader of the Folk," testified to this trait: "Chivalry is in Syria, eloquence is in al-Iraq, and sincerity is in Khurasan."

All of the above traits led Nishapur to be known as a center of formative Sufism. Here, the young al-Qushayri frequented the foremost scholars of his days in hadith, Shafi'i jurisprudence, and speculative theology (*'ilm al-kalām*). In this political, cultural, and intellectual center of Khurasan he also encountered and became the disciple of the renowned Sufi masters (shaykh) Abu Ali al-Hasan al-Daqqaq (d. 412/1021) and Abu Abd al-Rahman al-Sulami (d. 421/1021). The *Risālah* is thus a composite work that reflects a multi-faceted reality of intellectual discourse, of oral and textual tradition, and thus portrays in an intimate and personal manner Sufism's central role in Islamic society as the vehicle by which Islam's essential ideals and values were integrated into the cloth of the community's spiritual, intellectual, social, and political life. On the importance of the *Risālah*'s composite nature as being a key to its enduring nature, Karamustafa aptly remarks:

> This happy marriage between Sufism and legal-theological scholarship is the hallmark of the Treatise, and Qushayri's harmonious packaging of the two modes of learning and piety, along with his overall reputation among scholars (that is due, at least in part, to the persecution he suffered) as well as the astute inclusion of biographical notices into his survey of Sufism, goes a long way to explaining the Treatise's enduring popularity.[18]

Then, from another and perhaps a more academic perspective, one could say as well that Qushayri's *Risālah* will remain an essential reference work for scholars and students of Sufism and Islamic thought and theology, Muslim and non-Muslim alike; Sufi adepts and all those with an interest in "the great spiritual current present in all religions."[19]

Al-Risālat al-Qushayrīyah

In the light of the above, the *Risālah* is best understood as a lengthy manual or a missive based upon the fatwa tradition and, as fatwas are, intended for the benefit of the Muslim community as a whole. However, it surpassed the theological argumentation that had elicited his earlier fatwa, introduced at the beginning of this paper, as well his *Shikāyat Ahl al-Sunnah*. In his defense of Ash'ari and the Ash'ari school, Qushayri addressed the waywardness of his co-religionists and the corrupt attitudes that had afflicted them due to the divisive nature of their discourse. He wrote the first fatwa to meet the perceived need to correct error and, in so doing, to reaffirm ethical rectitude within the framework of the Muslim community as a whole. In the *Risālah* written in 437/1072, just a year after the fatwa, during a period of great trial and social upheaval, Qushayri issued, as it were, a mystical-ethical fatwa (*fatwā akhlāqī*), employing the format of a manual that, owing to its length, must have been in preparation well in advance of its completion date. This perception broadens our historical understanding of the term fatwa as going beyond any purely legal discourse. Qushayri composed his work at a time when "true Sufis" had become nearly extinct and Sufism was misunderstood among both its initiates and the Muslim community. The *Risālah* was therefore composed to rectify this misunderstanding and to affirm, while interpreting, Sufism's validity in light of the Qur'an and the Hadith literature. Its nature as a missive to the ummah is clear in the author's introduction:

> Since our age keeps bringing only more and more difficulties and the majority of our compatriots continue to adhere stubbornly to their ways … I have begun to fear that the hearts of men might think that this whole affair [Sufism] from the very beginning rested upon all those [faulty] foundations and its early adherents followed the same corrupt habits. So I have composed this epistle for you … that [it] might strengthen the followers.[20]

The *Risālah*, however, was written with a dual purpose: to remind Sufis of the authentic ancestral tradition and to vindicate Sufism against those who doubted its legitimacy. This aspect and its relevance today is the most important facet of this work's relevace to Muslim intra-faith dialog for, as Algar points out: "Sufis, however, were not the only intended audience of the book; al-Qushayri was also concerned to demonstrate to all the *shar'ī* appropriateness of distinctive Sufi practices (such as *samā'*) and to show that the creed of the Sufis was identical to that of the Ahl al-Sunnah (in its Ash'ari formulation)."[21] The author's introduction therefore concentrates on explaining the Sufis' beliefs concerning the fundamentals of religion (pp. 4-14) and the Sufis' creed, stressing their perception of divine unity (*tawḥīd*) and the relation of the divine attributes to the divine Essence (pp. 14-16). All of the narrations in the *Risālah* are provided complete with chains of transmission (*asnād*). In order to elucidate Qushayri's style and familiarize readers with this work's key facets, I will cite narrative examples from the text itself employing the translation of Alexander Knysh, unless otherwise noted.

In his introduction, Qushayri discusses the varying categories of knowledge. Among the scholars he draws upon are Abu al-Tayyib al-Maraghi, whose narration he cites from Abu Abd al-Rahman al-Sulami:

> Muḥammad b. al-Husayn told me: I heard Muhammad b. Abd Allah al-Razi say: I heard Abu al-Tayyib al-Maraghi say: "To the intellect (*'aql*), belongs argumentative proof, to wisdom (*ḥikmah*) allegorical allusion and to intimate knowledge of God (*ma'rifah*), direct witnessing. The intellect demonstrates, wisdom alludes, and *ma'rifah* witnesses directly the fact that the purest acts of worship can only be attained by the purest belief in God's oneness.[22]

He in this narration on *al-tawḥīd*, citing al-Junayd as the source, states:

> Someone asked al-Junayd about God's oneness. He answered: Rendering God one by realizing fully His unity through the perfection of His uniqueness (*infirād*), that is, that He is the one and only, Who has not begotten and has not been begotten (Q. 112:3) who has no opponents, rivals, likes, without likening Him [to created things], without asking, how [He is], without representing Him as an image or form, in accordance with [the verse] He has no likeness, He is the Hearing, the Seeing (Q. 42:11).[23]

The introduction's final section deals with the Sufis' beliefs as derived from dispersed and collected saying of the masters of the path, as well as their books, reads much like a short overview of Ash'ari theological text.

> God Most High – praise be to Him – is existent, eternal, one, wise, powerful, knowing, overpowering, compassionate, willing, hearing, glorious, exalted, speaking, seeing, proud, strong, living, one, everlasting and self-sustaining (Al-Ṣamad).
>
> He knows by [His] knowledge; He is powerful by [His] power; He wills by [His] will; He sees by [His] sight; He speaks by [His] speech; He lives by [His] life; He is everlasting by [His] everlastingness. He has two hands, which are His attributes and with which He creates whatever He wishes and gives it specific form. He has a face. The attributes of His essence are unique to it. One must not say that they are He or that they are not He. They are [His] eternal attributes and [His] everlasting properties. He is unique in His essence. He is not similar to any created thing, nor is any created thing similar to Him. He is neither a body, nor a substance, nor an accident….[24]

Chapter 1, "On the Masters of this path and their deeds and sayings that show how they uphold the Divine Law (*al-Sharī'a*)" (pp. 17-74), is a concise presentation of the biographies and sayings of eighty-three early Sufi mentors from the first generation up to al-Qushayri's time. Their presence testifies to the reality of an ongoing oral tradition and that Sufism never lost its oral quality as a narrative of its founders' teachings that gave rise to it originally and those who came after them.[25] It is this originality that we encounter in the *Risālah*'s narratives that affirms Sufism's centrality as a living oral tradition resonating with the textual tradition of Islamic scholarship. The following examples will present a succinct overview of the biographical style al-Qushayri employs in this oral tradition.

Abu Naṣr Bishr b. al-Ḥārith al-Ḥāfi (c. 152-227/c.766-841)

He came from the city of Marw. He lived in Baghdad, where he died. He was a son of Ali bin Khashram's sister. He died in the year 227/842. He was a man of great stature. The following [episode] became the reason for his repentance. He found on the road a small piece of paper upon which was written the name of God – may He be exalted. This sheet was trampled upon [by passer-bys]. He picked it up, purchased a dirham-worth of perfume, sprinkled the sheet with it and put it in the crack of a wall. Then he saw a dream as if someone told him, "O Bishr, you perfumed My name and I will perfume yours in this world and the next!"

I heard my teacher Abu Ali al-Daqqaq – may God have mercy on him – say: "Bishr was passing by a group of people who said, 'This man does not sleep all night and he breaks his fast only once in three days.' On hearing this, Bishr began to cry. When someone asked him why, he said: 'Verily, I do not remember ever saying that I keep vigil during the entire night. Nor have I said that after fasting during the day I do not break my fast at night. However, God, in His kindness and graciousness, has revealed to the hearts [of the people] more than His servant actually does – may He be blessed.'

I heard Shaykh Abu Abd al-Raḥmān al-Sulami say: I heard Muḥammad b. 'Abdallāh al-Rāzi say: I heard Abd al-Raḥmān b. Abi Hātim say: I came to know that Bishr b. al-Ḥārith al-Ḥāfi said: "In a dream I saw the Prophet – may peace and blessings be upon him! He asked me: 'Bishr, do you know why God has raised you above your contemporaries?' I said: 'I do not, Messenger of God.' He said: '[It is due to] your following my Sunna, your service to the righteous, your admonition of your brothers [in faith] and your love of my Companions and my family. This is what brought you to the stations of the most pious men.'"[26]

Among the biographies included in this chapter are:
Abu Ishaq Ibrahim b. Adham b. Mansur
Abu al-Fayd Dhu al-Nun al-Misri (d. 245/859)
Abu Ali al-Fudayl b. 'Iyad (d. 187/803)
Abu Mahfuz Ma'ruf b. Fayruz al-Karhi (d. 200/816)
Abu al-Hasan al-Sari b. al-Mughallis al-Saqati (d.257/865)
Abu Abd Allah al-Harith al-Muhasibi (d. 243/857)
Abu Ali Shaqiq b. Ibrahim al-Balkhi
Abu Yazid b. Tayfur b. 'Isa al-Bistami (d. 261/875)

He concludes this section:

> Here I have mentioned some of the masters of this community in order to show that all of them have a great respect for the Divine Law (*shari'a*), that they are committed to the paths of spiritual discipline, that they follow unswervingly the Prophet's Sunnah and that they never neglect a single religious rule. They all agree that whoever is remiss in the rules of proper conduct (*adab*) or in striving for perfection and does not build his or her life on scrupulous piety and fear of God lies before God in whatever he claims. Such a person is deluded. Not only has he perished himself, but also he has caused to perish those who were deluded by his lies.

Chapter 2, "An Explanation of the Expressions used by this [Sufi] Community and of their difficulties" (pp. 75-119), introduces the concept of a specific terminology for each science and the necessity for defining and elucidating each term within the context of its area of discourse. He writes:

> It is well known that each group of scholars has its own terms which it employs within its own field. These terms are unique to each group, which has agreed on them for its purposes, namely, (1) to bring these terms closer to the understanding of those to whom they are addressed, and (2) by articulating them, to help people of this science to better comprehend their meaning.
>
> The people of this community [the Sufis] use these terms among themselves with the goal of unveiling their meaning to one another, achieving concision and concealing them from those who disagree with their method, so that the meaning of their words would be hidden from outsiders. They have done so to protect their mysteries from being spread among those to whom they so not belong. For their realities cannot be collected by self-exertion or acquired by any deliberate action. They are subtle meanings that God deposits directly into the hearts of [His] folk, [after He has] prepared their innermost selves for [the reception of] these realities.

By this explanation we intend to facilitate the understanding of the meaning of these terms by those who want to follow their path and their custom.[27]

For example he explains the term *waqt* (moment) saying:

I heard that the master Abu Ali al-Daqqaq – may God have mercy on him – said: "The moment is what you are in [now]. If you are in this world, then your moment is in this world. If you are in the Hereafter, then your moment is in the Hereafter. If you are in joy, then your moment is in joy. If you are in sorrow, then your moment is in sorrow." By this he meant that a moment is a state that dominates a person.

The Sufis say: "The Sufi is the son of the moment (*al-waqt*)." They mean that he engages in the worship that is most appropriate for his current situation and performs what is required of him at this moment in time. It is said that the *faqīr* (the aspirant on the path) does not care about his past and future. All that matters for him is the moment in which he is now. Therefore, they say: "Anyone who preoccupies himself with the past moment wastes another moment."[28]

On the *nafs*, (ego-self) he writes:

In the Arabic language, a thing's *nafs* is its being. However, when the Sufis utter the word *nafs* they imply neither being nor a physical body. Rather, they imply the deficiencies of one's character traits as well as one's reprehensible morals and acts. The deficiencies of one's character traits fall into two categories: first, those which one acquires by oneself – namely, one's acts of disobedience and one's sins; second one's [inherent] base morals. They are blameworthy in and of themselves. However, when a man seeks to treat them and fight them, these blameworthy traits are extinguished in him through a strenuous and uninterrupted effort.[29]

He defines twenty-nine terms in all. Historically speaking, these terms are not found in the traditional works of Islamic jurisprudence (*fiqh*) and Qushayri's exposition in the *Risālah*, though not the first, is among earliest examples we have of a glossary for Sufism. It should be remembered, however, that he is narrating from a pre-existent scholarly tradition that had evolved with the circles of Sufi initiates during the generations prior to Qushayri's generation. These terms include *waqt* (the present moment), *maqām* (a spiritual station), *ḥāl* (a spiritual state), *qabḍ* (contraction) and *basṭ* (expansion), *haybah* (awe) and *uns* (intimacy), *jam'* (collectedness) and *farq* (separation), *fanā'* (annihilation) *baqā'* (subsistence), *'ilm al-yaqīn* (certain knowledge), *'ayn al-yaqīn* (essential certainty), *ḥaqq al-yaqīn* (the truth of certainty), *qurb* (proximity), *bu'd* (distance), *maḥw* (erasure), and *ithbāt* (affirmation).

Having defined *maqām* (station on the path to the intimate knowledge of God) in the previous section, Qushayri begins chapter 3, "The Stations of the Path (*maqāmāt*)" (pp.111-339), the longest and most detailed chapter with a detailed list and description of the various stations, beginning with repentance. It helps to recall again that historically speaking the discourse contained in this chapter is not to be found in the traditional works of Islamic jurisprudence (fiqh), nor does it originate from Qushayri himself. Among the stations he treats in this chapter are *mujāḥad* (striving), *khalwah* (spiritual retreat), *'uzlah* (seclusion), *taqwā* (God wariness), *zuhd* (renounciation), *ṣamt* (maintaining silence), *khawf* (fear), *rajā'* (hope), *ḥuzn* (sorrow), *khushū'* (awe before God), *tawāḍu'* (humility), *qanā'ah* (sufficiency), *tawakkul* (trust in God), *yaqīn* (certainty), and *ikhlāṣ* (sincerity).

He finishes the *Risālah* with individual sections on:

- How God protects the hearts of the path's shaykhs and on the necessity of not opposing them (pp. 339-42).
- The Sufi practice of audition (*samā'*) (pp. 342-57)
- The miracles of God's friends (*awliyā'*) (pp. 357-92)
- The vision of the Sufis (*ru'yat al-qawm*) (392-403)
- Spiritual advice for Sufi aspirants on the path (*waṣīyah li al-murīd*) (pp. 403-16).

Among his advice to the aspirants is that they should not ascribe infallibility to Sufi masters. Instead, they should concede their states to them, think well of them, and observe the limits set by God Most High in everything that the master instructs them to do. This is sufficient for them in distinguishing right from wrong.

Conclusion

The *Risālah al-Qushayrīyah fī 'Ilm al-Taṣawwuf* dates from Islam's classical period and is the product of a wide reaching intellectual discourse that comprised all of the fields of the Islamic intellectual pursuits of the time. It was written at a time of sociopolitical turmoil, when the Islamic community had separated into factions due to differing opinions along juridical, theological, and creedal and/or ideological lines – not unlike the situation today among a large segment of the community. The *Risālah* contextualizes for us the importance of maintaining intra-Muslim dialog along the broadest possible lines, which means that no areas of traditional discourse, including new ones, should be excluded. A careful study of it and its author's life and times will help us understand some of the following points.

1. *Iftā'* and fatwa are not the sole domain of jurists.
2. The domain of fatwa extends beyond matters of jurisprudence and legal discourse.
3. A given fatwa's relevance may extend beyond its individual socio-historical context. For example, the *Risālah* was addressed to all Sufis in the lands of Islam.
4. Theological and juridical discourse played an integral role in the formulation of what we know and understand of classical Sufism today.
5. The *Risālah* can be read as a virtue-based ethical fatwa (*fatwā akhlāqī*) that affirms and elucidates that Sufism is not an extraneous aspect of "mainstream Islam" that owes little to the authoritative sources of Islamic intellectual discourse or a sectarian development that occurred at a given point in Islamic history.
6. The *Risālah* testifies to a living oral tradition throughout the generations prior to its composition in 446/1054, in which the ethics of virtue was seen as a means to radically transform oneself.

Although Knysh's translation leaves something to be desired, particularly for the Arabist, but on the whole it is complete and faithful to the original text in form and content.[30] It reads very well and renders accessible, in its tone and content, this seminal work of formative Sufism to a broader audience than ever before.

Endnotes

1. See Hamid Algar's introduction to *Principles of Sufism* by al-Qushayri, translated from the Arabic by B. R. von Schlegell (Mizan Press: Berkeley, 1990) i-xvii.
2. Preserved in Subki, *Ṭabaqāt*, ed. Hulw and al-Tanahi (Cairo: 1386/1967), iii, 374; and in Ibn al-Asakir's (d. 571/1175) *Tabyīn Kidhb al-Futarī fī mā Nusiba ilā al-Imām Abī al-Ḥasān al-Ash'arī* (Damascus: 1347/1928), 113.
3. Subki, *Ṭabaqāt*, 399-423; Ibn al-Asakir in an abridged version, 109-10; and in a separate edition by Muhammad Hasan in *Al-Rasā'il al-Qushayrīyah* (Karachi: 1384/1964), 1-49.
4. Algar, *Principles of Sufism*, vi.

5. Abu al-Qasim al-Qushayri, *Al-Qushayri's Epistle on Sufism* (*Al-Risālah al-Qushayrīyah fī 'Ilm al-Taṣawwuf*), tr. Alexander D. Knysh (London: Garnet Publishers, 2007).
6. In Subki, *Ṭabaqāt*, iii, 374.
7. Algar, *Principles of Sufism*, vi.; also see H. Halm, "Der Wesir al-Kunduri und die Fitna von Nishapur," *Die Welt des Orients* (1971), 2:205-33.
8. Shaykh Abd al-Halim Mahud in his critical edition of the *Risālah Qushayrīyah.* "This state of affairs ended with al-Qushayri because he became, in the words of Imam Abd ul-Ghafir, the absolute imam (*al-imām al-mutlāqan*), jurist (*al-faqīh*), theologian (*al-mutakallim*), legist (*al-uṣūlī*), the interpreter of the Qur'an (*al-mufassir*), a man of letters (*al-adīb*), grammarian (*al-naḥwī*), writer/poet (*al-kātib al-shā'ir*), the master of his time (*lisān 'aṣrihu wa sayyid waqtihu*), God's secret among His creation (*sirr Allāh bayn khalqihi*), the axis of reality (*mudār al-ḥaqīqah*), source of happiness (*'ayn al-sa'ādah*), the pole of masterhood (*quṭub al-siyādah*), one who joined the Shari'ah and the Truth (*man jama'a bayn al-Sharī'ah wa al-ḥaqīqah*). He was knowledgable in the foundations of the Ash'ari creed and in the branches of the Shafi'i school of thought."
9. L. Silvers, *A Soaring Minaret: Abu Bakr al-Wasiti and the Rise of Baghdadi Sufism* (Albany: State University of New York Press, 2010), 2.
10. Ahmet T. Karamustafa, *Sufism: The Formative Period* (Edinburgh,UK: Edinburgh University Press, 2007), 97.
11. Ibid.
12. Al-Qushayri not only studied but also composed the two short compendiums of Ash'ari *kalām*. See Richard Frank, "Two Short Dogmatic Works of Abu al-Qasim al-Qushayri" ("Al-Fuṣūl fī al-Uṣūl and Luma' fī al-I'tiqād") in *Mélanges* 15 (1982): 53-74 and 16 (1983): 59-36.
13. Published in Cairo, 1981 (2d ed.) ed. Ibrahim Basyuni in three volumes.
14. Published in Beirut, 2006, ed. 'Asim Ibrahim al-Kiyali.
15. Published in Cairo, 1384/1968 ed. Ali Hasan Abd al-Qadir.
16. For the Malamatiyah see: *EI*[2], art. "MALĀMATIYYA," Fr. de Jong, Hamid Algar, and Colin Imber; Abdülbākī Gölpinarli, *Melāmīlik ve Melāmīler* (Istanbul: Devlet Matbaasi, 1931); al-Sulami, *Risālat al-Malāmatīyah*, ed. Abu al-Ala al-Afifi (Cairo: Dar Ihya' al-Kutub al-Arabiyyah, 1945); Sara Sviri, "Hakīm Tirmidhī and the Malāmatī Movement," in *Classical Persian Sufism: From Its Origins to Rumi*, ed. Leonard Lewis (London: Khaniqahi Nimatullahi Publications, 1993), 583-613; Fritz Meier, "Khurasān and the End of Classical Sufism," in *Essays in Islamic Mysticism and Piety*, trans. John O'Kane and Berndt Radke (Leiden: E. J. Brill, 2000), 215-217; Alexander, Knysh, *Islamic Mysticism: A Short History* (Leiden: E. J. Brill, 2000), 94-99; Hakim Tirmidhi, *Kitāb Ithbāt al-'Ilal*, ed. Khalid Zahra (Rabat: Muhammad V University, 1998), 24-25; also see the collected presentations from the International Conference on the Malamatiyya and Bayrami Orders held in Istanbul in June, 1987 in *Melâmis-Bayrâmis*, ed. N. Clayer, A. Popovic, and T. Zarcone (Istanbul: Les Editions Isis, 1998). For

a recent analysis of the Malamatiyyah and their role within the context of formative Sufism, see Ahmet T. Karamustafa, *Sufism: The Formative Period* (Edinburgh: Edinburgh University Press, 2007), citations throughout the work.

17. Karamustafa, *Sufism,* 49.
18. Ibid., 99.
19. Annemarie Schimmel, *Mystical Dimensions of Islam* (Chapel Hill: University of North Carolina, 1975) 4.
20. *Al-Qushayri's Epistle on Sufism*, 3
21. Algar, *Principles of Sufism*, xi.
22. *Al-Risālah*, 5.
23. Ibid., 5-6.
24. Ibid., 14-15.
25. One day in the souq of Marrakech, Morocco I encountered my respected friend, Sidi Ahmad Rabwabzi, who was among the more Salafi-oriented scholars of Marrakech, in his shop reading Abu Talib al-Makki's *Qūt al-Qulūb*. I asked him about this, and he said that in *Qūt al-Qulūb* there was the knowledge of the Companions of the Prophet – May the Peace and Blessing of God be upon him - (*'ilm al-Ṣaḥābah*).
26. *Al-Risālah*, 25-26.
27. Ibid., 75.
28. Ibid., 75-76.
29. Ibid., 109.
30. Several translations of Qushayri's *Risālah* appeared before the translation under discussion, such as von Schlegell's translation of al-Qushayri, *Principles of Sufism* (Mizan Press: Berkeley, 1990). He translated only chapter 3: "The Stations of the Path (*maqāmāt*)." Four sections not pertaining to states and stations were omitted: ("The Rules of Travel" and "Companionship" (*ṣuhbah*). The translation, therefore, goes from "Correct Behavior" (*adab*) to "Gnosis." In addition, the sections of "Backbiting" and "Envy" are included under the main heading "Failing of the self." The chains of transmission have been omitted; only the final narrator is cited. Von Schlegell's translation is accurate, eloquent, and reads well, but is not annotated. Algar's introduction contextualizes the *Risālah*'s place in Islamic scholarship and provides a concise biography of al-Qushayri and his works. Rabia Harris, *Sufi Book of Spiritual Ascent* (*Al-Risālah al-Qushayrīyah*), ed. Laleh Bakhtiar (ABC International Group, Inc., 1997). This is a translation of chapter 3, "The Stations of the Path (*maqāmāt*)," excluding "The Rules of Travel" and "Companionship" (*ṣuhbah*). Only the first and final narrators are mentioned in the chains of transmission. Harris' translation is accurate and reads well, but is not annotated. Rabia Harris, *The Risālah: Principles of Sufism*, ed. Laleh Bakhtiar (Great Books of the Islamic World, Inc., 2002). This complete translation contains a lengthy introduction by the translator and a forward by Seyyed Hossein Nasr. It cites the first and final narrators of each narration and, in the notes at the end of the translation, provides the missing links for each chain. The translation is well done and accurate.

Bibliography

Badur, Bassam Muhammad. *Tahdhīb al-Asrār fī Uṣūl al-Taṣawwuf.* Critical edition and notes by Abu Sa'd al-Kharqushi. Abu Dhabi: Isdarat al-Majma' al-Tamami, 1999.

Böwering, Gerhard. "Two Early Sufi Manuscripts." *Jerusalem Studies in Arabic and Islam* 31, 2006.

———. *Abū Khalaf al-Ṭabarī: The Comfort of the Mystics* (*Salwat al-'Ārifīna wa uns al-Mushtāqīn*). Critical edition and notes with Bilal Orfali. Leiden: E. J. Brill, 2013.

Bulliet, Richard. *The Partricians of Nishapur: A Study in Medieval Islamic Social History*. Cambridge, MA: Harvard University Press, 1972.

———. *Islam: The View from the Edge*. New York: Columbia University Press, 1994.

Chabbi, Jacqueline. "Remarques sur le développment historique des mouvements ascétiques et mystiques au Khurasan." *Studia Islamica* 57, 1997.

Chodkiewicz, Michel. *Le Sceau des Saints: Prophétie et sainteté dans la doctrine d'Ibn Arabī*. Paris: Gallimard, 1989.

Frank, T. "Taṣawwuf is ...; On a Type of Mystical Aphorism." *Journal of the American Oriental Society* 104, no. 1, 1984.

Ghamari, Abu 'Aṣim Nabil b. Hashim b. Abd Allah, al-. *Manāḥil al-Shifā wa Manāhil al-Ṣafā bi Taḥqīq Kitāb Sharaf al-Muṣṭafā* (with critical ed. and notes). Makkah: Dār al-Basha'ir al-Islamiyyah, 2003.

Godlas, Alan. "Influences of al-Qushayrī's *Laṭā'if al-Ishārāt* on Sufi Qur'anic Commentaries, Particularly Rūzbaihān al-Baqlī's 'Arā'is al-Bayān.'" *Journal of Sufi Studies* 2, no. 1, 2013.

Gölpinarli, Abdülbākī. *Melāmīlik ve Melāmīler*. Istanbul: Devlet Matbaasi, 1931.

Grandin, Nicole and Gaborieau, Marc (dirs.). *Madrasa: La Transmission du Savoir dans le Monde Musulman*. Paris: Éditions Argument, 1997.

Gril, Denis. "Adab and Revelation, or One of the Foundations of the Hermeneutics of Ibn 'Arabî." In *Muhyiddin Ibn 'Arabî: A Commemorative Volume*. Edited by Stephen Hirtenstein. Rockport: Element, 1993.

Halm, H. "Der Wesir al-Kunduri und die Fitna von Nishapur." *Die Welt des Orients* 2, 1971.

Ibn al-Asakir. *Tabyīn Kidhb al-Futarī fī mā Nusiba ilā al-Imām Abī al-Ḥasān al-Ash'arī*. Damascus: 1347/1928.

Ibn 'Ajiba, Ahmed. *Mi'rāj al-Tashawwuf ilā Ḥaqā'iq al-Taṣawwuf.* Edited by Abd al-Majid Khayali, Casablanca: Markaz al-Turath al-Thaqfi al-Maghribi, 2004.

———. *Kitāb Sharḥ Ṣalāt al-Quṭb Ibn Mashīsh*. Edited by Abd al-Salam al-'Imrani. Casablanca: Dar al-Rashad al-Hadithah, 1999.

Isfahani, Abu Nu'aym, al-. *Ḥilyat al-Awliyā'*. Edited by Mustafa Abd al-Qadir 'Ata. Beirut: Dār al-Kutub al'-Ilmiyya, 1997.

Kalabadhi, Abū Bakr Muḥammad Isḥāq, al-. *Al-Ta'arruf li Madhāhib Ahl al-Taṣawwuf.* Edited by Ahmad Shams al-Din. Beirut: Dar al-Kutub al-'Ilmiyyah, 1993.

Karamustafa, Ahmet T. *Sufism: The Formative Period*. Edinburgh: Edinburgh Univ. Press, 2007.

Kharqushi, Abu Sa'd, al-. *Kitāb Sharaf al-Muṣṭafā*. Critical edition and notes by Abu 'Asim Nabil b. Hashim b. Abd Allah al-Ghamari. Makkah: Dar al-Basha'ir al-Islamiyyah, 2003.

———. *Tahdhīb al-Asrār fī Uṣūl al-Taṣawwuf*. Critical ed. and notes by Bassām Muḥammad Badur. Abu Dhabi: Isdarat al-Majma' al-Tamami, 1999.

Knysh, Alexander, *Islamic Mysticism: A Short History*, Leiden: E. J. Brill, 2000.

———. (trans. and notes). *Al-Qushayri's Epistle on Sufism* (*Al-Risālah al-Qushayrīyah fī 'Ilm al-Taṣawwuf*). London: The Center for Muslim Contribution to Civilization, Garnet Publishers, 2007.

Lorry, Joseph E. (dir.). *Law and Education in Medieval Islam: Studies in Memory of Professor George Makdisi*. London: Gibb Memorial Trust, 2004.

Makdisi, George. *Rise of the Colleges: Institutions of Learning in Islam and the West*. Edinburgh: Edinburgh University Press, 1981.

Makki, Abu Talib, al-. Qūt al-*Qulūb fī Mu'āmalat al-Maḥbūb wa Waṣf Ṭarīq al-Murīd ilā Maqām al-Tawḥīd*. Edited by Sa'id Nasib Makarim. Beirut: Dar Sadr, 1995.

"MALĀMATIYYA." *EI*[2], art. Fr. de Jong, Hamid Algar, and Colin Imber.

Malamud, Margaret. "Sufi Organizations and Structures of Authority in Medieval Nishapur." *International Journal of Middle East Studies* 26, 1994.

Meier, Fritz. "Khurasān and the End of Classical Sufism." In *Essays in Islamic Mysticism and Piety*. Translated by John O'Kane and Berndt Radke. Leiden: E. J. Brill, 2000.

Nguyen, Martin. "*Al-Tafīr al-Kabīr*: An Investigation of al- Qushayrī's Major Qur'ān Commentary." *Journal of Sufi Studies* 2, no. 1. 2013.

———. "Al-Qushayrī and His Legacy." *Journal of Sufi Studies* 2, no. 1. 2013.

Nicholson, R. A. *Kitāb al-Luma' fī al-Taṣawwuf*. Critical edition and notes by Abu Nasr Abd Allah b. Ali al-Sarraj al-Tusi. London: Luzac & Co., 1914.

Orfali, Bilal. *The Comfort of the Mystics* (*Salwat al-'Ārifīna wa uns al-Mushtāqīn*). Critical edition and notes with Gerhard Böwering. Leiden: E. J. Brill, 2013.

Qushayri, Abd al-Karim, al-. *Risālat al-Qushayrīyah*. Edited by Abdel Halim Mahmoud and Mahmoud b. El-Sherif. Cairo: Dar al-Ma'ruf, 1995.

———. *Al-Qushayri's Epistle on Sufism* (*Al-Risālah al-Qushayrīyah fī 'Ilm al-Taṣawwuf*).Translated and notes by Alexander D. Knysh. Reviewed by Muhammad Eissa. London: The Center for Muslim Contribution to Civilization, Garnet Publishers, 2007.

———. *Principles of Sufism*. Translated from the Arabic (*Risālat al-Qushayrīyah*: part 3 only) by B. R. von Schlegell. Introductory notes by Hamid Algar. Berkeley: Mizan Press, 1990.

———. *The Risālah: Principles of Sufism*. Translated by Rabia Harris. Edited by Laleh Bakhtiar. London: Great books of the Islamic World Inc., 2002.

———. *Al-Fuṣūl fī al-Uṣūl* (*Two Short Dogmatic Works of Abu al-Qasim al-Qushayri*) Critical editing by Richard Frank. *Mélanges* 15, 1982.

———. *Kitāb al-Mi'rāj*. Edited by Ali Hasan Abd al-Qadir. Cairo: Dar al-Kutub al-Hadith, 1964.

———. *Laṭā'if al-Ishārāt bi Tafsīr al-Qur'ān*. Edited by Abd al-Latif Hasan Abd al-Rahman. Beirut: Dar al-Kutub al-'Ilmiyyah, 2000.

———. *Luma' fī al-I'tqād*, in (Two short dogmatic works of Abu l'Qasim al-Qushayri), Richard Frank (critical ed.), in *Mélanges* 16, 1983.

———. *Naḥwu al-Qulūb al-Ṣaqhīr.* Edited by Mursi Muhammad Ali. Beirut: Dar al-Kutub al-'Ilmiyyah, 2005.

———. *Naḥwu al-Qulūb al-Kabīr.* Edited by Ibrahim Basyuni and Ahmad 'Alam al-Din al-Jundi. Cairo: Maktab 'Alam al-Fikr, 1998.

———. *Al-Rasā'il al-Qushayrīyah*. Edited by Fir Muhammad Hasan. Pakistan: al-Ma'had al-Markazi li al-Bahithat al-Islamiyyah, 1384/1964.

———. *Sharḥ li Asmā' Allāh al-Ḥusnā*. Edited by 'Asim Ibrahim al-Darqawi. Beirut: Dar al-Kutub al-'Ilmiyyah, 2006.

Sands, Kristen Z. "On the Subtleties of Method and Style in the *Laṭā'if al-Ishārāt* of al-Qushayrī." *Journal of Sufi Studies* 2, no. 1, 2013.

Sarraj al-Tusi, Abu Nasr Abd Allah b. Ali, al-. *Kitāb al-Luma' fī al-Taṣawwuf.* Edited by Reynold A. Nicholson. London: Luzac & Co., 1914.

Schimmel, Annemarie, *Mystical Dimensions of Islam*. Chapel Hill: University of North Carolina, 1975.

Silvers-Alario, Laury. "The Teaching Relationship in Early Sufism: A Reassessment of Fritz Meier's Definition of the *Shaykh al-Tarbīyah* and the *Shaykh al-Ta'līm.*" *The Muslim World* 93, 2003.

———. *A Soaring Minaret: Abu Bakr al-Wasiti and the Rise of Baghdadi Sufism.* New York: State University of New York Press, 2010.

Subkī, Taj al-Din. *Ṭabaqāt al-Shāfi'īyah.* Edited by Ḥulw and al-Ṭanāhī. Cairo, 1386/1967. iii, 374.

Sulami, Abu Abd al-Rahman, al-. "Kitāb Adab Mujālasat al-Mashāyikh wa Ḥifẓ Ḥurumātihim." In *Collected Works on Early Sufism.* Edited by K. Honerkamp. Vol. 3, Nasrollah Pourjavady and Mohammed Soori. Tehran: Free University of Berlin, 2009.

———. "Kitāb Adab Mujālasat al-Mashāyikh wa Ḥifẓ Ḥurumātihim." *Ma'ārif* 20, no. 2 (Murdad-Aban 1382), series no. 59. Edited by K. Honerkamp. Tehran: Tehran University, 2004.

———. "Kitāb Fuṣūl fī al-Taṣawwuf." In *Collected Works on Early Sufism.* Edited by K. Honerkamp. 3:178-221.

———. "Kitāb Bayān Tadhallul al-Fuqarā'." In *Collected Works on Early Sufism.* Edited by K. Honerkamp. 3:33-61.

———. "Mas'alat Darajāt al-Ṣādiqīn fī al-Taṣawwuf." In *Collected Works on Early Sufism.* Edited by K. Honerkamp. 3:79-94.

———. "Kitāb Bayān Zallal al-Fuqarā'." Edited by Sulieman Ateş. *Tis'at Kutub li-Abī 'Abd al-Raḥmān Muḥammad b. al-Ḥusayn b. Mūsā*. N.p.: 1993, pp. 429-63.

———. *Mas'alat Darajāt al-Ṣādiqīn*. Edited by Sulieman Ateş. Tis'at Kutub li-Abī 'Abd al-Raḥmān Muḥammad b. al-Ḥusayn b. Mūsā, n.p, 1993, pp. 379-410.

———. *Al-Muqaddimah fī al-Taṣawwuf wa Ḥaqīqatihi*. Edited by Yusuf Zidan. Cairo: Maktabat al-Kuliyyat al-Azhariyyah, 1987.

———. *Jawāmī' Ādāb al-Ṣūfiyah*. Edited by Etan Kohlberg. Jerusalem: Jerusalem Academic Press, 1976.

———. "The Humble Submission of Those Aspiring" ("Kitāb Bayān Tadhallul al-Fuqarā'"). In *Three Early Sufi Texts*. Translated by Kenneth Honerkamp. St. Louis: Fons Vitae, 2009.

———. "The Stations of the Righteous" ("Mas'alat Darajāt al-Ṣādiqīn"). In *Three Early Sufi Texts*. Translated by Kenneth Honerkamp. St. Louis: Fons Vitae, 2009.

———. *Risālat al-Malāmatīyah*. Edited by Abu al-'Alā al-'Afīfī. Cairo: Dar Ihya' al-Kutub al-'Arabiyyah, 1945.

———. *Ṭabaqāt al-Ṣūfiyah.* Edited by Nur al-Din Shuraybah. Cairo: Maktabat al-Hanaji, 1969.

Sviri, Sara, "The Early Mystical Schools of Baghdad and Nīshpūr: In Search of Ibn Munāzil." *Jerusalem Studies in Arabic and Islam* 30, 2005.

———. "Hakīm Tirmidhī and the Malāmatī Movement." In *Classical Persian Sufism: from its Origins to Rumi*. Edited by Leonard Lewis. London: Khaniqahi Nimatullahi Publications, 1993.

Tabari, Abu Khalaf, al-. *Salwat al-Ṣārifīna wa Uns al-Mushtāqīn* (*The Comfort of the Mystics: A Manual and Anthology of Early Sufism.* Critical edition and notes by Gerhard Böwering and Bilal Orfali. Leiden: E. J. Brill, 2013.

Thibon, Jean-Jacques. "La Relation Maitre-Disciple ou les Elements de l'Alchimie Spirituelle d'apres Trois Manuscript de Sulamī ," In Gobillot, G. (dir.) *Mystique Musulmane: Parcours en Companie d'un Chercheur: Roger Deladrière.* Paris: Éditions Cariscript: 2002.

———. *L'oeuvre d'Abū 'Abd al-Raḥmān al-Sulamī (325/937-412/1021) et la formation du soufisme.* Damascus: Institut français du Proche-Orient, 2009.

Tirmidhi, Hakim, al-. *Kitāb Ithbāt al-'Ilal.* Edited by Khalid Zahra. Rabat: Muhammad V University, 1998.

Tusi, Abu Nasr, al-Sarrāj, al-. *Al-Lum'a*. Edited by Abd al-Halim Mahmud and Taha Abd al-Baqi Surur. Cairo: Dar al-Kutub al-Hadithah, 1960.

Discussion

Discussant: Mahmoud Ayoub

Islam is based on submission to God and not the ideas of human beings. The heritage that we attribute to the Sufi tradition – the ascetics, the "weepers" who wept when they read a verse dealing with paradise, for which they longed, or of Hell, which they feared – developed in the early days of Islam. Rabi'a al-Adawiyyah, the female mystical poetess, is generally considered to be the one who moved Sufism away from asceticism and toward spirituality. We should remember that with the esoteric influences on Sufism there came problems that led to the persecution of al-Hallaj, the Martyr of Love. He gave Sufism a bad name in the eyes of people in general, and thus the need for someone like al-Qushayri to rehabilitate Sufism, as described by our speaker. The *Risālah* explains the complete rootedness of Sufism in Islamic law and *'aqīdah*. I invite Dr. Honerkamp to compare the new translation with the partial translation by the earlier Barbara von Shlegel. Some fatwas are book-length, but in what way is the *Risālah* a fatwa rather than a manual of Sufism? Yes it contains criticism of people who adopt ideas or rituals not practiced by the first and second generation of Muslims. They were usually called Ahl al-Ahwa' wa al-Bid'ah. In the good-old days, and this says a lot about where we are now, people distinguished between good and bad *bid'ah*. I think the formulation that every new thing is a *bid'ah*, that every *bid'ah* is an act of going astray, and that every act of going astray leads to the fire probably is a harsh judgment on a civilization that gave so many new things to the world. I want to remind you that the only religion to produce a truly universal civilization has been Islam. If our ancestors believed in this notion of *bid'ah*, they would not have created the civilization that they did.

Discussant: Moustafa Kassem
This paper opens our eyes to important issues. I see two main themes: the actual fatwa that the Ash'ari tradition is founded in the Sunnah, and the discussion of the *Risālah* that Sufism is rooted in Ash'arism and thus also in traditional Islam. This paper relates to the politics of fatwas. Some opinions may reflect sociopolitical realities beyond the simple interpretation of text. The issue of labeling also comes up. Labeling often takes us off the path of knowledge by causing us to focus on the label rather than the content. I want to talk about interpretation. The right of people to their own knowledge, to not be bound by other people's ideas, is what will keep us free. Sufi scholars interpret traditions and verses in the light of their spiritual understanding. It was important that you reminded us that the Sufi masters are not infallible. Was al-Qushayri's authority to issue fatwas broadly recognized in his own time, or only among his followers? I was glad that you mentioned the chains of transmission in the book. It is important for freethinkers or any who wish to think for themselves that they have the ability to investigate and question the validity of these chains. The notions of good and bad *bid'ah* are essential for our concerns. We must not be scared in our scholarship that someone will accuse us of *bid'ah* because our conclusions differ from traditional scholarship or that one might be accused of guilt by association for communing with those who have unpopular ideas. We want to produce things that will benefit people. This requires us both to be brave and informed.

Honerkamp: Shlegel translated only the terminology, leaving out the biographies. There is another translation by Rabia Harris, partial in one edition and complete in the other. Although the footnotes were put at the end of the book in shortened form and are difficult to access, the translation is very good. I said that his fatwa was signed by the scholars of the day, recognized as an official hadith, and there was no doubt in Qushayri's community, not only among his followers, that he was *imām al-muṭlaq*. The intention behind the book seems to be to address Sufis and non-Sufis on his opinion and this makes it a fatwa. He says of God that "He knows by His knowledge; He is powerful by His power; He wills by His will; He sees by His sight" and this is straight Ash'ari *kalām*. He states very clearly in the introduction to the text that the Sufi creed is one with the Ash'ari creed.

Ayoub: That is what makes his book a manual. Its purpose is to lead people to the Sufi path.

Honerkamp: I think this fatwa is in a religious context. He says plainly that people define their terms in a way to make their meaning clear among themselves and to conceal them from those who disagree with their methods. I think he is attempting not to interpret, but to define, terms from the Sufi perspective. I agree with Br. Mustafa completely on the issue of interpretation. People too frequently say, "God said …" when they should say, "I believe that when the Qur'an says this it means this…." I think Muslims tend to turn off their critical faculties when they hear "God said …" or "the Messenger said…." People are not always quoting the Qur'an in Arabic when they say *qāl Allāh*.

General Discussion

- The challenge for us today is to try to bring spirituality to the discussion. We may need a new word besides "Sufi." We cannot help but label, because categorization is part of knowledge. Wisdom is about bringing knowledge to bear on life.
- *Fiqh* is not something to which western converts can necessarily relate. Not only in the West, but when you look at the spread of Islam all over the world *fiqh* is not the attraction. It is interesting that when converts speak of their conversion in a spiritual way they are immediately labeled "Sufi." That is why the suggestion that we may need a new term for spirituality is so interesting.
- The conclusion that the Risālah is a fatwa takes us back to the point that we need a serious discussion to come up with a clear sustainable definition of fatwa. Certainly *iṣlāḥ* is not the sole domain of jurists, but a fatwa is a matter of law. Otherwise there would be fatwas in politics, economics, and social science. We need more clarity. We don't want to face extremism in our material life, but what about in our spiritual life? Islam balances the spiritual and the material, and the challenge is to maintain that balance. The stronger our relationship with Allah, the stronger should be our relationships with our fellow human beings.
- We don't mind calling someone a *faqīh* or an *usūlī*, but as soon as someone is called a "Sufi" there is a problem. Sufism has its spokespeople, history, and methodology. There is in the world what might be considered an extremely effective de facto Sufi *ṭarīqah* that has had an enormous impact on the world; however, it is not called "Sufi" or even "Islam," even though it has a shaykh named Fethullah Gülen: the Gülen Movement. Islamic and Sufi principles deeply infuse it.

- However else the fatwa was received, the Hanbalis objected to refuting the Mu'tazilah on the grounds that to refute them would force you to repeat their arguments. Yet the scholars of his day identified it as a fatwa. Al-Qushayri said that you should not ascribe infallibility to the masters because so many critics of Sufism today say that to be a Sufi you must uncritically follow the master. He also says one should not be overly critical of them, but to think the best of them even when you don't understand them. Consider the case of the Moroccan shaykh Ahmad Zarouk, who saw his master sitting with a bottle of wine and a beautiful young girl. He walked out in disapproval, but the master called to him: "Come back! This is vinegar and this is my daughter." In other words, do not be so quick to criticize what you do not understand.
- There is no Arabic word equivalent to the English "mysticism." Sufism became a label that really refers to the initiate's clothing (course wool, or *sûf*), although some try to attribute it to other origins (like *sofia*). A fairly well-known ninth-century Sufi observed: "Sufism used to be a reality without a name, and now it is a name without a reality." Other terms, such as gnosis, can be used. It is about the love of God expressed through poetry or the knowledge of God. Sufism is a rich heritage mirroring a rich civilization. It is not, strictly speaking, a *madhhab*, but cuts across all legal schools. Although the Shi'a were hostile to Sufism in general, it developed in Iran prior to its becoming Shi'a and still prevails there.
- From the vantage point of the conference's theme, some dimensions are missing. A discussion of the methodology of fatwa from al-Qushayri's approach has already been mentioned. The main missing dimension, however, is the pressure as well as the coercion he was under not only from the authorities, but also the intellectual terrorism he faced from his opponents. All of this must be exposed. We must make the point that they are against the spirit of Islam. This addresses the issues of authority and legitimacy we face today.
- Sufism cuts across legal schools and sects. Sufism and *fiqh* have never been mutually exclusive. In saying that fiqh is boring or complicated or unattractive to new Muslims, we must be careful not to dismiss this important part of our intellectual tradition. Shaykh Ibn Baha'i al-'Amali from southern Lebanon was an architect, poet, theologian, and hadith scholar. The spiritual masters were also masters of *fiqh* and theology. For these people every act has a metaphysical value attached to it, and it is the scholar's duty to identify each act's metaphysical value.
- The *Risālah* is a coming together of all of these fields. Sufis don't call themselves Sufis. They usually call themselves *fuqarā'*. The negative aspect of the *nafs* in the *malāmātī* perspective is that it is like a piece of charcoal. No matter how much you wash it, it remains black. To change its color you have to put it in a brazier until it glows and turns red. There isn't a Sufi way of making a fatwa. Al-Qushayri gave his fatwa as an *'ālim*.
- One of the greatest Sufis, Abdul Qadir al-Jilani, belonged to the Hanbali *madhhab*, as did others.

- In some places the only thing people know about Islam is Sufism. Perhaps Sufism's origin is nothing more than a reaction against excessive legalism. Different groups emphasize different aspects of Islam. As soon as we name groups, we create opportunities for division and extremism. An excessive emphasis on some values undermines others. Islam is a balanced and harmonized teaching. The devotion in the West of certain days of the week to the spiritual and other days to the secular seems strange. Emphasizing the intellect at the university but not at the church seems strange.
- Good Sufis are very introspective; there are others, however, like one very well-known Sufi in the United States who has spoken against other Muslims and loves to be in the corridors of power. He doesn't know much about Islam or Sufism, but he is Sufi shaykh who is known to the people. Not all Sufis are *'ālim*s like Qushayri.
- Those coming out of Christianity see that Islam cuts across so many cultures. As soon as they become Muslim they have to ask: "What kind of a Muslim will I be?" It seems that you need a way to distinguish yourself among Muslims.
- Perhaps our negative attitude toward Sufism is in large measure a reaction against our nineteenth-century encounter with the West. We wanted to show it that we were more rational than the Christians, and Sufism became a victim of that desire.

The Guardians of the Islamic Marriage Contract and the Search for Agency in Twelver Shi'a Jurisprudence

Vinay Khetia

Abstract

The legal nature of the Islamic marriage contract and its guardians (*'awliyā' al-'aqd*) has been a source of discourse among both classical and contemporary Imami jurists.[1] Although *'awliyā al-'aqd* literally means "guardians of the contract," it is indicative of one or more individuals who have the authority to supervise the contractual matters of any non-*walī* subject.[2] This paper will attempt to examine the juristic debate over whether the mature virgin of sound mind (*al-bikr al-bālighah al-rashīdah*) is required to have the permission of her *walī* in order to get married.[3]

Introduction

Shi'i jurists of various generations have offered different opinions and rulings resulting from the differences that are attached to different streams of hadith and supported by an absence of any direct Qur'anic reference.[4] That being said, the focus of this study is largely limited to modern-contemporary discourse (nineteenth to twenty-fist century CE/fourteenth to fifteenth century AH). This undertaking is potentially substantial as it intends to demonstrate the inner-workings and performative function of the contemporary Imami *mujtahid*, as he attempts to grapple with intra-Imami *ikhtilāf*, all the while rendering a ruling on a matter of crucial social-religious importance.[5]

The primary texts of interest are works of demonstrative jurisprudence (*al-fiqh al-istidlāl*) in which jurists evaluate the textual sources (Qur'an and Hadith) through the matrix of *uṣūl al-fiqh* (principles of jurisprudence) in an effort to deduce a ruling on any *shar'ī* (legal) matter.[6] These works are often written in the form of commentaries upon earlier legal works such as *Sharā'i al-Islām* (eighth/thirteenth century), or *al-'Urwat al-Wuthqā'* (fourteenth/early-twentieth century), which then serve as traditional indicators of *ijtihād* and discourse among Imami jurists.[7] Although the jurists covered in this essay are primarily products of nineteenth to the twenty-first-century seminaries of Najaf and Qum, it becomes clear upon perusal of their work that these jurists make no mistake of recognizing and mentioning the Imami juristic tradition of the past millennia. However, as a part of these works they include the legal opinions of past scholars while being cognizant of the fact that in their role as *mujtahid*s they are not legally bound by the exegesis of those who preceded them.

The implications of this understanding is that, upon examiningf the juridical tradition, the *mujtahid* may break with the predominant opinion or choose to reify it. In the event that the jurist parts with the predominant opinion and/or generates a new ruling all together, new legal possibilities and alternative avenues of a conservative or liberal resonance are created for those Shi'is who adhere to the system of imitating the jurist (*taqlīd*). Furthermore, the creation of alternative avenues or rejection of the predominant contemporary outlook has the potential to create instability within the Shi'i legal hierarchy, where the jurist's credentials and credibility may come into question, in addition to stirring conflict within certain community settings where believers follow different jurists with diametrically opposing rulings.[8]

Contemporary jurists are of two opinions. The first group requires the consent of the *walī* (in most cases the father or grandfather), and the second group, the minority, does not require the consent of the *walī*. In the texts of demonstrative jurisprudence the conclusion of the first group is *tashrīk* (shared agency between father and daughter), and the position of the second group is *istiqlāl al-bint* (agency of the daughter).[9] All the texts consulted in this study set out to discover and define *istiqlālīyah*. The question arises: Why is there not a similar contention and discourse concerning the betrothal of a minor who is, in fact, legally bound by the marriage contract, with no choice in the matter, upon reaching the age of maturity? The lack of contention on this seemingly iniquitous situation is due to the conformity one finds in the corresponding hadith traditions, thus leaving the mujtahid with virtually no legally acceptable avenue of protest.[10]

By conducting a close textual analysis of Ayatullah al-Sayyid Abul Qasim al- Khu'i's (d. 1993) *Mabānī al-'Urwat al-Wuthqā'* (representing the first group) and Ayatullah al-Sayyid Sadiq al-Ruhani's (b. 1926) *Fiqh al-Ṣādiq* (representing the second group), I intend to explore some of the intricacies involved in *ijtihād*, which includes but is not limited to the hermeneutics of *uṣūl al-fiqh* and hadith sciences, while showing how these hermeneutical devices affect the eventual fatwa. Second, I will briefly explore the opinions of the four imams of the Sunni school and compare them to the various Shi'i positions. I do this for two reasons: (1) the Shi'i legal tradition employs the principle of *mukhālafat al-'āmmah* (opposition to the Sunnis) as a means of resolving contradictory reports[11] and (2) since the four schools are divided among themselves, how effective is *mukhālafah li al-'āmmah* as a tool for resolving bifurcation?[12]

An overarching concern throughout this essay is the dilemma surrounding *hujjīyah* (evidentiary or probative value), namely, which traditions and methodological devices constitute a sufficient degree of *hujjīyah*. As will be demonstrated, the answer to this question is tortuous and equivocal. Lastly, I will attempt to explore the social function of compatibility (*kafā'ah*) and *al-'aḍl* (prohibition from prevention of marriage) and its potential effects on power dynamics in the Islamic family structure.[13] While I do explore some notions of gender and social conditioning, this paper is chiefly concerned with describing and examining how Imami jurists approach the traditional sources of law (Qur'an, Sunnah, and reason), all the while making use of the elaborate mechanisms and potential of current scholarly exegesis through the live issue of contested notions of agency *a propos* the marriage contract.

The Hadith Tradition and Juristic Discourse

The Imami *akhbār* collection is replete with reports advocating three kinds of agency (*istiqlālīyah*): independence of the father, independence of the daughter, and joint agency.[14] I intend to show how the copious number of conflicting reports has generated extensive discussions, drawing upon the hermeneutics of *uṣūl al-fiqh* (principles of jurisprudence) and *dirayat al-ḥadīth* (the contextual study of hadith) to establish otherwise missing contextual evidences (*qarā'in*), reconcile seemingly disparate traditions (*al-jama'*), and/or prefer one or more textual or rational evidences over the other (*al-tarjīḥ*).[15]

There are nearly twenty-three *istiqlāl al-ab* traditions found in the four principal Imami hadith compendiums, which unequivocally assert the father's absolute authority.[16] Due to their copious number I shall cite two acclaimed reports:

(1) Ibn Abi Ya'fur - Imam Ja'far al-Sadiq: "Do not marry virgin daughters except with their fathers' permission."[17]
(2) Muhammad b. Muslim - Imam al-Baqir or al-Sadiq: "Do not seek the counsel (*lā tasta'maru*) of the *jārīyah* (spinster) when she has two fathers

> (biological father or paternal grandfather), she has no authority in the presence of her father, and he said: Everyone must seek her counsel (permission) except the father."[18]

Both of these traditions emphasize the father's privileged position within the family structure and enforce normative patriarchy in which only the father will do best for his daughter and no authority shall intervene in this process. Furthermore, hadith compilers such as al-Kulyani (d. 329 AH), al-Saduq (d. 381 AH), and even al-Tusi (d. 460 AH) often arranged and listed the *akhbār* in such a way to enunciate their own legal position. As Robert Gleave has aptly demonstrated, al-Saduq and al-Kulyani used the traditions as a means of asserting their legal opinions, and I see no predicament in extending and applying Gleave's analysis to this case.[19] Furthermore, Ibn Abi Ya'fur's tradition is listed first in both *furū' al-kāfī* and *man lā yaḥduruhu al-faqīh*, which is indicative of their repute and importance. Also, both al-Khu'i and al-Ruhani deem them to be *ṣarīḥ* (clear) and *ṣaḥīḥ* (authentic).[20] In fact, I do not hesitate to assert that nearly all Imami scholars consider them, in addition to six or seven others of similar genus, acceptable according to the standards of traditional hadith sciences, not only due to complete *isnād*s (chains of transmission) but also because their reporters include the likes of Muhammad b. Muslim, Zurara b. Ayan, Fudayl b. Yassar, and Ibn Abi Ya'fur, to name but a few.

From a *rijāl* perspective, reports carrying the names of these second-century Shi'i's are of significant value.[21] Also, Muhammad b. Muslim's tradition prohibits *ijbār* (compulsion) for all guardians except the father, indicating that everyone else is required to seek her permission (*yasta'maruhā kullu aḥadin mā 'adā al-ab*) prior to contracting a marriage on her behalf. The apparent signification of this would imply two things: (1) the father reserves the right to compel his teenage or young daughter (*al-jārīyah*) into a marriage of his choice, and (2) that he has a select position within the nuclear and extended familial network.[22] To further emphasize paternal agency, al-Khu'i cites a supporting tradition: "None can annul the marriage except the father."[23]

For al-Khu'i, this tradition is a clear indication that the marriage contract should be a joint venture and a process of consultation between the *walī* and his subject. But the question remains: Is the father above this call to *ishtirāk* (joint agency)? The answer to this question is no, because the *istiqlāl al-ab* traditions did not prevail for either al-Khu'i or al-Ruhani due to the presence of opposing (*mu'āriḍ*) traditions. It is at this juncture that the hermeneutics of jurisprudence and hadith become especially pertinent. The following are four examples of *mu'ārid* reports:

(3) Safwan b. Yahya sought the advice of Musa b. Ja'far (Imam Musa al-Kazim) regarding the marriage of his daughter to his nephew. The Imam said: "Go ahead with it, with her satisfaction for surely she has a propensity towards it within herself…"[24]
(4) Al-Fudala' - Imam Ja'far al-Sadiq: "The woman who controls-owns herself and is not feeble minded and has no guardian over her, she may marry without the permission of her guardian (*walī*)".[25]
(5) Zurara b. Ay'an - Imam Ja'far al-Sadiq: "If a woman controls her own affairs, [that is] she sells [goods], purchases, she is free, she acts as a witness, and she gives forth from her wealth as she wishes. Then surely her affair is acceptable, she may marry if she so wishes without the permission of her *walī*. If this is not the case, her marriage is not permissible except with the permission of her *walī*."[26]
(6) Sa'dan b. Muslim - Imam al-Baqir: "There is no harm in the marriage of a virgin if she is content (with the proposal) without the permission of her father."[27]

Both al-Khu'i and al-Ruhani accepted the third hadith as *ṣarīḥ* and *saḥīḥ*.That being said, al-Khu'i combined it with the contents of the previous two reports. This combination or harmonization between reports is described by al-Khu'i as *al-jam'ah* (reconciliation).[28] Consequently, by combining and reconciling them he arrived at the conclusion of *al-tashrīk* (joint agency) in which the father cannot compel his daughter into a marriage without her consent, and she cannot marry without his consent. Also, in harmonizing these traditions he is not required to reject one group over the other, but to consolidate the two positions; *istiqlāl al-ab* and *istiqlāl al-bint*, thus resulting in *ishtirāk*. Put another way, since both the aforementioned positions stem from "authentic" reports, al-Khu'i essentially harmonizes their content by allowing them to speak to each other by stating that the father does have a position of authority (*istiqlāl al-ab*) to authorize or reject a marriage contract for his virgin daughter, but at the same time the correctness of the *'aqd* (contract) relies upon her willful consent, thereby creating a position of *tashrīk*[29] This shared agency does not prevent her from contracting her own marriage, except that its validity relies upon the father's consent.[30] As far as al-Khu'i is concerned, he could only consolidate and rely upon traditions that he regarded as both *saḥīḥ* and *ṣarīḥ,* as per his exegetical estimation. Furthermore, for al-Khu'i, the position of joint agency is congruent with the Qur'an, the Sunnah, and stands in opposition to the predominant position of the Sunnis (*al- 'āmmah*). Therefore, with these supporting factors he reconciles the traditions and adopt the joint agency position.[31]

Keeping in mind the nuanced technicalities, joint agency essentially views marriage as a family matter requiring mutual respect between the father-grandfather and the daughter.[32] In keeping with patriarchal norms, the mother and brother have no legitimate claims to agency in this matter. Furthermore, al-Khu'i's intermediate position affirms the prevailing opinions of *akhbārī* and *uṣūlī* Imami jurists, among them al-Hurr al-'Amili (d. 1120 AH), Yusuf al-Bahrani (d. 1186 AH), Sayyid Muhsin Hakim, Muhammad Ali Araki, and Sayyid Sistani – al-Khu'i's own successor and most prominent legal authority in Najaf.[33] It should also be noted that al-Khu'i's eventual ruling, akin to that of Sistani, was that the mature virgin of sound mind must seek her father's permission to get married according to obligatory precaution (*ihtiyāt wujūban*). The validity of the marriage contract relies upon both father's and daughter's consent.[34] *Obligatory precaution* means that due to a lack of absolute certainty and the presence of clear *ikhtilāf*, al-Khu'i still considers *idhn* (consent) to be compulsory; however, in this case his followers are permitted to refer to another mujtahid if they so wish.[35]

Lastly, germane to the matter of *tashrīk* are the circumstances surrounding the marriage of Ali and Fatimah, of which Shaykh al-Tusi has provided an interesting rendition in his *Kitāb al-'Āmālī*. It is alleged that upon Ali's request for Fatimah's hand, the Prophet told Ali that other men had asked for her hand, but that each time he saw an expression of displeasure on her face (*ra'ytu al-kirāhah fī wajhihā*). Despite this, the Prophet explained to her the religious merits and divine approval of Ali's proposal. Then, noticing no displeasure (in her facial expressions) he said: "God is great, her silence is her acceptance."[36] This report expresses two notable factors: (1) the Prophet sought her permission and by doing so set a precedent for Muslims and (2) by emphasizing Ali's spiritual attributes he asserted that there was no other suitable or equal (*kafū'*) partner for her. Accordingly, this report delineates the importance of *kafā'ah* and its faith-based characteristics.[37] Furthermore, if this event is read through the developed notion of Prophetic authority (*walāyah*) in this instance, the Prophet would have had a dual *walāyah* over his daughter both in his capacity as her father and the Prophet. But despite this, he allegedly sought her consent.[38]

Reports four through six are the primary source of *ikhtilāf* and site of juristic discourse. What is intended by discourse here is that jurists approach these reports aware that their evidentiary value and authenticity have been debated in the past. Keeping this in mind, both Khu'i and Ruhani carry out their own evaluation of the material at hand. As will be demonstrated, at this point the *ijtihād* of the student (al-Ruhani) and that of the teacher (al-Khu'i) part ways.[39] There are two reasons for this, so to speak; *tashrīk* would not be viable in light of these two reports, and the *istiqlāl al-bint* position would arguably not exist without them.

Report four is deemed to have a complete chain of narrators, and thus is *ṣaḥīḥ* by *rijāl* standards. That being said, al-Khu'i and al-Ruhani disagree over its evidentiary value (*hujjīyah*). Put another way, it is the content (*matn*), at issue, not the *sanad*, thus emphasizing the importance of both content and chain in the process of demonstrative jurisprudence. Two problematic points arise upon analysis of its content: First, jurists are unsure of the implied meaning (*murād*) of *malakat nafasahā* and *lā mawlā 'alayhā*.[40] Similar complications concerning *hujjīyah* arise upon analysis of other *mālikah* reports, namely, *aḥādīth* that allow the *mālikah* woman to marry without the consent of her *walī*.[41] On this accord, al-Khu'i questioned its judicial value by stating that *mālikah*, as expressed in this report, could be rendered or interpreted as *al-jāriyah* (free or slave) virgin or non-virgin, hence leaving its application in doubt. Likewise, he is unsure as to what *lā mawlā 'alayhā* implies: Does it mean she does not have a father, or rather, that there is no guardian in general?

Therefore, by variegating the hadith's intended meaning he renders it *ṣaḥīḥ* but *ghayri ṣarīh* (unclear), and *muṭlaqah* (having a general and unrestricted meaning).[42] The primary reason al-Khu'i rejected the *hujjīyah* of these reports is because, in his view, the *istiqlāl al-ab* and *tashrīk* reports are *ṣ arīḥ* and *ṣaḥīḥ* and numerous, as opposed to the mālikah reports which are sparse in number and lack linguistic clarity. Likewise, al-Ruhani admits that the report is open to the same questions posed by al-Khu'i, but nevertheless insists that it is possible to interpret it as applying to the virgin (who controls her own affairs) and, second, *lā mawlā 'alayhā* could include her father thus rendering *mawlā* in a generic fashion.

But the question remains: How do we interpret malakat *nafsahā*? Put differently, does her right to enter into a marriage contract without her guardian's (father or grandfather) consent may only take effect in the absence of her *walī*? Or conversely, does her authority over the marriage contract remains even in the presence of her guardian, thus not obliging her to seek consent to ensure the marriage's validity (*ṣiḥa*)?[43] In the view of al-Ruhani the answer is the latter, since he cites report five in an effort to shed further light upon the contested *murād* of *mālikīyah al-'amr*.[44] The transmission from Zurara in the fifth report refers to the woman who controls her own affairs, engages in commerce, is a free woman (*hurrah*), and is financially independent. The three aforementioned functions serve to clarify the contested notion of a woman's *mālkīyah*.

Further, this tradition is of paramount importance in not only qualifying the virgin's agency in concrete terms, but also allowing her to demonstrate her independence by partaking in the mentioned activities (e.g., buying, selling, and witnessing) that constitute *mālikīyat al-'amr*. Therefore, in the view of such scholars as al-Ruhani this report acts as a *takhṣīṣ* (specification) of the previous *khabar*. Put another way, it has the potential to further clarify and define a contested *murād*, albeit the empowered woman in this report could be equally a virgin or non-virgin. Regardless, it sheds light on the function of *mālikīyah*.

Aside from the report being *ghayri ṣarīḥ*, al-Khu'i considers the chain of narrators to be *ḍa'īf* (weak).[45] In the *Mabānī al-'Urwa*, he rejects this report on two grounds: (1) he claims that he is unaware by which chain al-Tusi has transmitted from Ali b. Isma'il, although it is probable that he used the same *sanad* as Saduq, and (2) the reporter in question, Ali b. Isma'il, has not been authenticated.[46] *'Adam tawthīq* (absence of authentication) means that he is not known to have been among the principle sources or *mashāyakh* listed in the hadith books that have been authenticated, despite the fact that he is described as one of the earliest Imami-Badran theologians of the mid-second century *hijrī*.[47] Instances such as this demonstrate how al-Khu'i implements the enterprise of hadith-*rijāl* analysis and hermeneutics as way to reject the *sanad* of a report that has otherwise been accepted as authentic by the majority of his predecessors and contemporaries.[48]

The sixth report is the most *ṣarīḥ* of all the *mu'āriḍ* reports, as it clearly delineates that the virgin may marry whom she wills, provided that she is content (*raḍīyat*). However, despite its apparent clarity, its chain of transmission has been scrutinized by Imami *fuqahā'*.[49] Several of al-Khu'i's contemporaries consider the principal transmitter, Sa'dan b. Muslim to be unauthenticated and *majhūl* (unknown) and, as result, the report is by and large deemed be *ḍa'īf*.[50] Al-Khu'i, being cognizant of this, nevertheless stipulates that his reason for rejecting this *khabar* is not due to Sa'dan. In fact, al-Khu'i authenticates him by employing general authentication (*tawthiqāt al-'āmmah*) because Sa'dan is listed in the *isnāds* used by Ali b. Ibrahim al-Qummi (d. 310 AH) in his *tafsīr* and Ja'far b. Muhammad b. Qawlawayh (d. 369 AH) in his *Kāmil al-Ziyārāt*.[51] That being said, it should be noted that al-Khu'i altered his position toward the end of his life, when he only authenticated the *mashāyikh* (teachers) of Ibn Qawlawayh and Ali b. Ibrahim al-Qummi.[52]

However, in addition to Sa'dan being unauthenticated, Khu'i rejects the report by claiming that Sa'dan never transmitted any traditions to Abbas b. Ma'ruf, the second reporter in the chain hadith. On this note, al-Ruhani vehemently disagrees with his colleagues and claims that the charge of *'adam al-tawthīq* (absence of authentication) with regards to Sa'dan is without merit and the remaining part of the chain is in order.[53] Furthermore, the biographical works allege that Abbas b. Ma'ruf was a companion of the Eighth Imam (Ali b. Musa al-Rida'), thus leaving the period of the Seventh Imam remaining in between and leaving open the possibility that Abbas b. Ma'ruf may very well have transmitted from Sa'dan. This tradition serves as the axis upon which the discourse of *istiqlāl al-bint* revolves, due to it being the only clearly worded and "authentic" report of its kind.[54] Consequently it is of unquestionable importance for al-Ruhani to authenticate its text and chain, and by doing so he lends it a credible degree of *hujjīyah.*

The evaluation of the aforementioned hadith traditions reveal the nuances and performative nature of *dirāyat al-ḥādīth*. Put another way, hadith analysis and its usage as a means of *istinbāt* depends largely upon the individual *mujtahid*'s hermeneutical and rational assumptions. Moreover, the act of *istinbāṭ al-aḥkām* is the performance of careful and judicious *ijtihād* in which the *mujtahid* uses the necessary hermeneutical tools to validate his eventual conclusions. This validation is especially important for al-Ruhani, as his exegesis of the hadith and eventual conclusions represent a dissent from the predominant view of his colleagues.

Lastly, the complex and conflicting methods of hadith analysis are reflective of a highly advanced discourse with similar but not entirely parallel hermeneutical concerns in the pre-modern juristic tradition, as reflected in the works of al-Sayyid al-Murtada (d. 436 AH), Muhaqqiq (d. 672 AH), Allamah al-Hilli (d. 648 AH), and Shahid al-Thani (d. 966 AH). One example of divergence can be seen in the approach to the hadith tradition. Whereas previous scholars such as al-Tusi and al-Murtada considered the question of authenticity, contemporary *dirāyat al-ḥādīth* raises a greater number of concerns regarding both these reports' content and transmitters. In other words, as the discipline of hadith has evolved, the criticism and analysis has become sharper and more detailed.[55] On the same note, it has been shown that this development prompted jurists such as al-Khu'i to implement creative hermeneutics of authentication (*tawthīq*) and de-authentication of certain *rijāl* over others. Another example is that contemporary Imami jurists discuss the hermeneutics surrounding juristic preference and combination of reports as a way to resolve the *ikhtilāf* on this legal issue, whereas medieval Imami jurists such as Allama al-Hilli did not raise the same concerns while attempting to contend with the *ikhtilāf* concerning the *al-bikr al-bālighah al-rashīdah.*[56]

Juristic Preference (*al-Tarjīh*) and Opposition to the Sunnis (*Mukhālafah li al-'Āmmah*)

Juristic preference is the process of selecting one or a group of traditions with similar or identical content over all others.[57] Unlike Sayyid al-Khu'i and most others, al-Ruhani stipulates that upon realizing the impossibility of reconciling (*'adam imkān al-jama'*) the *istiqlāl al-ab* with *istiqlāl al-bint* reports he decided to prefer the *istiqlāl al-bint* reports above all others.[58] Thus in this case there are essentially three important factors to keep in mind; ideally the preference must be in accordance with the Qur'an and Sunnah, and be in opposition to the Sunnis.[59] To assert his *tarjīh*, Ruhani uses two hermeneutical devices in addition to the Qur'an: *al-shuhra al-fatwā'īyah* (the prevailing or most familiar legal judgment), and *qā'ādat tasalut al-nās 'alā anfusihim* (principle of governance over oneself).[60] As will be demonstrated, neither principle is traditionally among the *murajjihāt* (the established criteria for the preponderance of one tradition over another).[61]

In the case of *shuhra*, Ruhani asserts that the prevailing juristic opinions of past scholars have been *istiqlāl al-bint*, namely, the mentally mature virgin does not require her *walī*'s permission to get married. He also cites Sayyid al-Murtada's claim that there is a consensus (*ijmā'*) on this matter. Consequently, by implementing *shuḥra*, he is vesting the legal opinions of the past with a considerable degree of *ḥujjīyah* and implementing it as a part of his *ijtihād*.[62] Although a comprehensive examination of the opinions of al-Murtada and his Imami colleagues is beyond the scope of this study, al-Ruhani is not far-fetched in claiming that *istiqlāl al-bint* position was a predominant one among major thinkers such as al-Murtada and Allamah al-Hilli.[63] That being said, one would be hard pressed to characterize it as constituting the overwhelming position of both the *qudamā'* (early scholars) and the *muta'akhkhirūn* (later scholars).[64] Put differently, upon careful assessment of the Imami legal tradition from al-Saduq onward it would be hard to assert that this position is the most prominent one.[65] Furthermore, how are we to understand Sayyid al-Murtada's claim that the Imami jurists have an *ijmā' al-ṭāifa* (group consensus) regarding *istiqlāl al-bikr* to begin with?

Perhaps Murtada' used the term *ijmā'* to indicate the collective opinion of himself and those present within his scholarly circle. However, even in this case it cannot be known for certain whether his own esteemed instructor Shaykh al-Mufid (d. 413 AH) and the most senior student, Shaykh al-Tusi (d. 459 AH) would be included in this claim to consensus since they are alleged to have both held the position of *istiqlāl al-ab*. Furthermore, both al-Mufid and al-Tusi are said to have preferred the compromise position of *tashrīk* even if the daughter can show the ability to care for her own affairs.[66] This puzzlement arises from the fact that between the *Nihāya*, *Mabsūṭ*, and the *Tibyān*, al-Tusi is said to have held the *istiqlāl al-ab*, *tashrīk* and the *istiqlāl al-bint* positions, although Ibn Idris al-Hilli claims that al-Tusi retracted his initial ruling of *istiqlāl al-ab* as stated in the *Nihāya*, only to give complete agency to the *bikr*, as cited in the *Tibyān*, which Ibn Idris alleges was his final work and reflective of his final opinion. However this claim is also somewhat dubious.[67]

In the case of al-Mufid we encounter a similar uncertainty because according to his most infamous work on substantive jurisprudence, the *Muqnī'a*, he states clearly that not only does the daughter require her father's permission prior to marriage, but the validity of the marriage contract hinges upon his consent alone. Conversely in a treatise attributed to him, *Aḥkām al-Nisā'*, al-Mufid states that if the daughter were to marry without her father's permission, such a marriage would be in violation of the established practice (*al-sunnah*) of the Infallibles but nonetheless valid (*māḍiyan*).[68] Once again there is no compelling textual evidence to give absolute preference to one of these opinions over the other.[69]

Nevertheless, al-Ruhani contradicts himself at the very beginning of his discussion where he claims that *istiqlāl al-ab wa al-jadd* to also be the prevailing position among the earlier scholars.[70] Furthermore, al-Khu'i was explicit in his rejection of *al-shuhra l-fatwā'īyah*: "Aside from the most prevalent authentic and unauthentic traditions on a given subject, there is no other type of *shuḥra* when attempting to implement juristic preference."[71] In other words, the only kind of prevailing position or *shuhra* a jurist can hold fast to is that which is based on the consensus of the Imams' companions. But even in this case, it must be grounded upon a confirmed chain of narrators.[72] This is reflective of al-Khu'i's general concern and emphasis on discovering textual evidence, rather than predominant legal rulings of past jurists that, for him, do not constitute substantial enough evidence for *tarjīḥ*. This is also indicative of al-Khu'i's belief that the opinions of previous scholars, including any claims to *ijmā'*, should be considered but do not have significant probative value unless they unveil the opinion of an Infallible (*kāshif 'an ra'ī al-ma'ṣūm*). In the absence of this, these claims are to be considered to be *al-naẓar* (speculation).[73]

Interestingly enough, al-Ruhani expresses a similar theoretical sentiment with regards to both *al-shuhra* and *al-ijmā'*. In fact he states that *al-shuhra al-fatawāiyya* is the weakest form of *shuhra*, for it is one in which the jurist is not aware of the basis of the prevailing ruling. Furthermore in the case of its implementation as a means of juristic preference, the fatwa must, with perceptible certainty (*ḥass*), be grounded upon a transmission from an infallible and not arbitrary opinion (*rāy'ī*).[74] Despite the seeming theoretical congruity, the significant practical cleavage between these two Imami *mujtahids* indicates the subjective nature of elements of *uṣūl al-fiqh*, especially when it comes to the importance given to applying precedence to resolve a bifurcation in the tradition. For al-Ruhani, his perception of an overwhelming precedence of *istiqlāl al-bint fatāwā'* issued from such prominent authorities such as Sayyid al-Murtada' and Allamah al-Hilli is enough to vest the position with a weighty probative value, especially due to their close proximity to the period of the Imams and their companions in comparison to himself. For al-Khu'i and others, such as Muhammad Rida Muzaffar, a *mujtahid*'s reliance (*ta'wīl*) upon another jurist's rulings defeats the purpose of *ijtihād*, because according to their logic a *mujtahid* is a scholar who can perform *istinbāṭ* (extracting rulings from their sources), thus negating the purpose of imitating earlier scholars.[75] Consequently, one can say that the question of *walāyah* over the pubescent virgin is a question of competing earlier visions bringing forth the contested role that legal precedent plays in Imami demonstrative jurisprudence.

Al-Ruhani uses the second device, *qā'adat tasaluṭ al-nās 'alā anfusihim*, as a form of *sunnah* and thus claims that based on this principle *istiqlāl al-bikr* is in complete conformity with the *sunnah*. It should be mentioned that according to the texts of *qawā'id fiqhīyah* (legal maxims) there is no direct *nass* (explicit textual rulings) to support this principle.[76] Being fully aware of this, he cites *ijmā'* in order to establish it as an absolute *sunnah* (*al-sunnah al-qaṭ'īyah*), a matter of established practice beyond doubt supported, in principle, by the Qur'an and/or the Fourteen Infallibles.[77] Upon further examination, due to the absence of a direct *nass*, the contiguous juristic principles would be "the freedom to spend one's wealth as he or she wishes" and "no harm or injury" (*lā ḍarar wa lā ḍirār*). In other words, the jurist may extend the implications of these principles to serve as support for *tasalaṭ al-nās* due to absence of a direct *naṣṣ*.[78] Although there may be no direct textual indicator, jurists describe *tasaluṭ al-nās 'alā anfusihim* as an overarching *'aqlī* (rational) and *fiṭrī* (instinctual) concept that posits that humans and some animals have the freedom over their own bodies and hence have the right to act in their best interest.[79] Furthermore, he claims this *sulṭanah* over one's person is complete (*tāmma*) and absolute (*muṭlaqah*).[80]

As liberal and contemporary as this statement may seem, it is ripe with incongruity and essentialism for the simple reason that Islamic law gives much greater preference to responsibilities than to rights. In the Imami legal and doctrinal view, the rights of God, the Prophet, and the Imams outweigh the rights of the individual. Furthermore, his scenario has the potential to raise some foundational questions: If a virgin woman is free to marry whom she wills without her father's consent, then by the same token of *tasalut al-nās 'alā anfusihim* should she not have the freedom to divorce as she wishes or donate her organs? But the reality is that Ruhani is inconsistent and does not implement this principle as a way to allow either freedom.[81] That being said, al-Khu'i would certainly have rejected the principle of *sulṭanah 'alā al-nafs* (governance over the self) because, according to his understanding, an *'aqlī ijmā'* of this type is not among the *murajjiḥāt*.[82] Furthermore, al-Iraqi noted that a principle such as the freedom over one's person is a general overarching concept (*'umūm*) that cannot be included in the form of a condition (*sharṭ*) as a part of a marriage or financial contract. Hence, it has no applicability in this context.[83]

The debate and discourse over the applicability of such a principle in the context of marriage demonstrates the ever-present tension between *al-'aql* and *al-naql*: Just how far can a *mujtahid* extend and apply rational-philosophical concepts in the absence of a *muḥkam* (authoritative) hadith report? The answer is beyond the scope of this study and by no means straightforward, as it depends upon the individual *mujtahid*'s hermeneutical, epistemological, and social outlook. Nevertheless, the above analysis reveals the variegated nature of contemporary Imami *uṣūl al-fiqh* and the lengths to which jurists implement hermeneutical devices in order to resolve *ikhtilāf*.

The second element of an ideal *tarjīḥ* should ideally be *muwāfaq bi al-kitāb* (that which is congruent with the Qur'an).[84] In this case, the Qur'an does not mention the guardian and the virgin; however, the *iṭlāqāt* (general dispensation) of the verses forbid the guardian to prevent the divorced woman from marrying whom she wills or return to her husband after her waiting period ends.[85] Ruhani does not explore the verses in detail at all, but instead lists them as supporting evidence keeping in mind that they can be understood as general guidelines and not as having any specific and particular (*muqayyid*) evidentiary value. Although he does not explore these verses in detail, Muhammad Jawad Mughniyyah has done so in his *Tafsīr al-Kāshif* under the exegetical rubric of Q. 2:232: "And when you have divorced the women and they have ended their term (of waiting) then do not prevent them from marrying their husbands when they agree among themselves in a lawful manner..."[86] Although this verse concerns divorced women, Mughniyyah attempts to build a case for the virgin by stating that if she behaves in a way that demonstrates her maturity and ability to distinguish right from wrong, then she should have the right to decide what is best for her without outside interference. He contends that the guardianship surrounding marriage should be similar to other matters, that is, if she is independent (*mustaqillah*) in her other life affairs (e.g. education and wealth), then likewise she should be free to choose her own husband. This line of argumentation essentially draws upon rational-ethical ideals to extract *ḥujjīyah* from an otherwise muṭlaq verse.[87]

The final element of juristic preference is *mukhālafah li al 'āmmah* (opposition to Sunnis), in which the Imami jurist resolves an apparent contradiction by choosing the position that does not conform to the view(s) of Sunnis. Implementing this principle serves two purposes: (1) it affirms Imami sectarian identity as a legal school (*madhhab*) and devalues the views of the "other" and (2) enables Imami jurists to conveniently resolve contradictions within their own tradition by claiming that since the Infallibles (*ma'ṣumūn*) cannot contradict themselves or each other, those apparent contradictions must be as a result of dissimulation.[88] Thus in the event of contradictory reports, those reports which resemble the position of non-Shi'a must have been verbalized under duress by the Imam to protect himself and his followers by not attracting any undue attention from those who would wish them harm.[89] Keeping this in mind, both al-Khu'i and al-Ruhani claim their positions oppose the majority (*mashhūr*) Sunni position. In the case of al-Khu'i, the *tashrīk* position would be mukhālaf to al-Shafi'i and Malik, who state that a father is not required to seek the permission of his virgin intellectually sound (*al-'āqilah*) daughter, but that it would be preferable if he did so.[90]

As straightforward as this may seem, this *mas'alah* (case) is also a point of tension for al-Shafi'i and Malik. Al-Shafi'i is confronted with the traditions stressing the father's authority on one hand and Prophetic practice of seeking the virgin's *idhn* on the other. As a result, he recommends that the father seek her consent and take care not to select a partner displeasing to her.[91] Malik preferred the predominant Madinan custom, where al-Qasim b. Muhammad and Salim b. Abd Allah would give their virgin daughters in marriage without seeking their consent.[92] Muhammad Fadel argues that although this position has been ascribed to Malik, the father's role and function is not clear cut and, in reality, the virgin can circumvent *jabr* and even contract a marriage without the guardian's consent. As ideal as this may seem, one should keep in mind that this is a "reinterpretation" of Maliki law and not the predominant view.[93]

While al-Khu'i's conclusion is in line with the majority of his colleagues, it is also *mukhālaf* to the opinions of al-Saduq, Ibn Abi 'Aqil, and al-Tusi who, like Malik and al-Shafi'i, allow the father to compel his virgin daughter to marry.[94] Furthermore, Ibn Rushd also states that the Sunni jurists disagree as to whether the guardian's *idhn* is a condition for a valid marriage.[95] Aside from the Hanafis, Sunni jurists extend guardianship to the eldest brother, paternal uncle, and, in the event of their absence, the state.[96] This demonstrates that the opinions of Malik and al-Shafi'i were by no means monolithic and that the Sunni positions are also wrought with *ilkhtilāf* and debate over *hujjīyat al-akhbār* and the practice of the Tabi'un.

Among the four Sunni imams it is alleged that only Abu Hanifah did not require the pubertal virgin woman to seek her father's permission, although he deemed it would be preferable (*mustaḥabb*) for her to do so.[97] He supports this ruling by using the Qur'anic verses previously mentioned, supported by logical reasoning, that essentially states that if a woman is intellectually sound (*al-'āqilah*) and her behavior (*taṣarruf*) demonstrates her independence, then she should be given the agency to contract her own marriage.[98] Furthermore, an often overlooked similarity between the Imami *ikhtilāf* and that of their Sunni counterparts is the conflict over the inferred *'illa* (*ratio legis*). As it were, by means of speculative reasoning (*al-'aql*) and *ijtihād*, Abu Hanifah held that it is the minority (lack of *bulūgh*) that is the *ratio legis* behind allowing the father to compel his minor daughter or son to marry. On the other hand, al-Malik and al-Shafi'i held that the inferred *'illa* was not her minority but her virginity; so long as she is a virgin the guardians have *walayah al-ijbār* (coercive guardianship).[99] *Ijbār* can be described as a form of coercive force in which the father may marry off (*al-inkāḥ*) his virgin daughter (pubescent or otherwise).[100]

The Imami *madhhab* continues to disagree over the inferred *'illa* as well. In fact, this is why Sayyid al-Murtada' clearly points out that Abu Hanifah's position is *muwāfaq* with what he perceived to be the Imami consensus (*ijmā'*) or collective understanding, that is *istiqlāl al-bikr*.[101] Furthermore, a similar rationale led Muhaqqiq al-Hilli and al-Allama al-Hilli to assert the very same position as al-Murtada', contrary to the alleged *tashrīk* positions of al-Tusi and al-Mufid, in addition to later medieval jurists such as Zayn al-Din al-'Amili (al-Shahid al-Thani).[102] Correspondingly, while such contemporary Imami jurists as al-Khu'i, Sistani, and others do not permit *walāyat al-ijbār* upon the *bikr bālighah rashīdah*, they also do not allow her to marry without her father's permission due to her virginity, even if she is *rashīdah* (mentally sound and mature), because that is the governing *'illa* for the ruling. The essential distinction to be made here is that the father is not in a position to coerce his virgin daughter into marriage, hence *ijbār* is not permitted. In contrast, al-Ruhani, Mughniyyah, and Fadlallah do not require her to seek her guardian's permission because the operative *'illa* for their ruling is *bulūgh* (majority) and lack of *safah* (immaturity of mind).[103] Allama al-Hilli sums up the prevailing position of legal-philosophical divergence in a concise and pointed manner:

> If the free woman is of physical and mental maturity (*bālighah rashīdah*) she becomes empowered by means of her pubescence and mental maturity (*rushdihā*) in all aspects of her behavior (*jamī' al-taṣarrufāt*) with regards to contracts (entering into contracts) and other than that – (this is a matter) of consensus (*ijmā'*) among scholars collectively except for the act of marriage (*al-nikāh*).[104]

The *ikhtilāf* among the Imamis at least since the period of al-Mufid and al-Murtada', rests on analogy, whether the jurists can create a direct link between her ability to maturely and correctly enter into contracts of a financial nature or otherwise, and that of marriage. Can they legally and philosophically group them together? For those who do not discriminate between the various *tasārrufāt*, the question of disallowing parental coercive authority is not an issue because the virginal but pubescent girl is not legally required to seek her father's permission, let alone being subject to coercive authority, for she has demonstrated that she is mentally mature and able to independently conduct her affairs without recourse to any parental authority or otherwise.

Turing back to the jurisprudential process of *tarjīḥ* (preference) or *jam'ah* (reconciliation), as useful as *mukhālafah li al-'āmmah* may seem in its function as a hermeneutical tool, its functional application in this context is secondary at least due to the divergence of opinions both among Imamis and Sunnites. In the context of this *mas'alah* Shaykh al-Araki states that "in light of the contradictory *aqwāl* (statements and rulings) of the Sunnis it is not possible for us to carry out *tarjīḥ* from this point of view."[105] Furthermore, an often overlooked line of reasoning among traditional Imami *mujtahid*s here is that the *ikhtilāf* within the Imami *akhbār* could be a result of extra-Imami influences. Put another way, in the midst of sectarian disputes and dialogue both in Kufa and Madinah, it is inevitable that some Imamis would have transmitted and presented their own legal opinion while claiming to have heard it directly from the Imam. There is no conclusive evidence to support this, but Maria Dakake has aptly demonstrated that many Imami theological positions of the second Islamic century were evidently influenced by Hanafi-Murji'i doctrine of *ijrā'* (postponement of judgment).[106] Hence, in the process of debate and dialogue it is certainly possible, if not a foregone conclusion, that Muslims in fact influenced one another.[107]

This is not to say that the Ḥanafi position was the only influencing factor behind the proliferation of *istiqlāl al-bint* traditions, such as the one reported from Ja'far al-Sadiq through Sa'dan b. Muslim or the *mālikah* traditions transmitted by Zurara. Further yet, it could be asserted that Abu Hanifah and other Sunnis drew upon the traditions, either directly from the Fifth or Sixth Shi'i Imam, or indirectly through a transmitter. This scenario is not entirely implausible, for the Imami hadith creates analogies between a woman's ability to carry out various financial transactions and to contract a marriage on her own. If a woman possesses these characteristics and abilities, she should be given the freedom to marry without her guardian's consent. Consequently, the Imami oral tradition asserting the daughter's agency would have been seemingly more alluring to Abu Hanifah as opposed to the nearly exclusive *istiqlāl al-ab* traditions circulating among non-Imamis during this period.

It should be noted, however, that all of these hypotheses hinge upon the notion that a portion of the *istiqlāl al-bint* traditions can be ascribed to Imams al-Baqir or al-Sadiq and their accurate transmission from disciples such as Zurara b. 'Ayan, only to be included in the Imami hadith collection some 150 years later. Nevertheless, traditional scholars should not overlook the correlation between the jurisprudential dialectics of the formative period (second-third century AH) coinciding with the origin (*ṣuḍūr*) of the conflicting *akhbār* attributed to the Fifth and Sixth Shi'i Imams, especially in the case of this *mas'alah*.[108]

That being said, *mujtahid*s contemporary to al-Khu'i, such as Ayatullah Muhammad Ali Araki (d. 1994), are not sure as to when the conflicting Sunni position took shape. The reason for this concern is that ideally, in order for *mukhālafah li al-'āmmah* to be useful, it must be *mukhālaf* at the time of transmission and not retroactively. Therefore, the principle of opposing the Sunnis is not as simple as it may seem. There are complications and nuances involved that are often not mentioned at all by jurists due to their lack of cognizance or their far-reaching ideological commitment to their *uṣūlī* principles. Be that as it may, the probability of cross-pollination should not be ignored.

Kafā'at al-'Aḍl, and Power Dynamics in the Islamic Family Structure

Wael Hallaq describes the guardian's role as seeking the best interest of the family and its daughters. He adds: "Marriage was not an individualistic venture but a family matter."[109] His characterization is accurate and is equally compatible with the outlook of Imami law. This is why all of the Imami legal texts consulted in this study emphasize two things – respect owed to the biological father and the need for mutual consultation, despite the *mujtahid*'s eventual legal position. Even if he confirms the *walāyah* over the virgin, there is an emphasis upon mutual respect between father and daughter.[110] Therefore al-Ruhani deemed it *mustaḥabb* (preferable) that the daughter seek her father's permission before getting married.[111] Keeping this in mind, jurists have included two variable factors to be considered during the marriage proceedings: *kafā'ah*, and *al-'aḍl*. *Kafā'ah* (compatibility or suitability) is a prerequisite for the validity of the marriage contract. If a father attempts to compel his virgin daughter to marry, even though if it can be proven that the prospective spouse is not suitable for or compatible with her, she can opt out of the marriage. Likewise, if the father prevents her from marrying a man who satisfies the requirement of *kafā'ah*, his agency is terminated and the woman may marry without his consent.[112] Such stipulations indicate a cognizance on the part of jurists that paternal men do not always live up to their role in looking out for their female charges' best interest.[113] This is the overwhelming opinion of Imami jurists, including such past jurists as al-Tusi and Muhaqqiq al-Hilli.[114]

That being said, these caveats raise two important questions: What are the parameters of suitability, and how does one identify a case of *al-'aḍl*? Upon browsing the *aḥādīth*, one gets the impression that the equal partner should be righteous, not drink alcohol, be sound of mind, and have an affinity toward the family of the Prophet or preferably be Shi'i.[115] These are generally considered to be *shar'ī* descriptions of equality or compatibility. *'Urf* (common view) definitions of *kafā'ah* would be open to even greater interpretation but can include: genealogy (*naṣab*), socioeconomic class, and physical attraction. It immediately becomes apparent that suitability, equality, and compatibility in a partner can rest in the eye of the beholder, that is, provided the general legal guidelines are met, a father would find it hard to prevent his virgin daughter's marriage.[116] Once again, as the legal literature stresses, it is the woman who will be spending the rest of her life with that man; hence in her view he should be compatible.[117] Thus both past and present Imami jurists have used strong language when it comes to *al-'adl* (prevention of marriage). One such example is Muhaqqiq al-Hilli's statement:

> If the guardian prevents her (his daughter) from marrying and is not marrying her to someone of equitable status according to her wish, in that case it is permissible for her to marry even if he dislikes her (doing so). This is a matter of consensus.[118]

By doing so, they are attempting to communicate that agency is not some form of blind power but an intelligent authority. Within this dynamic, both the daughter and the father have certain responsibilities: the father must take care to not hastily accept or reject a marriage proposal, and the daughter should take into account the protective nature of her father's authority and the emphasis placed upon cordial and respectful conduct. The legal literature is complex and replete with nuanced language known primarily to those acquainted with this literature. However, within this process the jurists have expressed pastoral concerns of family unity and cordial relations between family members. Pastoral concerns such family unity and normative patriarchy reflect the influential social factors present in juristic literature. These social factors, although highlighted in the hadith tradition, can also be a product of common view (*'urf*) taken into account by the *mujtahid* when rendering his ruling.[119]

When scholars such as al-Ruhani and Mughniyyah dissent from the normative outlook, they lend a potential socially destabilizing agency to the *bikr*. because they challenge the normative patriarchal power structure in which the father reigns supreme. Furthermore, the purpose of including these two caveats is to remind all those involved that they have certain rights and responsibilities, so they should be foremost concerned with preventing any undue hardship upon the *bikr*.[120] Once again, terms such as *undue hardship* (*ḥaraj*) yield an array of interpretations relying upon one's evaluation of their individual situation.

To sum up, the pastoral concerns expressed by various scholars indicate their concern for emphasizing what they view to be the spirit of the law, which leans toward an Islamically conditioned individualism that entails a sincere young religious woman deserving of a sincere religious man. The role of patriarchal communalism should ideally be reserved for ensuring that, above and beyond any other concern, the daughter's religio-spiritual wellbeing must come first. A strict reading of the rulings independently do not always communicate these underlying concerns of those who wield authority in the Imami tradition, and it is for this reason that compatibility and other social-ethical imperatives are emphasized in addition to the literal wording of the fatwa or legal recommendation.

Conclusion

In this paper I investigated the process of deducing legal rulings from their sources using the live issue of guardianship and the marriage contract. I analyzed the relevant *aḥādīth* and their variant interpretations, interpretations that involved a nuanced, if not an abstruse, line of arguments, chiefly semantic, aimed at either accepting or rejecting the evidentiary value of a hadith report. These reports' rejection or acceptance determined the eventual rulings of both

Ayatullah Sayyid Abul Qasim al-Khu'i and Ayatullah Sayyid Muhammad Sadiq al-Ruhani in which they selected and sifted and, in the case of al-Khu'i, combined *aḥādīth*. Naturally, this raises questions concerning the epistemological position of the *mujtahid*s in their approach to the text: Did they interpret the reports in a way designed to reach the desired predetermined conclusion? An affirmative answer would essentially entail that the *mujtahid* manipulates the texts by means of exegesis for his own aims.[121] While this would be an unfair and sweeping characterization, it is not farfetched to assume that a *mujtahid*'s hermeneutical disposition and conviction certainly affects the outcome of his *ijtihād*. Even before he approaches a *mas'alah,* he has already decided how to authenticate or deauthenticate a certain *sanad*, or which *uṣūlī* principles he may prefer over others while interpreting the *matn*.[122] This predetermined hermeneutical disposition influences how he approaches the question of *ḥujjiyah*, for that which one *faqīh* may consider to have probative value may not be viewed in the same light by another. The divergent hermeneutical dispositions of al-Khu'i and al-Ruhani allowed them to both carry out *ijtihād* but arrive are different conclusions.

Since al-Ruhani could not combine or harmonize the traditions, he chose to prefer one set over the other (*tarjīḥ*). In doing so, he relied upon what he perceived to be the predominant position of both early and later Imami jurists. He also invoked *sulṭanat al-nās 'alā anfusihim* (human authority over one's self). In this context, neither of these principles is widely accepted by Imami jurists when used to support a juristic preference; however, the latter is cautiously included as one of the jurisprudential maxims (*qawā'id al-fiqhīyah*). Al-Ruhani's usage of a theoretical principle of this nature challenges the dominion of traditional hermeneutics, and by invoking such concepts as human freedom within this context he opens the door to multiple foundational questions, such as: How does one limit and/or apply such a principle, and who determines how and when it is used? Or as Makarem al-Shirazi states, the principle of human freedom to govern themselves must be limited by the Shari'ah. Otherwise, it would not make any sense.[123] However, in light of intra-Imami *ikhtilāf* on the matter of the virgin and her agency, al-Ruhani and others, such as Mughniyyah, are free to break loose from their contemporaries' conservative patterns and invoke the principle of human freedom to justify their dissent from the norm of *tashrīk*. This clearly demonstrates the variegated and nuanced nature of the principles of jurisprudence and *istinbāt al-aḥkām* (deduction of rulings from their sources).

In addition to this, both groups of scholars attempted to juxtapose their positions in opposition to those of the Sunnis (*mukhālfat al-'āmmah*) to further support their respective rulings. The operative value of this hermeneutical device is multifarious, at least in light of intra-Imami *ikhtilāf* and the ambivalent positions among the four Sunni imams. To sum up, there are two contemporary Imami positions: (1) *tashrīk*, held by al-Khu'i and the majority of contemporary Imami jurists, which states that by obligatory precaution the virgin daughter of mature mind must seek her father's permission or, in his absence, that of the paternal grandfather before getting married. Furthermore, the validity of the marriage contract relies upon both the father's and the daughter's consent and (2) *istiqlāl al-bint*, held by al- Ruhani and Mughniyyah, which states that the virgin mature daughter is not required to seek her father's permission to get married, although it is recommended that she do so, and the validity of the marriage contract does not rely upon her father's consent. The analysis of the hadith traditions and the methodological tools of *uṣūl al-fiqh* show that, at least within this context, jurists confront a dilemma of *hujjīyah* and have gone to great lengths to establish the viability of their respective conclusions via hadith, legal precedent, and, at times, broad-spectrum philosophical principles.

Lastly, I examined the two caveats of *al-kafā'ah* (equality or compatibility) and *al-'aḍl* (prevention of marriage by the guardian). Both of these forewarnings have been inserted into the rulings governing the virgin's marriage to express pastoral concerns dealing with family unity, the father's socio-religious precedence, and the need to prevent any undue harm or injury to the virgin girl or woman. In light of modern realities and the perceptible financially and intellectually independent Muslim woman in both the Muslim world and the "West," Muslim jurists will be forced to better explain and justify the laws governing agency and the marriage contract.

Endnotes

1. For the purposes of this paper, *jurist*, *Imami*, and *Shi'i* refer to Twelver Shi'i unless otherwise stated.
2. Within the context of this analysis, I define the *non-walī subject* as any individual who does not have the authority to contract a marriage without his/her guardian's consent.
3. In this paper, *virgin* implies an adolescent woman who has never had sexual intercourse but is of sound mind, able to discern right from wrong (*al-rashīdah*, *al-'āqilah* or *ghayri al-safīhah*). For those who have lost their virginity through fornication, the vast majority of contemporary jurists have ruled that although physically not virgins, they are classified as such insofar as they would not be afforded the agency offered to a divorced or widowed woman (*thayyib*). This includes the validity of a marriage contract executed without her *walī*'s permission.

4. In his *Kitāb al-Khilāf*, Shaykh al-Tusi (d. 460 AH) states *ikhtalafū aṣḥābanā* (our companions/Shi'a disagree) on this matter, that is to say from as early as early fifth century Twelver Shi'i scholars disagreed as to whether the *walī*'s *idhn* (permission) was required. He goes on to mention the disagreement between the Shafi'is and the Hanafis on the same matter. See Abi Ja'far Muhammad ibn al-Hassan al-Tusi, *Kitāb al-Khilāf* (Qum: Sharka Dar al-Ma'arif al-Islamiyyah, 1958), 2:358-59.
5. I use "he" because the vast majority (if not all) *mujtahid*s continue to be men. There may be female *mujtahid*s, but I have not come across any published work to indicate otherwise. This is perhaps further indicative that a great impediment to female authority within this tradition is the production of authoritative written texts, especially as regards positive and substantive Islamic law, logic, Qur'anic exegesis, and hadith studies. In Imami law, a *mujtahid* derives rulings from various sources, namely, the Qur'an, Sunnah, and reason. This process is known as *itjihād* (the exertion of effort).
6. This is commonly known as *iṣṭinbāt* (deduction of rulings from the appropriate sources).
7. These are normally substantial technical works often carried out once a jurist begins teaching advanced studies (*baḥth al-khārij*) covering the semantics and hermeneutics of demonstrative jurisprudence and principles of jurisprudence within which Qur'anic exegesis and ḥadith studies are included. *Sharā'i' al-Islām* is an early-mid seventh century work that outlines the fatwas of Muhaqiq al-Hilli who, along with his nephew al-Allama al-Hilli, were instrumental in developing a notion of *ijtihād* acceptable to Imami jurists that did not entail juristic opinion; rather, it provided a process of extracting the rulings from the Qur'an, Sunnah, and *al-'aql* (reason). They also laid the groundwork for the future epistemology of hadith analysis and shed further light on the acceptable use of solitary reports (*akhbār al-aḥād*) in deriving Islamic law. Numerous scholars have commented upon Muhaqiq al-Hilli's *Sharā'i' al-Islām,* and prior to the *'Urwah* it was a rite of passage for a *mujtahid* to either append his own notes to it or to compile a substantial commentary, such as Muhammad b. Ḥassan al-Najafi's forty-three volume *Jawāhar al-Kalām fi Sharḥ Sharā'i' al-Islām* (Dar Ihya' al-Turath al-'Arabi: 1984). On the other hand, the prominent early twentieth-century Imami *mujtahid* Sayyid Kazim al-Yazdi authored *Al-'Urwat al-Wuthqā*; his *aḥkām* work became a popular subject of commentaries and *ḥāshiyāt* by his students and later scholars. For a detailed overview of development of Imami *ijtihād* and hermeneutics, see Ahmed Kazemi Mousavi, *Religious Authority in Shi'ite Islam* (Kuala Lampur: ISTAC, 1996), 75-105. Also see Norman Calder, "Doubt and Prerogative: The Emergence of an Imami Theory of *Ijtihād*," *Studia Islamica* 70 (1989), 55-78.
8. Two examples come to mind: Ayatullah Khamene'i, following the groundbreaking ruling of his predecessor (Ayatullah Khomeini), allows the playing of chess (*al-shaṭranj*) providing no one gambles; on the other hand Sistani and the vast

majority of Shi'i jurists consider chess to be absolutely *ḥarām* (impermissible) and sinful. This is a significant cleavage between these two jurists, who have a significant number of *muqallidūn* (followers) in the Middle East (Iran, Iraq, Lebanon, and Bahrain) and India, Pakistan, Europe, and North America. Situations continue to arise where Khamene'i followers want to play chess and Sistani followers vehemently object. Both groups attend the same mosque. The imam of the center is usually called upon for an answer, only to insist that both groups show respect for one another's sources of emulation and learn to co-exist! This is a prime example of intra-Shi'i conflict. For rulings regarding chess, see al-Sayyid Abul Qasim al-Khu'i, *Ṣirāṭ al-Najāt with the notes of Mirza Jawad al-Ṭabrizi* (Qum: Maktab Nashr al-Muntakhab, 1995), 1:376, http://www.sistani.org/local.php?modules=nav&nid=5&cid=427&hl=chess, last assessed February 13, 2011 and http://www.leader.ir/tree/index.php?catid=23, last accessed February 13, 2011).

9. Throughout this paper, *father* includes the paternal biological father as well as the paternal biological grandfather, paternal great-grandfather, and so on.
10. See: Jawad Maghniyya, *Fiqh al-Imām Ja'far al-Ṣādiq* (Qum: Mu'assasah Sibtayn al-'Alamiyyah, 2002), 5:233-34. He states that the only way to interpret or discover *ikhtilāf* among the traditions is to invoke the principle of "no undue harm or injury" or a similar ethical basis for rejecting the traditions. The problem in calling upon such principles is that they are very general and can seldom, if ever, outstrip a series of confirmed and authenticated traditions (according to traditional Imami standards) of their legal and probative value. In such cases, these jurists may invoke certain ethical norms (e.g., family harmony or the need to ensure a healthy and religiously prosperous future for one's children), but such ethical precepts have little or no bearing on the eventual fatwa.
11. One method of resolving an apparent contradiction between two hadiths, both of which are believed to have been said by the Imam, is to reject the tradition that accords with or is closest to the Sunni position on the grounds that it must have been said in a state of dissimulation (*al-taqiyyah*). For a concise and complete discussion, see Sayyid Muhammad Taqi al-Hakim, *Uṣūl al-'Āmmah li al-Fiqh al-Muqāran*, 3d ed. (Qum: Majma' al-'Alimi li al-Ahlu l-Bayt, 1997), 355-56.
12. The principle disagreement between some Sunni jurists centers on the inferred *'illa* (*ratio legis*) of agency being virginity or physical and mental maturity (*al-bulūgh wa al-rushd*). See note 78 for more details.
13. Suitability (*kafā'ah*) indicates that the potential husband must be of a comparable socio-economic status and/or *tadayyun* (observes Islamic law and is not a drunkard, for example). The prevention of marriage (*al-'aḍl*) means the guardian attempts to prohibit his subject (*mawlā*) from accepting a marriage proposal.
14. Jurists describe these three positions as *istiqlāl al-ab*, *istiqlāl al-bint*, and *tashrīk* or *ishtirāk*. A fourth position, *tafsīl*, essentially distinguishes between permanent and temporary marriage: In some cases she would have agency to perform temporary marriage but not permanent marriage, and vice versa. I will not be dis-

cussing this because the vast majority of contemporary jurists do not differentiate between the two when issuing fatwas. For an extensive discussion concerning all the stated positions, see Muhammad Hassan al- Najafi (d. 1266 AH), *Jawāhir al-Kalām fī Sharḥ Sharā'i' al-Islām* (Beirut: Dar al-Ihya' Turath al-Arabi, 1981-84), 29: 174-83. For a brief overview, see Ja'far ibn al Hassan Muhaqqiq al-Hilli, *Mukhtṣar al-Nāfi'* (Qum: Mu'assasah Matbu'at Dini, 1997), 183.

15. Conflicting traditions or contradictory reports are known as *al-akhbar al-mut'āriḍah*. Textual evidences are described as *nuṣūṣ*.
16. These four compendiums are *Kitāb al-Kāfī, Man lā Yaḥḍuruhu al-Faqīh, Tahdhīb al-Aḥkām*, and *Al-Istibṣār fī mā Ikhtalafa al-Akhbār*. There exists minimal scholarly analysis of these four texts, as the field of Imami hadith studies remains in its infancy. For a general overview regarding these texts, see Jonathan Brown, *Hadith: Muhammad's Legacy in the Medieval and Modern World* (Oxford: Oneworld, 2009), 123-50.
17. Abu Ja'far Muhammad ibn al-Hassan al-Tusi, *Al-Istibṣār fī mā Ikhtalafa al-Akhbār* (Tehran: Dar al-Kutub al-Islamiyyah,1970), 3:235; 1. Also see Ibn Babawayh al-Qummi (a.k.a. Shaykh al-Saduq), *Man lā Yahḍuruhu al-Faqīh* (Beirut: Mu'asasah al-'Alimi al-Matbu'at,1986), 3:259, hadith no. 439; and Muhammad b. Ya'qub al-Kulyani, *Al-Furū' min al-Kāfī* (Beirut: Dar al-Ta'aruf, 1981), 5:393 hadith no. 1. Also, Shaykh al-Mufid cites this tradition verbatim in the form of a legal ruling without explicitly indicating that it is a hadith report. See Shaykh al-Mufid, *Al-Muqnī'a* (Beirut: Dār al-Mufid, 1993), 510-11.
18. Muhammad b. al-Ḥassan al-Hurr al-'Amili, *Wasā'il al-Shī'ah* (Qum: Dhu al-Qurba' 2007), 7:359, hadith no. 3. Also see Kulyani, *Al-Furū'*, 393, hadith no. 2, and Tusi, *Al-Istibṣār*, 235, hadith no. 5.
19. Robert Gleave, "Between Hadith and Fiqh: The Canonical Imami Collections of Akhbar," *Islamic Law and Society* 8 (2001): 358-364. Gleave draws attention to the arrangement, listing, and heading under which the *aḥādīth* are placed. Although this may vary from scholar to scholar, it is nevertheless important to take note of this, especially as regards Kulyani and Saduq.
20. Abu al-Qasim al-Khu'i, *Mabānī al-'Urwa al-Wuthqā' Kitāb al-Nikkāḥ,* vol. 2, and Sayyid Muhammad Sadiq Ruhani, *Fiqh al-Ṣādiq*, vol. 21 (Qum: Dar al-Kitab, 1992), http://www.imamrohani.com/arabic/kotob/fokh/21/02.HTM#fehrest18, last accessed April 2, 20011). The hardcopy of this work was not available to me during the writing of this paper; however, Imam Ruhani's office has uploaded the complete version of the cited edition online, including the footnotes from the original text.
21. See Liyakat Takim, "Offering Complete or Shortened Prayers? The Traveler's Salat at the Holy Places," *Muslim World* 96 (2006): 409-413. Takim provides an extensive discussion concerning the connection between jurisprudence and *'ilm al-rijāl* (science of the narrators of hadith). All three of the stated transmitters were among the most prominent students and companions of the Fifth, sixth, and Seventh Imams. All of these reporters, aside from Ibn Abi Ya'fur, are de-

scribed as belonging to the *aṣḥāb al-'ijmā'* (those companions known as jurists [*fuqahā' min al-aṣḥāb*] whose repute is beyond reproach). See Muhammad b. Umar al-Kashshi, *Rijāl al-Kashshi* (Karbala: Mu'assasat al-'Alimi, n.d.), 206 as cited in Ja'far al-Subhani, *Kullīyat fī 'Ilm al-Rijāl* (Qum: Imam al-Sadiq Foundation, 2006), 173-80. The idealization of these transmitters is in no way monolithic in the Imami tradition, for such later scholars as Mamaqani, Khu'i, and others engaged in a hermeneutics of idealization and rehabilitation of the *rijāl*. For a thorough discussion, see Liyakat Takim, *Heirs of The Prophet: Charisma and Religious Authority in Shi'ite Islam* (Albany: State of New York University Press 2006), 158-63.

22. *Al-jārīyah* has several meanings, one of them being a young woman or youthful woman, as well as a slave or free woman. The lexicons indicate the general usage of "unmarried" or "young woman," as opposed to *'ajūz* (older woman), and a virgin or non-virgin. Al-Khu'i and others tend to interpret this tradition and similar ones as applying to non-virgins because there are numerous and straightforward traditions that emphasize the *thayyib*'s (non-virgin) agency. See E. W. Lane, *Arabic-English Lexicon* (Cambridge: Islamic Texts Society, 2003), 1:416. Also see Fakhr al-Din b. Muhammad al-Turayhi, *Majma' al-Baḥrayn* (Najaf: Dār al-Thaqāfa, 1961), 1:82.
23. Khu'i, *Mabānī*, 266. Also see Kulyani, *Al-Furū'*, 392, hadith no. 8.
24. Hurr al-'Amili, 7:364, hadith no. 2 and Shaykh al-Tusi, *Tahdhīb al-Aḥkām* (Tehran: Dar al-Kutub al-Islamiyyah, 1988), 7:379, hadith no. 10. Al-Tusi lists numerous traditions stressing the need for seeking the virgin's permission and satisfaction before marrying her to future husband.
25. Kulayni, *Furū' al-Kāfī*, 7:391, hadith no. 1, as well as Saduq, *Man lā Yahḍuruhu*, 259 hadith no. 4397. It reads as follows: *Al-mar'ah alatī qad malakat nafsahā wa ghayri al-safīhah wa la mawlā 'alayhā, tazwīj bi-ghayri walī jā'iz.*
26. Hurr al-'Amili, 7:365, hadith no. 6. Shaykh Tusi, *Al-Istibṣār fī ma Ikhtalafa al-Akhbār* (Tehran: Dar al-Kutub al-Islamiyyah, 1969), 3:234, hadith no. 6. The tradition reads as follows: *Idhā kānat al-ma'rah malikah 'amruhā tabī'u wa tashtarī wa tu'taqu wa tushadu wa tu'ṭī min māliha ma shā'at fa-inna 'amrahā jā'iz tuzzauwiju 'in shā't bighayri idhni walīuhā, wa 'in lam takun kadhalika fa-lā yajūzu tazwījuhā 'illa bi-'amri walīuhā*. For traditions of a similar purport, see ibid, and Kulayni, *Furū' al-Kāfī* 7:391, hadith no. 1, as well as Saduq, *Man lā Yahḍuruhu*, 259 hadith no. 4397.
27. Shaykh al-Tusi, *Al-Istibṣār*, 3, 236, hadith no. 6 and Hurr al-'Amili, 7:365, hadith no. 4.
28. Al-Khu'i, *Mabānī*, 257.
29. As I mentioned earlier, al-Khu'i is by no means the first to construct this position based on reconciliation between these opposing traditions. But in his capacity as a *mujtahid*, he must go through the motions of once again surveying all of the traditions in order to delineate how he arrives at the position of joint agency also known as *tashrīk baynahumā*.

30. If her potential spouse is deemed to be suitable and equitable (*kafū'*), then his *idhn* is not an absolute must. I will return to the question of suitability in the paper's final section.
31. Ibid., 258. For al-Khu'i, the Sunnah constitutes the authenticated traditions of the Fourteen Infallibles. Also I should note that for al-Khu'i, the Qur'an only supports his position in a very general sense insofar as there is no objection to the *tashrīk* position. As a result, he places little or no emphasis on Qur'anic support for his ruling.
32. I will return to the family unit and social realities when discussing the function of *kafā'ah* and *al-'aḍl*. In the work of al- Khu'i, *father* implies both biological father and paternal grandfather (*al-ab wa al-jadd*). That being said, the *aḥādīth* appear ambivalent on the matter and the majority of jurists tend to the give the father priority in the case of a conflict. For example, after much debate the famous jurisprudent of Iraq, Kashif al-Ghita left the door open to *istiqlāl al-bint,* provided that she does not bring shame (*hatak*) upon her guardian. See Ja'far al-Subhani, *Niẓām al-Nikkāh* (Qum: Imam al-Sadiq Foundation, 1995), 192.
33. The joint agency position is famous among scholars from the tenth Islamic century onward. In one of the earliest commentaries on Muhaqiq al-Hilli's *Sharā'i' al-Islām,* under the section on marriage and agency, the author concluded the following: "*al-jama' bayna idhnihā wa idhn al-ab ṭarīq al-iḥtiyāṭ...*", the joining of her consent and that of the father is the way of precaution, and God knows best with regards to the realities of rulings." See Muhammad b. Ali al-'Amili, *Nihāya al-Marām fī Sharḥ Mukhtaṣar Sharā'i al-Islām,* vol. 1. (Qum: Jami'at al-Mudarrisin, n.d.); Sayyid Muhsin al-Tabatba'i al-Hakim, *Mutamasak al-'Urwat al-Wuthqā* (Qum: Manshurat Maktabat Ayatullah al-'Uzma al-Mar'ashi al-Najafi, 1983), 14:445-48; and al-Najafī, *Jawāhar al-Kalām,* 29:183-84, and Sayyid Ali al-Husayni al-Sistani, *Islamic Laws* (Stanmore: The World Federation of KS.I. Muslim Communities, 1994), 439. Sayyid Sistānī is considered to be the most popular source of emulation in Iraq if not the entire Shi'i world, in that he commands the largest number of *muqallidīn* (emulators).
34. Khu'i, *Manānī*, 270. Also see Sayyid Muhsin Hakim, *Minhāj al-Sāliḥīn*, ed. and comp. Sayyid Muhammad Baqir al-Sadr (Beirut: Dar al-Ta'aruf, 1980), 276.
35. A discussion surrounding the development and use of *ihtiyāt wujūban* in Imami jurisprudence is beyond the scope of this paper. It is restrictive but not absolute, because it allows a *muqallid* to refer to another jurist, provided that the jurist has a clear fatwa. Aside from Sayyid Muhammad Husyan Fadlallah and Sayyid Ruhani, the vast majority of jurists have made the same ruling as al-Khu'i. An example of this use of precaution can be seen in al-Khu'i's insistence that the hijab include face veiling. He considers this an obligatory precaution, thus allowing his followers to refer to "the next most learned jurist" with an alternative opinion.
36. Shaykh Tusi, *Kitāb al-'Āmālī* (Tehran: Dar al-Kutub al-Islamiyyah, 2001), 71-72, majlis 2, hadith no.13. There is also an interesting report, albeit without a

chain of narrators, in which Fatimah objects to marrying Ali, after which the Prophet explains the latter's spiritual merits in this world and the next, all of which were brought to his attention during his heavenly ascent, therefore leaving no other person *kafū'* (suitable) for her. She then agreed to the proposal. See Ali b. Ibrahim al-Qummi, *Tafsīr al-Qummī* (Qum: Dar al-Kitab, 1984), 2:336-37.

37. Both Muhammad b. Hassan al-Najafi and Sayyid Muhsin Hakim, who relate this incident, cite this same report in support of shared agency and thereby have infused it with legal value. That being said, neither of them mentioned Fatimah's *kirāha* to previous proposals. See Muhsin Hakim, 14:446, and Muhammad b. Hassan al-Najafi, 29:183.
38. "The Prophet has greater precedence over the believers than they have over themselves…" See Q. 33:6. For a mainstream Imami exegesis of this verse, see Abu al-Fadl al-Ḥassan al-Tabrasi, *Majma' al-Bayān fī Tafsīr al-Qur'ān* (Tehran: Nasr Khusraw Publication, 1993), 8:530.
39. Sayyid Muhammad Sadiq Ruhani was among the late Sayyid Abul Qasim al-Khu'i's most prominent students. This is quite a remarkable claim within contemporary Imami clerical circles. For a biography of Ruhani, see http://www.imamrohani.com/arabic/sira/01.htm, May 1, 2010.
40. Almost every work of demonstrative jurisprudence has cited this as central detracting factor in this report's *hujjīyah*. See Khu'i, *Mabānī*, 2:259. For other discussions, see Muhammad Ali al-Araki, *Kitāb al-Nikāh* (Qum: Nur Nagar, 1998), 46-47. For a concise overview, see Baqir Irwani, *Al-Fiqh al-Istidlāl* (Beirut: Dar al-Amirah, 2008), 2:299-203.
41. *Mālikah* can be rendered as "an empowered woman" or "a woman who governs herself."
42. For a discussion concerning the legal usage of *muṭlaq*, see Mahmud Abd al-Rahman, *Mu'jam al-Muṣtalaḥāt wa al-Alfāẓ al-Fiqhīyah* (Cairo: Dar al-Fadliyyah, n.d.), 3:308.
43. The implications of this question are enormous for those who assent to this system of law because if she marries despite her guardian's objections and assuming that the marriage was consummated, it may constitute fornication according to some interpretations.
44. Sayyid al-Ruhani describes this tradition as *tafsīr malikīyyah al-'amr* (a commentary of what it means to have control over one's life affairs). That being said, its exegetical function is debated and has been discussed at length by both past and present scholars. See Yusuf al-Bahrani, *Ḥadā'iq al-Nāḍirah fi Aḥkām al-'Itra al-Ṭāhirah* (Qum: Jami'at al-Mudarrisin, 1984), 23:222-23.
45. I have not come across a critique of this chain of transmission prior to al-Khu'i.
46. Khu'i, *Mabānī*, 260. Al-Khu'i is concerned with the transmitters who lie between Tusi and Ali b. Isma'il. This chain, which is often not disclosed, is what is meant by *bi isnādihi* when it is affixed at the chain's beginning.
47. The *rāwī* (reporter) in question has been widely described as one of the first *muttakalims* (theologians) among the Imamis. Al-Najashi describes him as being

min aṣhābinā kallama min al-Ḥudhayl wa al-Niẓām. Among other texts, he apparently also composed a treatise on marriage. See Ahmad b. Ali al-Najashi, *Rijāl al-Najashī* (Beirut: Dar al-Adwa', 1988), 2:72. Al-Khu'i corroborates much of what is found in Najashi, but does not mention the lack of his authentication in his *rijāl* compendium. See Sayyid Abul Qasim al-Khu'i, *Mu'jam al-Rijāl al-Ḥadīth* (Qum: Markaz al-Athar al-Shi'ah, 1990), 11:275-76.

48. Liyakat Takim provides an in-depth analysis of al-Khu'is methods of general and specific authentication of hadith transmitters. General authentication (*al-tawthīqāt al-'āmmah*) entails authenticating an entire chain based on the established *thiqah* of the text's compiler. For example, al-Khu'i believed that since Ibn Qulawah, who compiled *Kāmil al-Ziyārāt*, is trustworthy, this should imply that all of the transmission chains of which he is the final transmitter must be deemed authentic. An authentication of this type essentially deems the entire text to be *ṣaḥīḥ*. On the other hand, *al-tawthīqāt al-khāssah* implies that only Ibn Qawlawayh's principal sources of information (*mashāykh*; those of his teachers who transmitted directly to him) would be deemed authentic and trustworthy, thus leaving the remainder of the *isnad* open to critique. See Liyakat Takim, "The Origins and Evaluation of Hadith Transmitters in Shi'i Biographical Literature," *American Journal of Islamic Social Sciences* 24, no. 4 (2007): 35-37.

49. Ruhani points out that the last phrase, *bi ghayri idhn abīhā*, as recorded in the manuscripts and printed editions of al- Tusi's *Tahdhīb* and *Istibṣār* has also been rendered as *bi-gharyi idhn walīhā*. This alternative can be found in al-Khū'is *Mabānī* as well in Shahid al-Thani's *Masālik al-Ifhām*. This is most likely to due scribal error. See Ruhan, http:// www.imamrohani.com/arabic/kotob/fokh/21/02.HTM#fehrest18; Khu'i, *Mabānī*, 260; and Zayn al-Din b. Ahmad b. Ali al-'Amili, *Masālik al-Ifhām illā Tanqīh Sharā'i' al-Islām* (Qum: Mu'assasat al-Ma'arif al-Islamiyyah, 1992), 7:125. Also, the verb *raḍīya* (*r-ḍ-a*) implies an opposition to *al-sakhaṭ* (anger) and a high quality of consent or being well pleased. See Lane, *Arabic-English Lexicon,* 1:1099.

50. See Araki, *Kitāb al-Nikāh,* 46.

51. Ibn Qulawayh was said to have been one of Shaykh al-Mufid's teachers, and Ali b. Ibrahim al-Qummi was one of al-Kulyani's principal hadith instructors. See Muhammad b. Sulayman al-Tanakabuni, *Qiṣaṣ al-'Ulamā'* (Beirut: Dar al-Mahhajah al-Bayda', 1992), 454-55. The introduction to *Tafsīr al-Qummī* mentions some important biographical information. See al-Qummi, *Tafsīr al-Qummī,* 5-6.

52. See Takim, *Tafsir al-Qummi*, 43. Apparently it was brought to al-Khu'i's attention that by carrying out mass authentication he was, in turn, authenticating otherwise unknown and untrustworthy transmitters. Thus he changed his position from *tawthīqāt al-'āmmah* to *tawthīqāt al-khaṣṣah*. For al-Khū'is position on the authentication of *Tafsīr al-Qummī*, see Muslim al-Dawari, *Uṣūl 'Ilm al-Rijāl* (Qum: Mu'assasat al-Muhibin, 2005), 1:273-75.

53. The biographical texts allege that Abbas b. Ma'ruf was a trustworthy (*thiqah*) companion of the Eighth Imam, Ali b. Musa al-Rida. See Najashi, *Rijāl,* 5:120.

54. I use the term *authentic* in a relative fashion, as authenticity is interpretive and used in the context of Imami-Usuli hadith studies.
55. One may posit several hypotheses for this increase in complexity and intense critique: (1) the exigencies present due to the modern condition and society, which increasingly demand newer and more practical solutions to such socio-domestic matters as marriage and (2) the field's advancement is partly evolutionary insofar as Imami scholars, in addition to growing in number, are attempting to build upon the past's vast legal commentaries and not settle for its mere reproduction whether it be in the field of hadith studies, linguistics, history, or law. They may not always differ with past rulings; however, the justifications they provide for their rulings are often far more substantial and precise. This is especially true in the case of marital law, which continues to serve as a nexus point of competing social, legal, and cultural concerns for Muslim communities.
56. See al-Hassan b. Mutahar al-Hilli, *Mukhtalaf al-Shī'ah fī Aḥkām al-Shar'īyah* (Qum: Jami'at al-Mudarrisin, 1999), 7:114-15. What is meant here is that medieval jurists such as al-Hilli did not engage in the same discourse concerning juristic preference or harmonization of traditions in the context of this *mas'alah*.
57. Some jurists also describe this as *al-takhīr*, which entails the act of choosing one position over all others when confronted with opposing traditions.
58. The only prominent contemporary work of demonstrative jurisprudence, aside from that of al-Ruhani, that supports the virgin's agency is that of Jawad Maghniyya. See Jawad Maghniyya, *Fiqh Imām al-Ṣādiq*, 5:231-32.
59. See Taqi al-Hakim, *Uṣūl al-'Āmmah,* 354-56 and Muhammad Ishaq al-Fayad, *Muḥāḍarāt fī Uṣūl al-Fiqh: Taqrīran li Abḥāth Ayātullah Khū'ī* (Qum: Mu'assasah Ihya Athar al-Imam al-Khu'i, 2002), 3:221-23. *Sunnah* may imply any belief or position supported or practiced by an Infallible or accepted practice among Shi'i scholars, although the latter is not agreed upon. Imami jurists derive these three elements of juristic preference from following tradition: " When you are confronted with two conflicting traditions, compare them with the Qur'an. Take that which agrees with the book of God, and leave that which opposes it. If you do not find it (the answer) in the book of God, then compare them (the two traditions) to the reports of the *'āmmah* (non-Shi'as). Leave that which agrees with their reports and statements, and take that which opposes their reports." See al-Hurr al-'Amili, *Waṣā'il al-Shī'ah.* 10 vols. (Qum: Dhu al-Qurba', 2007), 27:118. Also see Saduq, *Man lā Yahḍuruhu,* 2:171.
60. I will address the contention over the evidentiary value of the Qur'an within the confines of this subject below.
61. This definition has been supplied by Liyakat Takim. See Takim, "Shortened Prayers," 406.
62. The entire process of *al-ta'ādal wa al-tarjīh* (comparison between traditions and juristic preference) is designed to produce a proof or *al-ḥujjah* (*taḥṣīl al-hujjah*) for a given legal ruling in the event that the traditional evidences oppose one

another (*'inda al-ta'āraḍ bayna al-'adillah*). See Muhammad Rida Muzaffar, *Uṣūl al-Fiqh* (Beirut: Mu'assasat al-'Alami al-Matbu'at, 1970), 181.

63. Maghniyya also uses *shahra* as a means of *tarjīḥ*. See Maghniyya, *Fiqh al-Imām Ja'far al-Ṣādiq*, 5:232. For al-Murtada, the virgin's agency hinges upon her being able to control her own affairs (*tammalaka amrāhā*) and of sound mind (*'aqlalat*) and complete (*kamalat*). I would assume that this implies she is both physically and mentally mature. See Ali b. al-Husayn al-Murtada, *Al-Intiṣār* (Najaf: Maktabat al-Haydariyyah, 1971), 120.
64. The *qudamā'* may include Shaykh al-Saduq, Tusi, and Murtada among others. the *mutā'khirūn* may include Shahid al-Awwal, Thani, al-Hurr al-'Amili, Yusuf al-Bahrani, and Muhammad b. Hassan al-Najafi (d. 1266 AH). For a summary of the various legal opinions, see al-Hassan b. Mutahar al-Hilli, *Mukhtalaf al-Shī'ah fī Aḥkām al-Shar'īyah* (Qum: Jami'at al-Mudarrisin, 1999) and Ja'far Subhani, *Niẓām al-Nikāḥ*, 173-75. For a summary of both early and later opinions, in addition to an extensive analysis of the various positions and historical trajectory of this *mas'alah*, see Shaykh Murtada' al-Ansari, *Kitāb al-Nikāḥ*, (Qum: al-Mu'-tamar al-'Alami li Takhlid Dhikra' Shaykh al-'Azam, 1995), 108-28.
65. For instance, Jawad Maghniyya goes further to claim the following: Most of the Imamis (hold) that the physically mature and mentally sound woman, by means of her physical maturity (*bulūgh*) and mental soundness (*rushd*) possess agency (*tamalak*) in all aspects of her behavior (and endeavors) with respect to (commitment to and fulfillment) of contracts and otherwise. This (agency) extends to marriage, regardless of whether she is a virgin or non-virgin. Thus, she can contract (a marriage) for herself (*ta'qadu li nafsihā*) or for someone else (*ligharihā*) directly or via proxy, and may respond (*ījāb*) and accept (*qubūl*) the marriage proposal (without necessary recourse to a guardian). This is equally allowable if she has a father, a grandfather, other male blood relatives, or none at all. Furthermore, it does not matter if the father is pleased or displeased (with her marital arrangement). And it is all the same whether she is of elevated (*rafī'ah*) or lower (*waḍī'ah*) social status, or if she marries a man of high status or low status. See al-Mughniyya, *Al-Fiqh 'alā Madhāhib al-Khamsah*, 2:322.
66. See note 18.
67. Ibn Idris (d. 598 AH) states the following: "*Wa raja'a 'ammā dhakarahu fī nihāyatihi wa sā'ir kutubihi li'anna kitāb al-tibyān sannafahu ba'da kutubihi jamī'ihā wa istiḥkām 'ilmihi.*" He then extracts a gloss from al-Tusi's commentary on Q. 2:237, stating that there is no *wilāyah* except that given to the father or grandfather upon the non-pubescent virgin (*'alā al-bikr ghayri al-bāligh*). See Ibn Idris al-Hilli, *Al-Sarā'ir al-Ḥāwī li Tahrīr al-Fatāwī* (Qum: Jami'at al-Mudarisin, 1990), 2:563. However, this selection must be scrutinized further because upon referring to the *Tibyān*, al-Tusi follows this gloss by stating the following: "*wa fīhi khilāf bayna al-fuqahā' dhakaranāhu fī al-khilāf wa qawaynā mā akhbararnāhu hunāka*" which translates as "and in it (the issue of guardianship over the marriage contract) there is disagreement between the jurists. We

have discussed it in *Al-Khilāf* (al-Tusi's work on comparative jurisprudence) and supported what we have reported there." This statement could be interpreted as meaning that the full explanation of his position vis-à-vis the Sunnis can be found in the *Khilāf.* Upon referring to this book, al-Tusi clearly states that the pubescent virgin of sound mind does not have the authority to contract a marriage without the consent of her father(s). See al-Tusi, *Al-Tibyān fī Tafsīr al-Qur'ān* (Beirut: Dar al-Ihya' Turath al-'Arabi, 1989), 2:273; al-Tusi, *Al-Khilāf*, 358. Despite all of these apparent incongruences, Ibn Idris cites another of al-Tusi's opinions from *al-Mabsūṭ*, in which after noting the intra-Imami *ikhtilāf* he states: "*idhā tazawwaja man dhakarnāhu gibhayri walīn kāna al-'aqd saḥīḥan*" which translates "as if whom we mentioned (the pubescent virgin) was to marry without the *walī* (without his permission), the contract would be valid." See al-Tusi, *Al-Mabsūt fī Fiqh al-Imāmīyah* (Qum: Jami'at al-Mudarrisin, 2006), 3:387. Now, the question as to which statement best reflects his final position is subjective, at least for the reason that if the *Tibyān* was really his final work (which most biographies confirm), then the shaykh himself is giving preference to what he has mentioned in the *Khilāf.* Therefore what is found there can be considered his most authoritative opinion on the matter. However, this may only be limited to comparative jurisprudence since the *Khilāf* is a comparative work and his more profound work is without doubt, the *Mabsūṭ*. Nevertheless, any conclusions drawn from this or claims to *shuhra* are speculation at best.

68. Al-Mufid, *Al-Muqni'a*, 510-11, and al-Mufid, *Aḥkām al-Nisā'* (Qum: Collection of Shaykh Mufid's Works, 1992), 36.
69. The reason for such uncertainty lies in the fact that we are not sure if the *Aḥkām al-Nisā'* was written before or after the *Muqni'a*, especially since al-Najashi, while mentioning both of these works, does not mention when they were completed. Furthermore in al-Tusi's canonical hadith collection, namely, *Tahdhīb al-Aḥkām fī Sharḥ al-Muqni'a*, he does not mention this alternate position of Mufid, but rather supports the *istiqlāl al-ab* position. Further yet, Yusuf al-Bahrani and Muhammad Mahdi Niraqi (d. 1245 AH) have both taken issue with and attempted to grapple with the apparent contradictory or variant opinions of early jurists such as al-Tusi, al-Mufid, and al-Murtada' in addition to questionable claims to *ijmā'*. Al-Bahrani cites a partial treatise in his possession, written by Zayn al-Din al-'Amili (Shahid al-Thani), in which al-'Amili cites seventy occasions in which al-Tusi states one legal position only to contradict himself (*mukhālafat al-shaykh li nafsihi*). See al-Bahrani, *Ḥadā'iq al-Nāḍirah,* 4:98. Sayyid Muhammad Husayni al-Husayni al-Jalali kindly gave me a copy of the original manuscript of this unpublished treatise attributed to Shahid al-Thani, in which he lists in detail the numerous occasions in which al-Tusi seems to contradict himself from the chapters of marriage and divorce to foodstuffs. In it, Shahid al-Thani provides no explanation for these except to state the shaykh (al-Tusi) has made claims to *ijmā'* only to oppose these very same claims elsewhere, and therefore the jurist cannot establish two opposite claims to consensus and,

"in doing so *faqad waqa'a fī al-khaṭa'* (he falls into error)." However, he does not cite guardianship and the marriage contract as instances of conflict, perhaps because al-Tusi never claims consensus on the matter. See Zayn al-Din al-'Amili, *Risālah 'ala Masā'il Da'a'fīhā al-Shaykh al-Ijmā' wa Khālafa Idā' al-Ijmā' fīhi* Collection of Sayyid Muhammad Husaynī al-Husaynī al-Jalālī, Chicago, MS# unknown. On the other hand, Niraqi cites Shahid al-Awwal as stating that these apparent conflicting *ijmā'āt* (pl. *ijmā'*) are in fact not contradictions at all, but merely attestations to the *riwāyat* of the *ḥukm*, meaning that the ruling has been reported and there exists evidence for it within the corpus of *akhbār* and upon this there is consensus. See Muhammad Mahdi Niraqi, *'Awā'id al-Ayyām* (Qum: Maktabat Basirati, 1980), 693-95.

70. "*Wa huwa thubūt al-walāya lahumā mustaqillan muṭlaqan bal huwa al-mansūb ilā al-mashūr bayna al-qudamā'*," which translates as " and it (this legal position) consists of the confirmation of guardianship to both of them (father and paternal grandfather(s)." See Ruhani, http://www.imamrohani.com/arabic/kotob/fokh/21/02.HTM#fehrest18
71. Khu'i, *Muḥādarāt*, 223. "*Ama al-shuhra, lam tudhakir fīhā 'adā al-marfū'ah wa al-maqbūlah.*"
72. Muhammad Rida Muzaffar describes this as *al-shuhra fī al-riwāyah*, when the "large" number of reporters is not sufficient to be described as constituting *al-tawātur*. See Muzaffar, *Uṣūl al-Fiqh*, 2:143.
73. Khū'i's representative told me that the *mujtahid*s do not do *taqqadus* of past scholars, meaning that they do not sanctify their legal judgment. This disposition can be described as applying to the vast majority of contemporary Imami *mujtahid*s. One example can be found in al-Khu'i's *Mābānī al-'Urwat al-Wuthqa*, in which he critiques Sayyid al-Murtada's claim to consensus that if a couple commits adultery they are forbidden to each other permanently. Credit for this key reference goes to Sayyid Muhammad Rizvi, who lent me his copy of al-Khu'i's lecture notes notes. See al- Khu'i, *Mabānī*, 1:280-81.
74. Al-Ruhani, *Zubdat al-Uṣūl* (Qum: Amin Publishers, 2004), 4:186-87; Ibid, 6.
75. These are strong words, insofar as al-Muzaffar is accusing those who vest *al-shuhra al-fatwāiiyyah* with *hujīyah* to essentially be guilty of performing a form of unacceptable *taqlīd* and thus not living up to their commitments as bona fide *mujtahid*s. See al-Muzaffar, *Uṣūl al-Fiqh*, 2:144.
76. I have used Wolfart Heinrichs' analysis of *qawā'id fiqhīyah.* After stating this concept's contested definition, he cites Taj al-Din al-Subki (d. 771 AH) as describing the *qawā'id* in the following way: "The *qā'idah* is the generally valid rule with which many particular cases [*juzīyāt*] agree whose legal determinations can be understood from it [the *qā'idah*]." Therefore jurisprudential maxims can be understood as overarching theoretical concepts that may potentially make sense of individual rulings and cases. See Wolfart P. Heinrichs, "*Qawā'id* as a Genre of Legal Literature," in *Studies in Islamic Legal Theory*, ed. Bernard Weiss (Leiden: Brill Publications, 2002), 401-02. The most common example cited is that

if anything causes undue harm, then it can be rendered as non-compulsory or even impermissible, or that everything is considered pure unless it is proven that it is impure. This is one of the juristic principles behind *ṭahārah* (purity). See Baqir Irwani, *Al-Qawā'id al-Fiqhīyah* (Qum: Dar al-Fiqh, 2006), 2:96-98. In Shi'i jurisprudence, the term *naṣṣ* carries superior evidentiary value that is described as being a direct textual ruling in the form of Qur'anic verses or a hadith deemed to be authentic. See the glossary of Muhammad Baqir al-Sadr, *Principles of Islamic Jurisprudence*, tr. Arif Abdulhussein (London: ICAS Press, 2003), 137.

77. Shi'is consider the Fourteen Infallibles to include Muhammad, Fatimah, Ali, al-Hassan, al-Husayn, and the remaining nine Infallible Imams who are select descendents of al-Husayn.
78. For a discussion concerning *qa'ādat sulṭanat al-nafs*, see Irwani, *Al-Qawā'id al-Fiqhīyah*, 2:96-113. The closest synonymous principle I could discover is *qā'adat min al-milk* (the principle regarding authority), namely, the endowed authority given to every free and sane human being to willfully enter into financial contracts and purchase slaves and *iqrār al-'uqalā'* (affirmation of those with intelligence). This has similar implications indicative of the freedom to spend one's wealth as one pleases, witness in court, loan money to others, as well as accept the responsibility of taking a loan and paying it back. See al-Tusi, *Al-Mabsūṭ*, 3:4-6.
79. Nasr Makarem Shirazi, *Al-Qawā'id al-Fiqhīyah* (Qum: Madrassah Ali b. Abi Talib, 2004), 2:20-22.
80. Jawad Maghniyya makes a similar argument in his *Al-Fiqh 'alā Madhāhib al-Khamsah*, 322. Allama al-Hilli has also used a similar concept, namely, *iqrār al-'uqlā'*: "*law aqārat al-hurrah al-bālighah al-'āqilah bi al-nikāh, siḥḥah iqrārahā 'inda 'ulamā'inā 'ajma'a* (If the free pubescent and mentally sound woman decides to marry, her decision is vaild in the view of our scholars by consensus)." He then states that Abu Hanifah used a similar rationale to support the same viewpoint. See Allama al-Hilli, *Tadhkīra*, 2:583-84.
81. The vast majority (if not all) of Imami scholars forbid abortion unless the mother's life is at risk, as well as organ donation after death. They also do not give a woman the unadulterated right given to men to divorce at will.
82. Khu'i, *Muḥāḍarāt*, 221-23.
83. See Araki, *Kitāb al-Nikāḥ*.
84. This *muwāqafah* entails that which could be described as *iṭlaqāt al-ayāt* or *muṭlaq*, meaning that the verse may not directly address the issue at hand, but it nevertheless implies a general ethic or ethos of understanding
85. See Q. 5:2 and Q. 2:232, 235.
86. Q. 2:232. See Jawad Maghniyya, *Tafsīr al-Kāshif* (Tehran: Dar al-Kutub al-Islamiyyah, 2003), 1:354-55. While Maghnīyya's use of this verse and others to assert the virgin's agency is novel from a contemporary perspective earlier scholars (e.g., al-Murtada', Ibn Idris al-Hilli, and Allama al-Hilli) used the same verse and others, despite their exceedingly unrelated content. In fact, Ibn Idris states that if the verse's open meaning stands, in order to specify or limit it a proof

must be brought forward. See al-Murtada, Ibn Idrīṣ al-Hilli, 541-43, Allamah al-Hilli, *Tadhkīra*, 2:585, and al-Murtada, 1*Al-Intiṣār,* 19-20.

87. Sayyid Muhammad Husyan Fadlallah has a very similar line of argument. See http://english.bayynat.org.lb/se_002/womenfamily/partner.htm. Similar sentiment has been expressed via email from his office. Maghniyya draws upon similar ethical arguments in his legal work *Al-Fiqh 'alā Madhāhib al-Khamsah* (Beirut: Dār al-Jawad, 2001), 321-22.
88. For an extensive discussion, see Takim, "Shortened Prayers," 403-04. I use "apparent" because Imami jurists only consider it *ta'ārad* in an apparent (*ẓāhir*) manner and because one of the purposes of *uṣūlī* hermeneutics is to discover the reality and resolve this bifurcation.
89. *Taqīyah* became especially popular under the Abbasids, when Imami Shi'ism entered a stage of quietism. See Lynda Clarke, "Taqiyya in Twelver Shi'ism" in *Reason and Inspiration in Islam*, ed. Todd Lawson (London: I.B. Tauris, 2005), 43-63.
90. Susan Spektorsky, *Women in Classical Islamic Law* (Leiden: Brill Publications, 2010), 67-68.
91. See Muhammad b. Idris al-Shafi'i, *Kitāb al-Umm* (Cairo: Maktaba al-Kalimat al-Azhariyyah, 1961), 7:171-73. Also see Spektorsky, 67-68.
92. Ibid. Also see Muhammad Fadel, "Reinterpreting the Guardians Role in the Islamic Marriage Contract: The Case of the Maliki School," *The Journal of Islamic Law* 3, no. 1 (1998): 3.
93. Ibid.
94. For the opinions of al-Saduq and al-Tusi, see Fadel, "Reinterpreting the Guardian's Role," 3.
95. See Ibn Rushd al-Qurtubi al-Andalusi, *Sharḥ Bidāyat al-Mujtahid*, ed. Abdullah al-'Abari (Cairo: Dar al-Sala, n.d.), 3:1248. That is, if the virgin marries without her guardian's consent, is the marriage valid or not?
96. The Imamis hold that only the father and the paternal grandfather have compelling authority or agency.
97. The contemporary Imami jurists that share this position are Ruhani, Maghniyya, and Fadlallah.
98. See Abi Zayd Abd Allah b. 'Umar al-Dabusi al-Hanafi (d. 430 AH), *Kitāb al-Nikāh min al-Asrār* (Beirut: Dar al-Manar, 1993), 191-201. Also see John L. Esposito, *Women in Muslim Family Law*, 2d ed. (Syracuse: Syracuse University Press, 2001), 15.
99. Muhammad Hashim Kamali, *Principles of Islamic Jurisprudence* (Cambridge: Islamic Texts Society, 2003), 466. For an extensive discussion regarding the variant Sunni positions, see Kecia Ali, *Marriage and Slavery in Early Islam* (Cambridge: Harvard University Press, 2010), 33-41.
100. Muhammad b. Idris al-Shafi'i, *Kitāb al-Umm* (Beirut: Dar al-Wafa', 2001), 6:47.
101. Al-Murtada', *Al-Intiṣār,* 120 and Muhaqiq al-Hilli, *Mukhtaṣar al-Nāfi'*, 183.
102. See note 29. For a detailed discussion regarding Allama al-Hilli's *istidlāl* and

his contention that the *'illa* for agency is her physical and mental maturity, see al-Allamah al-Hilli, *Tadhrīkat al-Fuqahā'* (Tehran: Maktabat al-Murtadawiyyah li Ihya' al-Athar al-Ja'fariyyah, 1968), 2:568-88.

103. Imami scholars still debate the age of majority.
104. Ibid., 585.
105. "*Naqala al-ikhtilāf al-'āmmah fīhi wa la na'lamu annahu fī zamān suḍūr al-khabar ayḍan, kāna ilā ayī man al-'aqwāl qdātahum amīlun, la yumkin lanā al-tarjīḥ bihadhā al-wajh*. See al-Araki, *Kitāb al-Nikāh* (Qum: Nur Nagar, 1998), 43.
106. Maria Dakake and others have posited the notion that either the Fifth or the Sixth Imams and their companions formed parts of their theological doctrines in dialogue with Hanafis-Murji'is and Mu'tazalis. One example is the doctrine of postponing opinion, which essentially states that the non-Shi'a sinner has a middle position and it is not known whether he will benefit from salvation or not. Hence it is better to postpone judgment upon him. See Maria Dakake, *The Charismatic Community* (Albany: State University of New York Press, 2007), 128-39.
107. *Liyakat* Takim, *Heirs*, 101-07.
108. Muhammad Taqi al-Hakim states that it is entirely possible that the *sā'il* (the one posing the question to the Imam) transmitted what he chose (or what was in his best interest) from the Imam, essentially procuring a fatwa for himself. Meanwhile, the imam's actual fatwa does exist. Furthermore, al-Hakim states that due to the prevelaence of divergent legal opinions, including that of the Imam, he (the *sā'il*) would select what he feels is nearest to the Imam's views, which may in reality oppose their actual viewpoint, hence creating opposing reports. This is as far as the traditional scholar will go, because accusing the Imam of double speak or contradictory juristic positions would compromise the tenet of infallibility (*'iṣmah*). This is not included within the *mujtahid*'s exegetical temperament. See Muhammad Taqi al-Hakim, *Uṣūl al-'Āmmah,* 356.
109. Wael B. Hallaq, *Sharī'a* (Cambridge: Cambridge University Press, 2009), 275-76.
110. This respect and obedience owed to the father extends through the paternal line.
111. For a few examples, see Araki, *Kitāb al-Nikāh,* 48. al-Ruhani, http://www.imam-rohani.com/arabic/kotob/fokh/21/02.HTM#fehrest18; Khu'i, *Mabānī*, 269; Najafi, 183-84; al-Hilli, *Mukhtalaf al-Shī'ah*, 7:116; and Maghniyya, *Fiqh al-Imām al-Ṣādiq*, 5:232.
112. See Sistani, 439 and Subhani, *Niẓām al-Nikāḥ*, 193. Sayyid Murtada has claimed that Abu Hanifah held that even if the virgin posseses agency and marries someone (*bi ghayri kafū'*), the father has the right to intervene and stop the marriage or annul an completed marriage contract. See: al-Murtada, *Intṣār*, 120. With regards to Abu Ḥanifah's position, he states: "*laysa li walīuhā al-'itirāḍ alayhā illa idhā waḍa'at nafsahā fi ghayri kafū'*".
113. I owe this insight to Lynda Clarke.

114. Tusi, *Istibṣār*, 3:144. Tusi attempts to interpret the Sa'dan b. Muslim tradition as either applying to temporary marriage or a case of *al-'aḍl*. Also see Muhaqqiq al-Hilli, *Sharā'i' al-Islām*, 2:220. Hilli also claims there is *ijmā'* on this matter.
115. For a list of related traditions, see Kulyani, *Al-Furū'*, 347-54.
116. That is, his task would be difficult in legal terms.
117. Subhani, 193-95.
118. Muhaqqiq al-Hilli, *Sharā'i' al-Islām*, 221. The Arabic reads as follows: "*Ammā idhā 'aḍalahā al-walī wa hūwa an la yuzawijuhā min kafu'in ma'a raghbatihā fa-innahu yajūzu lahā an tazawwaja nafsahā wa law karhan ijmā'an.*" Al-Ruhāni expresses a very similar (if not identical) sentiment. http://www.imam-rohani.com/arabic/kotob/fokh/21/02.HTM#fehrest18; Sayyid Sistani, *Minhāj al-Ṣāliḥīn* (Beirut: Dar al-Muarrikh al-'Arabi, 2003), 3:28.
119. Upon examining the positions and reports concerning the *bikr*, al-Allamah al-Hilli states that even if we were to give her agency, she would be unaware of the nature and functioning of men (*lā ta'rifu aḥwāl al-rijāl*). Such statements are not universal; rather, they are based upon his common view of the *bikr* and perhaps those in his region of southern Iraq. See Allamah al-Hilli, *Mukhtalaf al-Shī'ah*, ibid.
120. Ibid. Also see Ruhani, http://www.imamrohani.com/arabic/kotob/fokh/21/02.HTM#fehrest18. Both Subhani and al-Ruhani emphasized the need to prevent any undue hardship as the underlying purpose of the *nahī al-'aḍl* clause. I should also note that terms such as *undue hardship* or *haraj*, when used in the context of this ruling, are particularly modern. I have not come across it in medieval compendiums on marital law written by Muhaqqiq al-Hilli, Shahid al-Thani, Shaykh al-Tusi, or other jurists.
121. Such a scenario is not implausible; however, each case would have to be evaluated on its own merit.
122. This line of reasoning would indicate the interconnectedness of positive and substantive law in contemporary Imami Shi'ism.
123. *Makārim al-Shīrāzī*, 2:25-26.

Bibliography

Unpublished Work(s)

Zayn al-Din al-'Amili (Shahid al-Thani). *Risālah 'alā Masā'il Da'a'fīhā al-Shaykh al-Ijmā' wa Khālafah Idā' al-Ijmā' fīhi*, Collection of Sayyid Muhammad Husayni al-Husayni al-Jalali, Chicago, MS# unknown.

Published Works

Abd al-Rahman, Mahmud. *Mu'jam al-Muṣtalaḥāt wa al-Alfāẓ al-Fiqhīyah* v. 3. Cairo: Dar al-Fadliyyah, n.d.

Ali, Kecia. *Marriage and Slavery in Early Islam*. Cambridge: Harvard University Press, 2010.

Al-'Amili, Muhammad b. Ali. *Nihāya al-Marā'im fī Sharḥ Mukhtaṣar Sharā'i' al-Islām*. 2 vols. Qum: Jami'at al-Mudarrisin, 1992.

Al-'Amili, Muhammad b. al-Hassan al-Hurr. *Waṣā'il al-Shī'ah*. 10 vols. Qum: Dhu al-Qurba', 2007.

Al-'Amili, Zayn al-Din Ahmad b. Ali. *Masālik al-Ifhām illā Tanqīh Sharā'i' al-Islām*. 10 vols. Qum: Mu'assasat al-Ma'arif al-Islamiyyah, 1992.

Al-Andalusi, Muhammad b. Hassan ibn Rushd al-Qurtubi. *Sharḥ Bidāya al-Mujtahid wa Niḥāya al-Muqtaṣid*, ed. and commented on by Abdullah al-Abari. 4 vols. Cairo: Dar al-Salam, n.d.

Al-Araki, Muhammad Ali. *Kitāb al-Nikāh*. Qum: Nur Nagar, 1998.

Al-Ansari, Shaykh Murtada'. *Kitāb al-Nikāḥ*. Qum: al-Mu'tamar al-Alami li Takhlid Dhikra' Shaykh al-'Azam, 1995.

Al-Bahrani, Yusuf. *Ḥadā'iq al-Nāḍirah fī Aḥkām al-'Itra al-Ṭāhirah*. 25 vols. Qum: Jama'at al-Mudarrisin, 1984.

Calder, Norman. "Doubt and Prerogative: The Emergence of an Imami Shi'i Theory of *Ijtihād*." *Studia Islamica* 70 (1989).

Clarke, L. and Cross, P. *Muslims and Canadian Family Laws: A Comparative Primer*. Toronto: Canadian Council of Muslim Women, 2006.

Clarke, Lynda. "Taqiyya in Twelver Shi'ism." In *Reason and Inspiration in Islam*. Edited by Todd Lawson. London: I.B. Tauris, 2005.

Dakake, Massi Maria. *The Charismatic Community: Shi'ite Identity in Early Islam*. Albany: State University of New York Press, 2007.

al-Dawari, Muslim. *Uṣūl 'Ilm al-Rijāl*. 2 vols. Qum: Mu'assasat al-Muhibin, 2005.

Delong-Bas, Natana J. and Esposito, John L. *Women in Muslim Family Law*. 2d ed. Syracuse: Syracuse University Press, 2001.

al-Fayad, Muhammad Ishaq. *Muḥāḍarāt fī Uṣūl al-Fiqh: Taqrīran li Abḥāth Ayatullah Khu'i* v. 3. Qum: Mu'assasah Ihya' Athar al-Imam al-Khu'i, 2002.

Fadel, Mohammad. "Reinterpreting the Guardian's Role in the Islamic Contract of Marriage." *Journal of Islamic Law* 3, no. 1 (1998).

Gleave, Robert. "Between Hadith and Fiqh: The Canonical Imami Collections of Akhbar." *Islamic Law and Society* 8 (2001).

———. "The Imami Shiite Conception of the Madhhab." In *The Islamic School of Law: Evolution, Devolution, and Progress*. Edited by Peri Bearmen, Rudolph Peters, and Frank E. Vogel. Cambridge: Harvard University Press, 2005.

Al-Hakim, Muhammad Taqi. *Al-Uṣūl al-'Āmmah li al-Fiqh al-Muqāran*. 3d ed. Qum: Majma' al-'Alimi li al-Ahl al-Bayt, 1998.

Al-Hakim, Sayyid Muhsin al-Tabataba'i. *Mutamasak al-'Urwat al-Wuthqa'*. 14 vols. Qum: Maktabat Ayatullah al-Mar'ashi al-Najafi, 1983.

———. *Minhāj al-Ṣāliḥīn*. 2 vols. ed. Sayyid Muhammad Baqir al-Ṣadr. Beirut: Dar al-Ta'aruf, 1980.

Hallaq, B. Wael. *Sharī'a: Theory, Practice, and Transformations*. Cambridge: Cambridge University Press, 2009.

Heinrichs, P. Wolfart. "*Qawā'id* as a Genre of Legal Literature." In *Studies in Islamic Legal Theory.* Edited by Bernard Weiss. Leiden: Brill Publications, 2002.

Al-Hilli, Ja'far Muhammad b. al-Hassan Muhaqiq. *Mukhtṣar al-Nāfi'*. Qum: Mu'assasah Matbu'at Dini, 1997.

———. *Sharā'i' al-Islām*. 4 vols. Qum: Mu'assasat al-Isma'iliyan, 1988.

al-Hilli, Ibn Idris. *Al-Sarā'ir al-Ḥāwī li Tahrīr al-Fatāwī.* 3 vols. Qum: Jami'at al-Mudarisin, 1990.

Al-Hilli, Ibn al-Mutahhar al-Hassan b. Yusuf. *Mukhtalaf al-Shī'ah fī Aḥkām al-Shar'īyah*. 10 vols. Qum: Jami'at al-Mudarrisin, 1999.

———. *Tadhīkat al-Fuqahā'*. 12 vols. Tehran: Maktabat al-Murtadawiyyah li Ihya' al-Athar al-Ja'fariyyah, 1968.

Al-Hanafi al-Dabusi, Abi Zayd 'Abdullah b. 'Umar. *Kitāb al-Nikāh min al-Asrār*. Beirut: Dar al-Manar, 1993.

Al-Irwani, Baqir. *Al-Fiqh al-Istidlāl 'alā al-Madhhab al-Ja'farī*. 3 vols. Beirut: Dār al-Amirah, 2008.

———. *Al-Qawā'id al-Fiqhīyah*. 2 vols. Qum: Dar al-Fiqh, 2007.

Kamali, Mohammad Hashim. *Principles of Islamic Jurisprudence*. Cambridge: Islamic Texts Society, 2003.

Al-Khu'i, Sayyid Abul Qasim. *Mabānī al-'Urwat al-Wuthqā'*, 3 vols. Najaf: Manshurat Madaris al-'Ilm, 1984.

———. *Mu'jam Rijāl al-Ḥadīth*. Qum: Markaz al-Athar al-Shi'ah, 1990.

Al-Kulyani, Muhammad b. Ishāq. *Al-Furū' min al-Kāfī*. 5 vols. Beirut: Dar al-Ta'aruf, 1981.

Lane, Edward Wiliam. *Arabic-English Lexicon*. 2 vols. Cambridge: Islamic Texts Society, 2003.

Moussavi, Kazemi Ahmad. *Religious Authority in Shi'ite Islam: From the Office of Mufti to the Institution of Marja'*. Kuala Lampur: The International Institute of Islamic Thought and Civilization, 1996.

Al-Murtada', Ali b. al-Husayn. *Al-Intiṣār*. Najaf: Maktabat al-Haydariyyah, 1971.

Muzaffar, Muhammad Rida'. *Uṣūl al-Fiqh*. 2 vols. Beirut: Mu'assasat al-'Alami al-Matbu'at, 1970.

Al-Najafi, Muhammad Hassan b. Baqir b. 'Adl al-Rahman. *Jawāhar al-Kalām fī Sharḥ Sharā'i' al-Islām*. 43 vols. Beirut: Dar al-Ihya' Turath al-'Arabi, n.d.

Al-Najashi, al-'Abbas Ahmad b. Ali. *Rijāl al-Najāshī*. 2 vols. Beirut: Dar al-Adwa', 1988.

Niraqi, Muhammad Mahdi. *'Awā'id al-Ayyām*. Qum: Maktabat Basirati, 1980.

Al-Mughniyyah, Muhammad Jawad. *Fiqh al-Imām al-Ṣādiq*, 5 vols. Qum: Mua'ssasah Sibtayn al-'Alamiyyah, 2002.

———. *Al-Fiqh 'alā l-Madhāhib al-Khamsah*, 2 vols. Beirut: Dar al-Jawad, 2001.

———. *Tafsīr al-Kāshif*, 7 vols. Tehran: Dar al-Kutub al-Islamiyyah, 2003.

Al-Mufid, Muhammad b. Muhammad al-Nu'man. *Al-Muqni'a*. Beirut: Dar al-Mufid, 1993.

———. *Aḥkām al-Nisā'*. Qum: The Collection of Shaykh al-Mufid's Works, 1992.

Ruhani, Sayyid Muhammad Sadiq. *Fiqh al-Ṣādiq*. 26 vols. Qum: Dar al-Kitab, 1992.

———*Fiqh al-Ṣādiq*. http:// www.imamrohani.com/arabic/kotob/fokh/21/02.HTM# fehrest18 (last accessed April 1, 2011).

———. *Zubdat al-Uṣūl*. 6 vols. Qum: Amin Publishers, 2004.

Al-Sadr, Muhammad Baqir. *Principles of Islamic Jurisprudence*, tr. Arif Abdul Hussein. London: Islamic College for Advanced Studies Press, 2003.

———. *Durūs fī 'Ilm al-Uṣūl: Ḥalaqah al-Awwal*. Qum: Munzamat al-Hawzat al-'Ilmiyyah al-Buldan, 2004.

Al-Saduq, Muhammad b. Ali al-Husyan. *Man Lā Yaḥḍuruhu al-Faqīh*. 4 vols. Beirut: Mu'aassat al-'Alami al-Matbu'at, 1986.

Spectorsky, Susan A. *Women in Classical Islamic Law*. Leiden: Brill Publications, 2010.

Al-Seestani, Ayatullah al-Uzama Syed Ali al-Husaini. *Islamic Laws: English Version of Tauhihul Masa'el*. London: World Federation of KSIJ, 1994.

Al-Sistani, Sayyid Ali al-Husayni. *Minhāj al-Ṣāliḥīn*. 3 vols. Beirut: Dar al-Muarrikh al-'Arabi, 2003.

Al-Shafi'i, Muhammad b. Idris. *Kitāb al-Umm*. 7 vols. Cairo: Maktabat al-Kalimat al-Azhariyyah, 1961.

Al-Subhani, Ja'far. *Irshād al-'Uqūl ilā Mubāḥath al-Uṣūl*. Beirut: Dar al-Adwa', 2001.

———. *Kulliyāt fī 'Ilm al-Rijāl*. Qum: Imam Sadiq Foundation, 2006.

———. *Niẓām al-Nikāḥ fī al-Sharī'ah al-Islāmīyah*. Qum: Imam Sadiq Foundation, 1995.

al-Tabrasi, Abu al-Fadl b. al-Hassan. *Majma' al-Bayān fī Tafsīr al-Qur'an*. 10 vols. Tehran: Nasr Khusraw Publications, 1993.

Takim, Liyakat. "Offering Complete or Shortened Prayers? The Travelers Salat at the Holy Places." *Muslim World* 96 (2006): 401-22.

———. *The Heirs of the Prophet: Charisma and Religious Authority in Shi'ite Islam*. Albany: State University of New York Press, 2006.

———. "The Origins and Evaluations of Hadith Transmitters in Shi'i Biographical Literature," *The American Journal of Islamic Social Sciences* 24, no. 4 (2007).

Al-Tunakabuni, Muhammad b. Sulayman. *Qiṣaṣ al-'Ulamā'*. Beirut: Dar al-Mahajjah al-Bayda', 1992.

Al-Ṭurayhi, Fakhr al-Din Muhammad. *Majma' al-Baḥrayn*. 11 vols. Najaf: Dar al-Thaqafah, n.d.

Al-Tusi, Abu Ja'far Muhammad b. Hassan. *Istibṣār fī mā Ikhtalafa al-Akhbār*. 4 vols. Tehran: Dar al-Kutub al-Islamiyyah, 1969

———. *Kitāb al-Khilāf*. 3 vols. Qum: Sharikat Dar al-Ma'arif al-Islamiyyah, 1958.

———. *Kitāb al-Āmālī*. Tehran: Dar al-Kutub al-Islamiyyah, 2001.

———. *Al-Mabsūṭah fī Fiqh al-Imāmīyah*. 6 vols. Qum: Jami'at al-Muddarisin, 2007.

———. *Tahdhīb al-Aḥkām*. 7 vols. Qum: Dar al-Kutub al-Islamiyyah, 1988.

———. *Al-Tibyān fī Tafsīr al-Qur'ān*. 10 vols. Beirut: Dar al-Ihya' Turath al-'Arabi, 1989.

Discussion

Discussant: Mahmoud Ayoub

These are real, not just theoretical, issues. Whatever the jurists say among themselves, the people in southern Lebanon are not aware of it and the father assumes complete authority. If the daughter does not submit, she will get the beating of her life. There have been cases where daughters asked to consent have refused, even if it meant they would be killed … and some have been. You can attribute whatever you want to *taqīyah*, so it is not a helpful tool. The clear injunction of Ja'far al-Sadiq is that the Shi'a may not turn to Sunni scholars. Anyway, there is no *ijmā'* among the Sunnis. We have no choice but to give people authority over themselves. The Lebanese scholar Shamsuddin wrote that the ideal state of the Righteous Caliphs is impossible today, as is the divine rule of the infallible Imam, and thus people must have authority over their own affairs. This minimizes the jurists' authority over people in their own affairs. *Wilāyat al-faqīh* is not a new concept. It goes back to the Twelfth Imam; however, it was a moral and juridical authority. All Khomeini did was add a political aspect, which led to the Iran of today. I believe that two kinds of people should never be allowed to rule: the military and the religious. Ja'far al-Sadiq said: "The scholars are God's trustees over His revelation until they knock at the doors of the ruling authority; when they do, suspect them." I ask, then, what happens when the ulama themselves become the ruling authority?

Discussant: Mohamed Adam El-Sheikh

This is my first opportunity to learn about the Shi'a schools. According to the Sunnah, by my own investigation it has not reached that level. All the hadith on this subject have some defect, even the most commonly applied ones. According to Imam Malik, the ability of the guardian to force belongs to the father or grandfather, or, if they are not present, to another man from the father's side. It might be justified because daughters or sisters were pledged to marriage at a very early age, thirteen or fourteen, and were unable to negotiate their dowries or conditions. Thus it was for the protection of minors. In Egypt or my own country of Sudan – even though it is Maliki in other respects – people now adopt Abu Hanifah's position as being well thought out. His opinion is also applied in America: A woman of mature mind, whether virgin or previously married, has the right to marry without her guardian's consent, although obtaining her consent is preferred. We used to ask the imam to be a woman's *walī*, but that led to some collusion and so we found it better to let the woman be her own *walī*. Marriage must be a contract between two competent individuals. The most acceptable Sunni hadith, in my opinion, is the one of the woman who told the Prophet, "My father has given me in marriage to his nephew." The Prophet asked her father to justify his action. The daughter then told the Prophet that she consented to the marriage; she only wanted his confirmation that her consent was required.

General Discussion

- Imami can mean Ja'fari or Isma'ili, but in my paper it refers only to the Twelvers (or Ja'fari). The view that we have called the position of Abu Hanifah may have been the custom of Iraq that may have been attributed to him retroactively.
- During the mid-tenth to the mid-eleventh century ("the Shi'a Century"), the Shi'as were completely open to Sunni ideas. Only after the fourteenth century did that change. The whole idea of *mukhālafah li al-'āmmah* must be used with caution.
- Kecia Ali's *Marriage and Slavery in Early Islam* (Cambridge, MA: Harvard University Press, 2010) is commendable. During that period, as in rabbinic Judaism, marriage and slavery had much in common. There is no agreement, however, as to whether a girl's emancipation is achieved by majority or by marriage.
- Anyone can represent a woman, including herself. The question is not who represents her, but "Who is her guardian?" This is the difference between the *wakīl* and the *walī*.
- In very conservative families we send the *walī* and two witnesses to ask: (1) "Does she accept this man?" (2) "Does she accept the advanced and deferred dowries?" and (3) "Does she have conditions that she wants to be mentioned?" Sometimes we might ask if there is a prenuptial agreement.
- Tabari maintained that a woman can lay down any conditions she wishes in the marriage contract, even refusing to do housework, with only one limit: She cannot refuse sex, because that is the point of the marriage.
- Some imams will refuse to marry a couple if they have not negotiated a contract.
- This conversation is interesting, but seems out of place, out of time, and very literal. Does the woman have agency? Can women control their own bodies? Young American-born women hearing this conversation might be driven away by it. How can we say women can be judges or even rulers and still ask whose permission they need to marry? If people who care about Islam continue to return to those arguments, Islam will continue to be marginalized. The *fuquhā'* are approaching the text with a preconceived conclusion in mind.
- We cannot just jump out of what we know into something that is foreign to our background. Change will come, but gradually.
- The jurists have serious pastoral concerns almost to the brink of defending women's rights. It is so simple for a woman to marry whomever she wishes. Marriage has always been a family enterprise instead of an individualistic one. Scholars emphasize their fear of a father being high-handed with his daughter and categorically reject such behavior. Maybe there should never have been a ruling giving the guardian agency in the first place; however, in all fairness, someone like Allamah al-Hilli, a contemporary of Ibn Taymiyyah, gives so many reasons for allowing the woman absolute agency while at the same time cautioning that she be protected from the possible machinations of her intended.

- Islam liberates, of course, but our history is open for everyone to study. Either we study it or we end up in apologetics, which leads nowhere. Academic freedom is important, and the study of history and culture is important even if we must study things that, from the perspective of the twenty-first century, seem lacking. Intention aside, in the end avoiding our history doesn't work.
- This study is appropriate in the context of this scholarly meeting. It would be inappropriate for a public lecture in a mosque.
- It is valuable to integrate the best of this history and integrate it into the thought of our time.
- This is not the time to go back in time.
- The first thing we should learn from this is that it is not an easy matter. The compilation of the hadith has still not been resolved. Second, this paper shows the relevancy of such debates to those of us in the West to formulating a methodology. The great scholars are the liberal scholars: the more you know, the more you know that you don't know. Our approach is family-oriented, but we live in a society that is not family-oriented. Our concern is to protect the family, which is a society's founding unit.
- It is important for the fatwa to be relevant to our times. The presentation comes from the lecture notes of their students. In the *fiqh* books they give their one-sentence conclusions, which is not enough. The presentation doesn't support anyone, but only exposes the reality to which we must face up. We must not water down the patriarchal history of the Abrahamic religions. We must recognize that there are patriarchal and misogynistic hadith, even if we wish to reject them.
- Virginity is sexual; maturity is psychological.
- When we speak of the virgin of sound mind, we speak of a woman who is unmarried but who knows the ways of the world. This is why these texts are relevant to modern society, where unmarried working and educated women are common.
- A young convert received three marriage proposals through women (mothers) at an extremely conservative mosque; all of the questions put to her by women through her friend. Her husband never received a single question from the prospective husbands' menfolk, usually the fathers, who seemed to play no role at all. It seemed to be totally controlled by the women. Is this case unusual?
- Like rabbinic jurisprudence, these academic analyses can be very divorced from social reality.
- There have been real efforts among Shi'a ulama to come closer to Sunni thought. We should bless and work with such efforts, because above all we need unity. Legal jargon in Islam makes a distinction between a virgin and a non-virgin, one that is applied to both men and women in different ways. Virginity is a marker of immaturity, as girls in that society usually married early. Many of early female Muslims, including the Prophet's daughters, died young because they got pregnant before their bodies were ready. It was a cultural problem.
- In a manuscript of all the claims to *ijmā'* among the early Shi'a, there is the case of a shaykh who contradicted his own claim to *ijmā'* seventy times. This raises

the question of what *ijmāʿ* means in such a case. As some of the early scholars rejected solitary traditions, some of the claims of *ijmāʿ* may have referred not to literal consensus, but rather to a tacit consensus that such an opinion exists and has some support or evidence. Whether we agree with this or not, it is there.

- For the Shiʿa, the Imam is the safeguard of the society's integrity. In his absence scholars can err. And if each scholar can err individually, it is possible that all can err collectively, which means that you can have no *ijmāʿ*. If the entire Shiʿa community were to agree on an error, that would be a cause for the Imam to return.
- Was anyone ever attracted to Islam by *fiqh* or *ʿaqīdah*; people are attracted by the heart in the community or because of Sufism. As far as women being the agents of the marriage contract, Moroccan women do everything and the men are informed at the end. Perhaps the scholars have distanced themselves from the ummah.
- Harvard published a wonderful book devoted to the Islamic marriage contract: *The Islamic Marriage Contract: Case Studies in Islamic Family Law* (2008). According to Shiʿa law, couples can amend the contract by mutual consent regardless of the terms included by the *walī*.

Islam, Healthcare, and Spirituality

Abdulaziz Sachedina

Abstract

Contemporary moral discourse has been aptly described as a minefield of incommensurable disagreements. Such disagreements are believed to be the result of secularization marked by a retreat of religion from the public arena. To provide an overall sense of Islamic ethical discourse in the complexity of bioethical pluralism in the Muslim world, in this chapter I have followed principle-rule based deontological-teleological ethics that serves as the foundation of Islamic legal-ethical investigation. The deontological ethical norm in Islamic jurisprudence determines the rightness (or wrongness) of actions without regard to the consequences produced by performing such actions (Killing is wrong.). By contrast, the teleological norm determines the rightness (or wrongness), of actions on the basis of their consequences produced by performing these actions (Saving life is commendable.). Deontological-teleological ethics undergirds Muslim legal-ethical methodology in resolving moral dilemma in social ethics. In Islamic jurisprudence ethical values are integral to the prescriptive action guide that the system provides to the community. No legal decisions are made without meticulous analysis of various factors that determine the rightness or wrongness of a case under consideration.

Healing through Spiritual Morality

Given that suffering can result from either natural or moral evil, we are obliged to examine the concept of good health in Islam, especially insofar as it is regarded as part of a person's obligation to avoid undue pain and suffering. The Arabic word *ṣiḥḥah* ("sound" or "health") is rich in connotations. Like the word *salāma* (also "sound" or "health"), it conveys the wholeness and integrity of a being that generates a sense of security. Further, it connotes a life of balance and moderation that avoids behavioral extremes. Disturbing this balance causes physical ailment. The Qur'an lays down the golden rule about moderation: "O children of Adam [and Eve], . . . eat and drink the good things you desire, but do not become wasteful" (Q. 7:31).

Imbalance or overindulgence in the enjoyment of God's bounty leads to both physical and moral suffering. In the moral sense, human volition may result in the overconsumption of certain foods because of sensual indulgence rather than attention to good health. The Prophet is reported to have advised his Companions to avoid overeating and recommended that one stop eating before feeling full.[1] Another tradition traces all sickness to a lack of moderation in eating. On this view, those physical or psychological conditions beyond one's own control dictate lifestyle adjustments in the interest of physical wellbeing.

The Qur'an prescribes the pursuit of self-knowledge as a part of maintaining good health. Physical and psychological health cannot be taken for granted – they are a divine benefaction that depends on human moderation in food and drink and regular physical activities, including swimming and horse riding, as the Prophet instructed his followers.[2] Yet there are people who suffer from genetically inherited illnesses about which they have no choice whatsoever. This kind of suffering raises questions about God's will and the existence of evil in the world.

Islamic Spirituality

God's omnipotence is the most important idea in Muslim theology. God is the creator of all things, including human destiny on Earth and rewards and punishments in the hereafter. Such a deterministic concept of human action gives rise to the problem of reconciling the divine predetermination of human action with divine justice, which entails God punishing the wicked and rewarding the righteous. This aspect of the problem of theodicy arose out of statements from the Qur'an and Sunnah. In the context of health care, the idea of God's omnipotence has enormous implications, for it breeds a quietism that discourages the ill from prying into His unfathomable ways and encourages resignation to suffering.[3] With modern medicine's enormous strides in healing the sick and alleviating suffering, the inexorability of God's decrees provides little comfort to those who want to see an end to the agonies of incurable diseases.

Yet despite the phenomenal advancement in medical treatment, people need to come to grips with what I constantly hear in my duties as a hospital chaplain: undeserved suffering. The need to understand the divine decree and cultivate necessary faith in God's goodness brings me face to face with the role of Islamic spirituality.

In Islam, the realm of spirituality is located within the human experience of transcendence. It does not matter whether one is anchored in an organized religious tradition or not. The experience of transcendence is positioned in the depth of the human heart, which needs to be explored by each individual through the natural endowment with which all humans have been created. This endowment – the innate capacity (*fiṭrah*) to incline toward transcendence – is the source of that human spiritual and moral awareness (*taqwā*) that is created the moment they are fashioned as humans (Q. 97:7-10).

At various points in their journey toward spiritual and moral perfection, humans receive portents that are present both in their own selves (*anfus*) and in the environment (*āfāq*) for them to realize the stages of their journey toward becoming perfected (Q. 16:78). In this sense, their personal perfection is tied to the perfection of the environment, which requires humanity's undivided attention because its own preservation and beautification are existentially connected to humanity's own survival and internal beauty. The more one understands this indispensable connection between the internal and external sources of human spiritual and moral development, the more one commits oneself to achieving the equilibrium generated by this understanding in actual life situations. This is the universal dimension of one's nature as well as one's spiritual and moral journey.

In this sense, spirituality and morality are intertwined because the former is the internal dimension of the being's identity and thus individual and subjective; the latter is the external aspect and grounds for a person's overall performance in corporate existence, and hence collective and objective. Claims of being spiritual are bereft with the calamity of self-righteous attitudes in faith communities, since they are ultimately inaccessible to outsiders for scrutiny. This is why, in Islam, morality (doing what is right and avoiding what is wrong) must accompany spirituality as its consequence and take the form of being objective and accessible to others for evaluation to establish the validity of the claim to be moral.

If spirituality generates peace and confidence, then morality becomes its objective manifestation when one deals with other humans as equals endowed with the same dignity, regardless of one's faith connection. In this estimation, then, spirituality is not only a precondition of one's inner peace and healthy state of mind; it is functionally indispensable to develop the moral sensibilities that enable a person to deal with others in fairness and justice.

However, this morality-oriented spirituality is overshadowed by the exclusionary Muslim theology that finds its major application in Islamic law. The juridical tradition is founded upon this theology, which, paradoxically, also advances the idea of a common human family that can be traced back to the first human couple: Adam and Eve. Human beings need one another to enable them to live in peace and harmony – the very foundation of human wellbeing. Hence the critical need for spirituality is underscored by Islam's mystical tradition, namely, Sufism, which neutralizes this exclusionary theology by emphasizing the Prophetic teaching that the Children of Adam are like one body because they share the same essence in their creation.

One of the striking features of religiously based spirituality is its emphasis on human relationships and the ethics that govern them. By its very emphasis on an ethics of relationship, this spirituality is dialogical. It is not only in dialogue with other humans, something to which it inevitably leads; it also leads to dialogue with all of nature. It requires humans to engage in beautifying nature in a reciprocal mode (if I am beautiful, so is my environment) and mandates its preservation in the same way as it treats one's own preservation as a moral and religious duty.

Dialogue allows the relationship of equality to emerge, one that potentially can confront the sources of conflict generated by the culturally advanced dichotomy of superiority/inferiority, saved/damned theology. To defeat the negative forces of this cultural theology, human endeavors need to be equipped with the spirituality that orients a person toward ethical action. When the Prophet was asked about the meaning of religion, he is reported to have replied: "It is obedience to God and kindness to creation (*makhlūq*)." "Creation" is used here in its generic sense to include all created beings and not just humans. This is why fractured human relationships need to be mended through the healing that comes by reaching out to fellow humans qua humans.

The correlation between spirituality and morality provides a unique way of estimating the relationship between faith and law. Law is certainly connected with the human experience of living with one another and in community. In Islam, God's will is expressed in God's commandments delivered through the supernatural medium of revelation. God's law guarantees salvation to those who obey them. In some unique sense, fulfilling the legal-ethical rulings restores total human wellbeing and leads to a blissful hereafter. In order to fully appreciate this interdependent relation between spiritual and moral wellbeing, we need to turn our attention to Islam's normative legal system, which functions as a divinely ordained scale of what it means to be a spiritually and morally healthy community.

The Islamic Legal Tradition

Islamic law covers all the actions performed by humans, whether toward one another or toward God. The Shari'ah, the norm of the Muslim community, grew out of Muslim endeavors to ensure that Islam pervaded all of life. Two essential areas of human life define its scope: acts of worship, both public and private, that are connected with the pillars of faith; and acts of public order that ensure individual and collective justice. The first category of actions, undertaken with the intention of seeking God's pleasure, is collectively known as "ritual duties" toward God (*'ibādāt*, literally "acts of worship"). These include all religious acts such as the daily prayers, fasting, alms-giving, and so on. The second category of actions, undertaken to maintain social order, is known as "social transactions" (*mu'āmalāt*, literally "social intercourse").

The religious calibration of these two categories depends upon the meticulous division of jurisdiction based on the ability of human institutions to enforce the Shari'ah and to provide sanctions for disregarding its injunctions. According to Islamic law, all actions should be performed to secure divine approval; however, human agency and institutions have jurisdiction only over the social transactions that regulate interpersonal relations.

In order to create such an all-comprehensive legal system founded upon revealed texts, Muslim scholars went beyond the Qur'an to the person of the founder and the early community. The Qur'an required obedience to the Prophet and those invested with authority, which included the idealized community made up of the elders among the first and second generations. In this way, the Qur'an opened the way for extending the normative practice beyond the Prophet's earthly life. Such an understanding of the normative tradition was theoretically essential for deriving the legal system, which saw its validity only in terms of its being extracted from the Prophet's own paradigmatic status. Hence, his life as understood and reported by the early community became an ethical touchstone for what the Muslims call the Sunnah. The intellectual activity surrounding the interpretation of God's will as expressed in the Qur'an and the evaluation of the hadith (reports ascribed to the Prophet and the early community) became the major religious-academic activity among Muslims and thereby laid the foundation for subsequent juridical deliberations – what became known as *fiqh* ("understanding"), or jurisprudence.

By the ninth and tenth centuries, the Muslim community was affiliated with one or another of the leading scholars in the field of juristic investigation. The legal school that followed the Iraqi tradition was called Hanafi, after Abu Hanifah (d. 767), the imam (teacher) in Iraq. Those who adhered to the rulings of Malik ibn Anas (d. 795) in Arabia and elsewhere were known as Malikis. Al-Shafi'i, who is credited with being a profound legal thinker, founded a legal school in Egypt whose influence spread widely to other Muslim regions. Another school was associated with Ahmad ibn Hanbal (d. 855), who compiled a work on hadith-reports that became the source for the juridical decisions of those who followed him. The Shi'a developed their own legal school, the Ja'fari school, whose leading authority was Imam Ja'far al-Sadiq (d. 748). Normally, Muslims accepted their region's prevailing legal school. Today most Sunnis follow the Hanafi or Shafi'i rite, whereas the Shi'a follow the Ja'fari school. In the absence of an organized "church" and ordained "clergy," the Islamic legal rite is inherently pluralistic. The determination of valid religious practice is left to the qualified scholars of religious law, collectively known as the ulama.

Muslim legal theorists were thoroughly aware of the moral underpinnings of the religious duties that all Muslims were required to fulfill as members of the faith community. In fact, the validity of their research into Islam's foundational sources (viz., the Qur'an and Sunnah) for solutions to practical matters depended upon their substantial consideration of the different moral facets of a case that could be discovered by considering conflicting claims, interests, and responsibilities in the precedents preserved therein. What ensured the validity of their judicial decision regarding a specific instance was their ability to deduce such universal moral principles as "there shall be no harm inflicted or reciprocated" (*lā ḍarar wa lā ḍirār*),[4] which flowed downward from their initial premise to support their particular conclusion without relying upon the circumstances that would have rendered the conclusion circumstantial at best. However, the power of these conclusions is contingent on the ethical considerations that were operative in the original precedents as well as the agreement of the scholars who sought to relate the new case to the original rationale and rules.

Customarily, when faced with a moral dilemma juridical-ethical deliberations are geared toward a satisfactory resolution in which justifications are based on practical consequences, regardless of applicable principles. For instance, in deciding whether to allow the dissection of a cadaver to retrieve a valuable object swallowed by the deceased, Muslim jurists have given the permission by simply looking at the consequence of forbidding such a procedure. The major moral consideration that outweighs the respect for the deceased's dignity is the surviving orphan's ownership through inheritance of the swallowed object. Islam forbids this procedure, and yet the case demands an immediate solution based on consequential ethics.

Or, in the case of a female patient who, as prescribed in the Shari'ah, must be treated by a female physician; in an emergency situation the practical demand overrides this prohibition because the rule of necessity (*ḍarūrah*) extracted from the revealed texts outweighs the rule of sexual segregation extracted from rational consideration. Numerous instances clearly show the cultural preferences involved in solving pressing healthcare problems in Muslim societies in which communitarian ethics considers the consequence of any medical decision on both the family and the community's resources and interests.

Health-related Beliefs and Values

People with different backgrounds approach suffering through illness and death with a wide range of diverse attitudes about its causes and consequences, attitudes that often have been cultivated and transmitted by their respective cultures and religions. Sometimes these attitudes undermine the efficacy of those treatments that require the patient to have the necessary will to fight the disease. A holistic medical approach, which treats both psychosomatic and physical conditions, necessitates that clinicians be aware of the patient's emotional condition and cultural background in order to formulate an accurate diagnosis and successful treatment plan.[5] What should the healthcare worker know about her Muslim patient's religious and moral presuppositions about the nature of suffering?

Generally a situation that is negatively described as suffering refers to an objective state of affairs ("It is unbearable!") and the subjective response ("It is harmful for the patient!") of a judging individual. In other words, when one assesses suffering as a form of evil, either objectively or subjectively, one needs to take into account the agent, the act of suffering, and the resultant harm that is objective enough for a positive or a privative understanding of evil. When both elements are present, suffering in the context of illness is described as an experience that is undesirable and maleficent. Both physically and morally, this description immediately captures an objective standard that most people would judge as tragically harmful to the agent, without any reference to any ontology or complex metaphysical or theological explanation. We are, in a realistic way, able to assert that a person is suffering unrequited pain and destruction. Evil then reveals the undesirable and maleficent aspects of human suffering. Understood in this way, we can now probe into theodicy and begin to unfold the divine mystery regarding the infliction of destruction of innocent life through natural evil.

The quest to unfold this divine mystery paves the way for a meaningful conversation between the religious beliefs and medical aspects of illness, where metaphysical and physical dimensions of medical care struggle to come to terms with the human condition and the limitations of human undertakings to alleviate that suffering. The difference between religious and medical assessment of the situation is stark. Faith in divine will nurtures humility and reveals human limitations in comprehending the ways of the all-powerful God who gives and takes life. Medicine, on the other hand, which assumes the responsibility for removing the evil of pain and suffering, continues its search to find the cure and prolong the impending death unabated.

This stark difference is further underscored by how religion inculcates personal piety in dealing with illness, which is to inculcate faith in God's goodness and accept suffering as part of the overall divine plan for humanity's spiritual and moral development. Although medical professionals enter the field of human suffering with enormous confidence and determination to treat ailments by undertaking the necessary training and research, religion emphasizes the finitude of human life and reminds humanity not to arrogate God's functions of taking life at a fixed point in history, for that knowledge rests only with God.

"How fortunate you are that you died while you were not afflicted with illness." Thus said the Prophet to the person whose funeral rites he was performing. Such an assessment of death without illness indicates the value attached to a healthy life in Muslim culture. To be sure, good health is God's blessing for which a Muslim, whenever asked, "How are you (lit. "How is your health?")?" responds, "All praise is due to God." However, this positive appraisal of good health might seem to suggest that illness is an evil to be eliminated at any cost. No doubt illness is regarded as an affliction that needs to be cured by every possible legitimate means. In fact, the search for a cure is founded upon the unusual confidence generated by the divine promise that God has not created a disease without creating its cure.[6]

Hence, the purpose of medicine is to search for a cure and provide the necessary care to those afflicted with diseases. The Muslim physician's primary obligation is to provide care and alleviate the patient's suffering. Decisions about ending the life of a terminally ill patient at her/his request are beyond his moral or legal obligations. The Qur'an states its position in no uncertain terms: "[I]t is not given to any soul to die, save by the leave of God, at an appointed time" (Q. 3:145). Moreover, "God gives life, and He makes to die" (Q. 3:156) and, hence, "A person dies when it is written" (Q. 3:185, 29:57, 39:42).

Death, then, comes at the appointed time by God's permission. In the meantime, humans are faced with the suffering caused by illness. How does

Islam view suffering? Is it part of the divine plan to cause suffering? To what end? These general questions about the meaning and value of suffering should lead us to appraise the suffering caused by prolonged illness to an individual's personal and family life. The need to take a decision to end one's life arises precisely at that critical point when the sick person is undergoing severe discomfort and desperation, and when all forms of advanced medical treatments have failed to restore her/his hope in getting better.

Closely related to such a consideration on the part of the sick person is whether the unbearable circumstances caused by one's interminable illness make existence worthwhile at all. Does such an existence, which is almost equivalent to non-existence because of the intense sense of helplessness in managing one's life, possess any value for its continuation? Beneath these concerns remains a deeper question about the quality of life that individuals and society regard as worth preserving.

The discussion about the quality of life points to the cultural and religious attitudes regarding human existence and the control over life and death decisions when an individual is overcome by suffering. Furthermore, it underscores the view that a human being has the stewardship, but not the ownership, of his body so that he can assert his right to handle it the way he pleases. He is merely the caretaker, the real owner being God, the Creator. As a caretaker, it is his duty to take all the necessary steps to preserve it in a manner that would assist him in seeking the good of both this world and the next. In light of such a stipulation about human duty toward his earthly existence in Muslim theology, the problem of human suffering through illness assumes immediate relevance. The Qur'an provides an essential philosophy behind human suffering by pointing out that it is a test or trial to confirm a believer's spiritual station:

> O all you who believe, seek your help in patience and prayer; surely God is with the patient. ... Surely We will try you with something of fear and hunger, and diminution of goods and lives and fruits; yet give thou good tidings unto the patient who, when they are visited by an affliction, say, 'Surely we belong to God, and to Him we return'; upon those rest blessings and mercy from their Lord, and those – they are the truly guided. (Q. 2:153-57)

In this situation, suffering is caused by a divinely ordained trial. More pertinently, it functions as an instrument in revealing God's purpose for humanity and reminding it that ultimately it belongs to God and will return to God. Accordingly, from this perspective it cannot be regarded as evil. In a well-known tradition, the Prophet is reported to have said: "No fatigue, nor disease, nor sorrow, nor sadness, nor hurt, nor distress befalls a Muslim, even if it were the prick he received from a thorn, but that God expiates some of his sins for that."[7]

Hence, understanding suffering is central to Islamic understandings of health and illness. As pointed out earlier, human suffering in any form raises the question of God's power and knowledge over what befalls human beings. God's overwhelming power is the most important doctrine in Muslim theology. God is not only the Creator of all things, including human destiny (*qadar*), but also determines the ultimate outcome of human decisions. Such a deterministic theology primarily gives rise to the problem of reconciling God's justice with existing evil. It also has tendencies toward resignation and almost passivity in dealing with illness and other forms of affliction. Our everyday experience with death and disease provides us with plenty of grounds to complain about the sad fact that, in view of what modern medicine promises to do for the sick, faith in the inscrutable ways of God's decree offers little comfort to those who want to see an end to the agonies associated with incurable diseases.

Muslim theologians have done their best to comprehend the rationale of suffering, for instance, of children and even animals. Explaining why bad people suffer, even though unconvincing, has been easier because of the causal link drawn between sin and suffering by majority of Muslim theologians. But what sins can one count for the suffering of innocent children? The suffering of children in reproductive technologies and genetics, as well as the unprecedented devaluation of a defective fetus in contemporary biomedical advancements, await a full accounting of the ethics of fertility clinics and prenatal genetic screening.

Islamic Biomedical Ethics[8]

Secular bioethics in the Muslim world today has severed its partnership with faith communities in resolving the moral problems that have arisen in clinical situations and public health around the world. International bodies like the WHO and UNESCO, which support local efforts in developing culturally sensitive bioethical curriculum, still appear to be unaware of the essentially religious nature of the Muslims' bioethical discourse and the need to engage religious ethics in the Muslim context to better serve those whose cultures take religion more seriously. An examination of the emerging literature on Muslim bioethics, mostly authored by interested Muslim physicians, shows that those who represent Muslim bioethics do not take local cultures and their religious ingredients seriously enough to speak with the necessary acumen and sensitivity about Muslim culture-friendly bioethics. Thus secular bioethics, with its emphasis on liberal western values, does not fully resonate with local and regional Muslim values.

The Fundamental Principle of Public Good in Islamic Bioethics

The principle of public good consists of each and every benefit that has been made known by the purposes stated in the divine revelation. Given that some jurists have essentially regarded public good as safeguarding the Lawgiver's purposes, they have discussed this principle in terms of both the types and the purposes they serve. The Shari'ah is instituted in the interests of Muslims, whether these interests pertain to this life or the next. In order to safeguard these interests and achieve God's purposes for humanity, it seeks to promote three universal goals. These goals are discussed under the following universal principles, whose authority is based on a number of probable instances and supporting documentation in the revelation:

1. **The Essentials or Primary Needs (*al-Ḍarūriyāt*).** These are indispensable things promulgated for the good of this and the next world, such as providing healthcare to the poor and downtrodden. Such actions are necessary for maintaining public health and the good of people in this life and for earning reward in the next. Moreover, without them life would be threatened, thereby resulting in further suffering for people who cannot afford even the basic necessities of life. According to Muslim thinkers, the necessity to protect the essentials is also felt across traditions among the followers of other religions. The good of the people is such a fundamental issue that there is a consensus among all people that when one member of a society suffers, others must work to relieve the afflicted.[9]
2. **The General Needs (*al-Ḥājiyāt*).** These enable human beings to improve their life and remove those conditions that lead to chaos in one's familial and societal life in order to achieve high standards of living, even though these necessities do not reach the level of the essentials. These benefits are such that, if not attained, they lead to hardship and disorder but not to corruption. This kind of common good is materialized in matters pertaining to performing one's religious duties, managing everyday life situations, maintaining interpersonal relationships, and upholding a penal system that prevents people from harming others.[10]

3. **The Secondary Needs (*al-Taḥsīnāt*).** These are commonly regarded as praiseworthy deeds that lead to the avoidance of those things regarded as blameworthy. They are also known as "noble virtues" (*makārim al-akhlāq*).[11] In other words, although they do not qualify as "primary" or "general" needs, their goal is to improve the quality of life, to make them easily accessible to the average member of a society, and even to embellish them in order to render these noble virtues more desirable.[12]

One of the issues in the Muslim world that is assessed in terms of public good is assisted reproduction in sex selection, defined as any practice, technique, or intervention intended to increase the likelihood of the conception, gestation, and birth of a child of a specific sex. Some Muslim parents prefer one sex for cultural or financial reasons. Some jurists have argued in favor of sex selection as long as no one, including the resulting child, is harmed. However, others have disputed the claim that it is possible for no harm to be done in sex selection by pointing to violations of the divine law, natural justice, and the inherent dignity of human beings.[13]

The principle of public good has also been examined in terms of collective or individual goodness. When the juristic rule of *istiḥsān* (i.e., choosing between two possible solutions of a case within the context of recognized sources of Islamic law) is evoked to justify a legal-ethical solution, the actual rationale is based on considering the common welfare that is unrestricted and reaches the largest number. However, it is sometimes likely that an individual benefit could become the source for a ruling that could clash with another ruling that entails morally superior consequences. To put it differently, the only criterion for legislation on the basis of public good is that the ruling must lead to the common good, even when it is prompted by a specific individual good.

The underpinning of the Qur'an's primary ordinances (e.g., saving human life or maintaining just order) is this kind of good. However, the consideration of individual welfare is provided by the context of change for a ruling from primary to secondary (e.g., prolongation of life without any hope for cure), so that it can benefit a particular individual in a particular situation. To be sure, any elimination of the primary ordinance that requires saving life and its change to a secondary ruling that allows discontinuing extraordinary care takes place in the context of a particular situation. In this sense, common interests function as criteria for legislation, whereas individual interests function as the context for secondary rulings. This change from common to individual good causes disagreement among Muslim jurists trying to determine the benefits and harms of the situation under consideration.[14]

Autonomy and Piety

The international community has shown a growing interest in Islamic perspectives in bioethics. It is important to keep in mind that autonomy, as the patient's overriding right, found institutional and legal-ethical support in the West. Western notions of universal human rights rest on a secular view of the individual and of the relations between such individuals in a secularized public sphere. The idea of individuals as bearers of something called "rights" presupposes a very particular understanding and reading of the self essentially as a self-regulating agent. This modern idea of the autonomous self envisions social actors as self-contained matrixes of desires who direct their own interests.

In Islamic communitarian ethics, however, patient autonomy is far from being recognized as one of the major bioethical principles. Islam's universal discourse conceives of a spiritually and morally autonomous individual capable of attaining salvation outside the nexus of the community-oriented Shari'ah, with its emphasis on integrated system of law and morality. The Shari'ah did not distinguish between external acts and internal states because it did not regard the public and the private as unrelated in the totality of individual salvation. Islam's communal discourse sought to define itself by legitimizing individual autonomy within its religiously based collective order by leaving the individual free to negotiate his/her spiritual destiny, while requiring him/her to abide by a communal order that involves the play of reciprocity and autonomy upon which a regime of rights and responsibilities are based in the Shari'ah.

Practical piety and reliable character are emphasized in connection with all professions. Although a physician does not have to be pious in order to be competent, because a physician's work is essentially to take care of his/her patient, piety and good character nevertheless aid in the general acceptance of the physician's advice and bad character detracts from its value. A physician should be a cultured person, one aware of the sensibilities of the people among whom he/she works. In Muslim culture, a physician has to work hard to gain the patient's trust and cultivate professional confidence.

Islam places a great emphasis on virtue and obligation in connection with the medical profession because medicine deals with the most valued aspect of existence: the preservation of human life. Bad character in a physician is seen as a mortal poison and a sure path to perdition. The sicknesses of the heart and the diseases of the soul are regarded as a great threat to the normal professional role assumed by a physician. Moreover, the society and institutions that provide medical care have certain expectations from a person to whom they entrust their physical wellbeing. Muslim ethicists lay down canons by which virtues become ingrained in a skillful physician's practice.

Techniques of meditation and prayers are suggested for medical professionals to focus their attention on the wholeness of human care, and not simply to their physical condition. In this way, each medical professional in a Muslim community is expected to learn not only the origins and causes of sicknesses that cause the loss of corporeal life, but he/she also begins to pay attention to the diseases of heart and soul. In this latter diagnosis, Muslim physicians go beyond the role-related technical skill and equip themselves with a character built on virtuous life in order to understand the profession's religious/psychological dimensions. The two most important virtues emphasized in Islamic professional ethics are spiritual and moral consciousness (*taqwā*) and patience (*ṣabr*). The physician must cultivate these two virtues by leading a balanced and moderate life and not waste time and energy indulging in pleasure and amusements.

The question of professional ethics is directly connected to a religious problem of the relationship between action and its impact upon human conscience. To state it briefly, human acts have a direct impact upon the development of the conscience, which, in the Islamic tradition, is regarded as the source of determining the rightness or wrongness of human undertakings. The conscience must be constantly guarded against corruption. When it becomes corrupted as a result of neglecting ethical matters related to the production of daily sustenance, no moral safeguard is left to prevent these professionals from engaging in more serious acts that would lead to the destruction of the very fabric of social relations founded upon the divinely ingrained sense of justice and fairness. Both intention and reflection must precede all human acts that infringe upon the spiritual and physical wellbeing of others.

Here it is important to keep in mind that Islam requires both patient and physician to observe ethical discipline. Patients should respect their physicians, strictly follow their orders, and regard them better than their best friends. Patients should have direct contact with their doctors and fully confide in them regarding their sickness. In fact, it is better for people to stay in touch with a physician who can advise them about their health before they actually need treatment.

Conclusion: The Spiritual Care of Muslim Patients

Spiritual care begins by providing settings that permit, and preferably encourage, religious observance and follow the rules of interpersonal behavior in providing care and carrying out interventions. Spiritual care, however, also involves supporting appropriate decision making. Healthcare practitioners have to be able to provide patients and families with information that is appropriate to religious, communitarian ethical decision making, and to respect the process that such decision making must take. As part of this process, it may be necessary for the patient and family to consult a trusted physician and/or imam, and communication protocols may need to be adapted to include these key people. The negotiable and local character of Islamic communitarian ethics should be a reminder to healthcare practitioners that a "fact file" approach to care is, at best, inadequate.

Endnotes

1. The major compilations of Prophetic traditions consist of hadith-reports that advise Muslims on dietary laws and permissible foods and drinks. Among these traditions are those that teach the followers of the Prophet to be moderate in eating. For instance, in Ibn Maja, *Sunan* (Beirut: al-Maktabat al-'Ilmiyyah, n.d.), 2:1111, in the section on foods, one reads the subtitle: *Bāb al-Iqtiṣād fī al-Akl wa Kirāhat al-Shib'* (Section on Moderation in Eating and Reprehensibility of [Eating] with Satiation). This section contains traditions in which the Prophet declares explicitly that those who have full stomachs in the world shall suffer hunger for a longer period on the Day of Judgment.
2. The tradition is reported on the authority of Umar, who said: "The Prophet instructed to teach the children swimming, archery, and horse riding."
3. A number of traditions to this effect have been cited in George F. Hourani, "Ibn Sina's 'Essay on the Secret of Destiny,'" in *Bulletin of School of Oriental and African Studies*, University of London (1966): 25-48.
4 Literally: "There shall be no harming, injuring, or hurting, [of one person by another] in the first instance, nor in return, or requital, in Islam" (See Edward William Lane, *An Arabic-English Lexicon*, off-print edition [Beirut: Librairie du Liban, 1968], part V, 1775). This is the rule of "No harm, no harassment."
5. Peter Antes, "Medicine and the Living Tradition of Islam," in *Healing and Restoring: Health and Medicine in the World's Religious Traditions*, ed. Lawrence E. Sullivan (New York: Macmillan, 1989), 173-208, discusses the problem of assessment and diagnosis of culturally diverse individuals in Germany, and underscores the importance of understanding Muslim patient's religious and cultural backgrounds for a successful diagnosis and treatment.
6. *Saḥīḥ al-Bukhārī, Kitāb al-Mardā* (Chicago: 1979), vol. 7, hadith no. 582.
7. Ibid., hadith no. 545.
8. For a detailed discussion on the subject, see Abdulaziz Sachedina, *Islamic Biomedical Ethics: Principles and Application* (New York: Oxford University Press, 2009).

9. Abu Hamid al-Ghazali, *Kitāb al-Mustaṣfā min 'Ilm al-Uṣūl* (Cairo: Bulaq, 1904-7), 174ff., Ibrahim b. Musa al-Shatibi, *Al-Muwāfiqāt fī Uṣūl al-Sharī'ah* (Beirut: Dar al-Jil, n.d.), 2:8ff.; Ibn Badran al-Dimashqi, *Al-Madkhal ilā Imām Aḥmad b. Hanbal* (Beirut: Mu'assassah al-Risalah, 1401/1981), 295; Abd Allah b. Ahmad Ibn Qudama, *Rawḍat al-Nāzir wa Jannat al-Manāzir* (Riyadh: Jami' al-Imam, 1399/1978), 3:170.
10. Muhammad b. Umar al-Razi, *Al-Maḥṣūl fī 'Ilm al-Uṣūl al-Fiqh* (Riyadh: Jami' al-Imam, 1400/1979), 6:220 quotes al-Ghazali regarding the lack of authoritativeness of the principle of *maṣlaḥah* in the area of the Necessities. In general, Ghazali maintains that to derive a legal decision only on the basis of the public good, without any reference to another principle based on the revelation, is not appropriate. However, he adds, such a ruling is necessary in positive law, and it is for this reason that it is possible that a jurist's final judgment may end up citing this principle without any proof from the revelation itself (*Al-Mustaṣfā*, 175). In other words, he does admit the possibility of independent reasoning based on public good to derive a legal-ethical ruling.
11. Shatibi, *Al-Muwāfiqāt*, 2:9.
12. Ghazali, *Al-Mustaṣfā*, 175.
13. Shatibi, *Al-Muwāfiqāt*, 2:9-10; Muhammad Sa'id Ramadan al-Buti, *Ḍawābiṭ al-Maṣlaḥah fī Sharī'ah al-Islāmīyah* (Beirut: Mu'assassat al-Risalah, 1401/1981), 219.
14. For instance, after explaining the good of this and the next world, Shatibi opens up a new section and states very clearly: "As for the public good and corruption, if they happen to be outside customary law, then it requires further investigation [before any ruling can be given]." He provides examples of eating a dead body or other contaminated foods under certain circumstances out of necessity, cutting a limb that has been affected by irremediable disease, and so on, on the basis of disagreement between the good the potential corruption that might occur while adopting one or the other course of action. See: *Al-Muwāfiqāt*, 2:23-25.

Selected Bibliography

Antes, Peter. "Medicine and the Living Tradition of Islam." In *Healing and Restoring: Health and Medicine in the World's Religious Traditions.* Edited by Lawrence E. Sullivan. New York: Macmillan, 1989.

Al-Ghazali, Abu Hamid. *Kitāb al-Mustaṣfā min 'Ilm al-Uṣūl.* Cairo: Bulaq, 1904-07.

Hourani, George F. "Ibn Sina's 'Essay on the Secret of Destiny.'" *Bulletin of School of Oriental and African Studies* (1966).

Ibn Maja. *Sunan*. Vol. 2. Beirut: al-Maktaba al-'Ilmiyyah, n.d.

Lane, Edward William. *An Arabic-English Lexicon*. Off-print edition. Beirut: Librairie du Liban, 1968, part V, 1775.

Sachedina, Abdulaziz. *Islamic Biomedical Ethics: Principles and Application*. New York: Oxford University Press, 2009.

Discussion

Discussant: Ebrahim Moosa

I am struggling very hard to find a problem with your presentation. You raise the issue of Shaykh Atia's breast-feeding fatwa, but he does not understand human biology. Women do not lactate all the time. I find the trend is away from the deontological discussion to an ethical discussion. The inquirer should not be treated as a child. The Qur'an and Sunnah are supposed to push us forward, but instead we are always looking backward and so we are held back. We are anxious about the Qur'an and the Prophet. *Tawṣīah* rather than *ḥukm*, recommendation rather than judgment, pushes the patient into a morally autonomous zone. A patient needs resources to make that decision. Doesn't this require patient literacy? You gave examples from traditional *fiqh* on the necessity for the individual to decide. Al-Ghazali requires that the individual have minimal knowledge, even if it is just to know who is the better-informed *faqīh*.

You introduced an important point about conscientious decision making. This could be a real opening as to what kind of literacy is required. You also clarify individual vs. communitarian decision making. Traditional *fiqh* is based on understanding the relationships that inform inheritance and kinship relationships and so on. The anxiety in Muslim circles is that the traditional kinship model will be reduced to the genetic model. When technology reveals new dimensions of the body and the self, how is the traditional model affected? I can empathize with the permissibility of sperm donation because adultery is an impermissible physical act.

Sachedina: There is a tension in how Muslims define relationships. Communitarian ethics is not the only way to define Islamic ethics. I only say that relationships are very important and that autonomy assumes a position below communal concerns. The role of conscience is important in a way to which *iftā'* has not given any attention. The empowerment of the individual has not taken place in the Muslim world. The Qur'an is not only iconoclastic, but also against claims of special position by certain people; however, in the culture that is not the case. There is the desire to let others make the decision.

Discussant: Imad-ad-Dean Ahmad

What is at the heart of this talk is the fundamentals of the consideration of ethics in *iftā'*, rather than bioethics per se. Understood this way, I agree with its thrust. Like you I am a chaplain at a hospital. But in my case it is an Adventist Hospital, which emphasizes the spiritual as well as the material aspects of healing. The Shari'ah is more than just the revealed law. We know it means "path," because like the path to the well it is divine given and humanity's job is not to invent it but to discover it.

If you take two passages together, the Qur'an does identify the time of personhood (ensoulment). One passage says that the time of a child's full dependency on its mother is thirty months; elsewhere it says the full term of weaning is twenty-four months. Simple arithmetic says there is an additional six-month period apart from the time of breast feeding covered by the term "full dependency." If this six-month period follows weaning, then I have no idea what it means. However, if it precedes weaning, then it implies that the fetus is a person during the last six months of pregnancy. Therefore, during the first three months it is not a person. This places ensoulment at about ninety days rather than the 120 days mentioned in the hadith. This is not a problem for me, as I always prefer the Qur'an over the hadith. When you try to obtain a purely rational or a purely scientific answer to the question, things get messy. Many atheists concerned with abortion have tried to define when personhood begins, and their answers diverge widely: at conception, at birth, when the heart is audible, when brain waves appear, and so on. They are trying to obtain a physical answer to what is a metaphysical question.

I question the statement that argument of permission by necessity is based on prohibiting difficulty in religion. Rather, I think it is based on multiple Qur'anic verses that give explicit consent to eating otherwise *ḥarām* food on the grounds of necessity (Q. 2:173, 6:119, 6:145, and 16:115).

The argument that a woman can sidestep the problem of being in an adult male co-worker's physical presence by suckling him is not an example of the contradiction between reason and revelation so much as of poor reasoning. The hadith on which it is based (e.g., *Ṣaḥīḥ Muslim*, hadith no. 3427), as you imply, should be dismissed due to the text's moral weakness.

On the question of whether sexual intercourse is necessary for adultery, I think we must remember that adultery comes from the root of adulteration, meaning of the "bloodline." Substituting genes for blood does not alter the principle. I am not saying that sperm donation is necessarily evil; I am only saying that we should approach it the same way we approach adoption, of which it seems to be a variety.

I would like to apply your point on the difficulties caused by an absence of moral explanation more broadly. The problems become the most difficult when the Qur'an gives no reason, such as the distinction between riba and trade, and the restrictions on beating women.

General Discussion

- What did Khamenie do with the Qur'anic verse "Know them by their fathers" and the hadith "the child belongs to the marriage bed" when he allowed a third-party sperm donation? Kinship is through *raḥm* (the womb) not the blood.
- Khamenie rescinded his fatwa in the next edition. Perhaps senior *mujtahid*s drew his attention to his error. He often has a committee sit with him and advise him on *iftā'*. Khamenie was politically promoted; his scholarship is managed by others. The senior (first tier) *mujtahidīn* disagreed with him on this issue. Khamenie is in the third tier.
- What happens to those who followed his first edition?
- Is not a false accusation of adultery an example of psychological harm? Khaled Abul Fadl says that law and ethics do not always correlate. It has been argued that the Mu'tazilis and the early Ash'aris started with deontological ethics and shifted to consequentialist ethics.

- Slander is a public crime, but rape, which is a trauma, was not necessarily recognized as a public crime until Bosnia. There rape was used as a weapon of war. Imam Khomeini declared rape to be a harm that would permit abortion in the first thirteen days, but others disagree. I think our criticism is introducing the subject of moral reasoning into *fiqh*.
- Most Mu'tazilis accepted the deontological, but the Ash'aris did not because they think only God knows good and evil. The medical community respects chaplains, but the ultimate decision is made by the hospital's ethics committee. Our influence depends on how much faith they have in us.
- Are Indonesians unrestrained by the four *madhhab*s because they have a different culture?
- As for rethinking *fiqh* in a cultural context, *fiqh* means to understand and so *fiqh*, as an activity, is different from the Shari'ah. It is a growing body of knowledge and thus will differ according to culture.
- I am trying to clarify *ḥukm* and *tawṣīyah*. I believe morality has always been there, but there has been a lack of understanding the issues.
- *Fiṭrah* is not sufficient; we need revelation. The texts have many references to conscience. The Qur'an emphasizes *īmān* more than *iḥkām*, because once you have submitted Allah's guidance is sufficient for you.
- In rural areas of Morocco women openly nurse their infants by the side of the road, and no one is shocked or even surprised. It is doubtful if our current Puritanism was the norm when the *aḥkām* were established. Giving an illegitimate child the name of ibn *abīhī* (child of his father) today would mark the child for life. We have to find a *maṣlaḥah* for the individual because we know that the blame for the illegitimate child cannot be put upon him.
- Even in the time of the Prophet there were different interpretations of the Qur'an and Hadith, such as the people who were told to pray when they reached the Bani Qurayzah. Umar ibn al-Khattab suspended the *ḥadd* of theft, to much controversy. The stages of the fetus are mentioned in the Qur'an, and I like what al-Ghazali said: Life starts at fertilization and is thus like the contract of buying or selling in that destroying the embryo at any of its three stages has a specific monetary penalty: *'arsh* = 10 dinar, or double or triple. There is also the question of who dies first and who dies second as regards taxing the inheritance.
- I understood there is an enforcing body for *ḥukm*, whereas the mufti is dependent upon the one who follows him. Khamenie's fatwa (which was requested by doctors) was not adopted by the government. *Akhlāq* (morality) is essentially intertwined with *fiqh*. The Prophet's language was *akhlāq*, but that was before you had an Islamic empire. Conscientious objection is not developed in fiqh. For me, *uṣūl al-fiqh* is ethical. *Al-waḥy awlā min al-'aql*. There is clearly a link, but it has not been well developed. I am not saying that all Muslim jurists ignore ethics.
- The Companions saw the Qur'an as the Prophet and the Prophet as the Qur'an, because it was not there in a manuscript form. Thus *īmān* in the Qur'an required submission to the Prophet. Today it is a struggle to keep the two together.

- Our *fuquhā'* said when the father's identity is unknown the child must be known by the mother's name specifically to avoid such stigma. People who were called ibn *abīhī* or such were being insulted, sometimes for political reasons.
- We are teaching the *waṣīyah* (Islamic will) today.
- How does the contrast of the western focus on the individual with the Muslim focus on the individual as part of a family or community affect Muslim immigrants?
- Why is the individual's opinion more important than that of the family? Sometimes the illness is such that the person cannot make that decision and thus we empower the family to do so. When a patient needs a stent in Iran, the doctors do not accept his approval before consulting his family.